pause & AFFECT

A Shabbat Outlook

Printed in the United States of America

The Rohr Jewish Learning Institute
822 Eastern Parkway, Brooklyn, NY 11213

(888) YOUR-JLI/718-221-6900
www.myJLI.com

ROSHCHODESH society

pause & AFFECT

A Shabbat Outlook

The Rohr Jewish Learning Institute acknowledges the generous support of the following individuals and foundations:

PRINCIPAL BENEFACTOR

GEORGE ROHR
New York, NY

ADVISORY BOARD OF GOVERNORS

YAAKOV AND KAREN COHEN
Potomac, MD

YITZCHOK AND JULIE GNIWISCH
Montreal, QC

BARBARA HINES
Aspen, CO

DANIEL B. MARKSON
S. Antonio, TX

DANIEL AND ROSIE MATTIO
Seattle, WA

DAVID MINTZ
Tenafly, NJ

DR. STEPHEN F. SERBIN
Columbia, SC

LEONARD A. WIEN, JR.
Miami Beach, FL

DR. VERA KOCH GROSZMANN
S. Paulo, Brazil

HERSCHEL LAZAROFF
Baltimore, MD

JENNY LJUNGBERG
New York, NY

DAVID MAGERMAN
Gladwyne, PA

DR. MICHAEL MALING
Deerfield, IL

YITZCHAK MIRILASHVILI
Herzliya, Israel

LARRY SIFEN
Virginia Beach, VA

YAIR SHAMIR
Savyon, Israel

PILLARS OF JEWISH LITERACY

KEVIN BERMEISTER
Sydney, Australia

PABLO AND SARA BRIMAN
Mexico City, Mexico

YOSEF GOROWITZ
Redondo Beach, CA

PARTNERING FOUNDATIONS

WILLIAM DAVIDSON FOUNDATION

MEROMIM FOUNDATION

KOHELET FOUNDATION

CRAIN-MALING FOUNDATION

WORLD ZIONIST ORGANIZATION

AVI CHAI FOUNDATION

OLAMI WORLDWIDE—WOLFSON FOUNDATION

RUDERMAN FAMILY FOUNDATION

THE ESTATE OF ELLIOT JAMES BELKIN

SPONSORS

MARK AND REBECCA BOLINSKY
Long Beach, NY

DANIEL AND ETA COTLAR
Houston, TX

ZALMAN AND MIMI FELLIG
Miami Beach, FL

SHMUEL AND SHARONE GOODMAN
Chicago, IL

FRANK (A"H) AND FRUMETH POLASKY
Saginaw, MI

DR. ZE'EV RAV-NOY
Los Angeles, CA

CLIVE AND ZOE ROCK
Irvine, CA

ZVI RYZMAN
Los Angeles, CA

ALAN ZEKELMAN
Bloomfield Hills, MI

JLI
JEWISH LEARNING INSTITUTE

THE ROHR JEWISH LEARNING INSTITUTE

gratefully acknowledges
the pioneering support of

GEORGE AND PAMELA ROHR

Since its inception,
the Rohr JLI has been
a beneficiary of the vision, generosity,
care, and concern
of the Rohr family.

In the merit of
the hundreds of thousands of hours of Torah study
by JLI students worldwide,
may they be blessed with health,
Yiddishe nachas from all their loved ones,
and extraordinary success
in all their endeavors.

DEDICATED BY

MOSHE, REBECCA, AND SARA BOLINSKY

in loving memory of their parents and grandparents

ELEANOR BOLINSKY

אסיא בת בנציון ע"ה

and

NATHAN BOLINSKY

נחום חיים בן מנחם מענדל ע"ה

May their selfless dedication, devotion, and love for Jewish education during their exemplary lives serve as an everlasting foundation upon which thousands of Jewish homes around the world will be built, educated, and inspired.

May the light of Torah and Judaism kindled by the Rosh Chodesh Society chapters across the globe bring eternal merit to their souls, and may their memories be for a blessing.

אילן במה אברכך . . .
אלא יהי רצון שכל נטיעותיך יהיו כמותך.

תלמוד, תענית ה, ב - ו, א

"Tree, wherewith can I bless you? That your fruit may be sweet—it is already sweet; that you afford plenty of shade—it is already plentiful; that a spring of water passes under you—that too is so. Rather, may it be His will that all your offspring will be as fruitful as you are."

—*Talmud, Ta'anit* 5b–6a

As their progeny, Moshe, Rebecca, and Sara are this fruit.

May their goodness of heart and partnership with JLI stand them in good stead, propelling them from strength to strength, toward health, happiness, nachas from their loved ones, and success in all their endeavors.

ENDORSEMENTS

What a wonderful benefit to know that each and every week we are guaranteed sanctified family time! Equally special are the moments spent in preparation for this unique gift of rest, called Shabbat.

Having the good fortune of traveling around the world and teaching women to bake their own challah, I'm blessed to witness the mundane become holy. As yeast raises flour and water, so too does Shabbat elevate the rest of the week. Sift, stir, and knead the ingredients of life during the week, then set them aside—allowing them rest—to the setting of the sun each Friday evening.

Keep the Shabbat holy. That is the greatest all-star lifetime achievement one can wish for. This course from the Rosh Chodesh Society, is guaranteed to bless you with the greatest award of all!

SARA BRIMAN
Recipient, American Academy of Hospitality Sciences Five Star Diamond Lifetime Achievement Award for Best Challah in the World

In today's world of confusion and loss of direction in life, which manifests in young people adopting self-destructive habits, this excellent course is a beacon of light that can guide people to the safe haven of true happiness.

RABBI ABRAHAM J. TWERSKI, MD
Psychiatrist, Founder and Medical Director Emeritus of Gateway Rehabilitation Center, Pittsburgh, PA; Author of 60 books on self-esteem, personal growth, dependency recovery, and Torah commentaries

As an Orthodox woman, wife, mother of five, and entrepreneur, my life is filled with the spirit of doing. Keeping Shabbat has given me the exhale to a week of holding my breath: the space to reconnect, recharge, and escape to an island of time where connecting to spiritual affairs allows me to actively participate in my life rather than just hold it all together. In this goal-oriented time in humanity where people chase dollars, titles, recognition, and perfection, the Rosh Chodesh

Society cuts through the noise to provide an honest and multidimensional look at this infinite gift that is Shabbat—and how the ultimate goal is as simple as coming back to self and home every week. Whether you view the Shabbat with the innocence of a child who tastes a new food for the first time, proclaiming he didn't like it before he even tried it, or whether you observe it every week and want to reconnect with the why: this course will lift you up, inspire you and give you the sparkle that comes from swallowing it up and realizing you are in love with what you just tasted.

JOYCE AZRIA
CEO / CCO, Avec Les Filles

The French theorist Bernard Stiegler has written that in today's technological age we are experiencing a collective loss of savoir faire and savoir vivre: the loss of an understanding of how to be and how to live. Communication technologies orient us to the urgent and the efficient, rather than to the meaningful and the humane. The *Pause & Affect* course promises to provide a much-needed respite. Drawing upon ancient traditions, the immersive and contemplative experiences of this program can help us to develop the much-needed habits of mind and spirit necessary to address ourselves to these troubled times. I am pleased to recommend it.

LYNN SCHOFIELD CLARK, PH.D.
Professor and Chair; Department of Media, Film & Journalism Studies; and Director, Estlow International Center for Journalism and New Media, University of Denver; Author with Regina Marchi, Young People and the Future of News: Social Media and the Rise of Connective Journalism *(Cambridge University Press, 2017)*

My parents always told me, "If you take care of Shabbat, Shabbat will take care of you." Shabbat has charted the course of my life. It has been the backbone of my energy and my power throughout my basketball career. I encourage you to attend the Rosh Chodesh Society's upcoming course, *Pause & Affect,* and learn how Shabbat can provide direction and motivation to use your talents to create a better, more spiritual world.

TAMIR GOODMAN
Professional basketball player (retired)

Shabbat is a very special time of the week that we observe. When I was younger, emigrating from a post-*Shoah* time, there were no *shomer Shabbat* (Shabbat observant) individuals so we celebrated with our family, as my father was the rabbi of a small town in Massachusetts. As I grew and found more people celebrating Shabbat, I experienced the strength and beauty in communal meals and rituals. Joe and I have experienced many occasions and campaigns where we have celebrated the beauty of Shabbat. Chabad has so frequently assisted us with procuring challahs, candles, and food, not only around the country but also around the world. I sincerely endorse this important Shabbat course in all its important efforts!

HADASSAH LIEBERMAN
Health care professional, dedicating much of her life's work to health issues, assisting nonprofit organizations, improving educational standards, and promoting international understanding. Married to U.S. Senator Joseph Lieberman of Connecticut, Democratic vice-presidential candidate in the 2000 presidential election.

In our techno-driven society, we often worry that we are building different relationships and often distant relationships because of our use of screens. Shabbat allows us to reconnect, to fully be present with one another, and rediscover our relationships. I highly recommend that we all study this Rosh Chodesh Society course. We can all do well with a Shabbat outlook.

KIMBERLY S. YOUNG, PSY.D.
Founder and Director, The Center for Internet Addiction and Netaddiction.com
Author: Internet Addiction in Children and Adolescents: Risk Factors, Treatment, and Prevention.

TABLE OF CONTENTS

pause
& AFFECT

LESSON 1

Gift of Rest

ROSHCHODESH society

THE PURPOSE OF SHABBAT

ORIGINS

Text 1

EXODUS 20:8–10

זָכוֹר אֶת יוֹם הַשַּׁבָּת לְקַדְּשׁוֹ.
שֵׁשֶׁת יָמִים תַּעֲבֹד וְעָשִׂיתָ כָּל מְלַאכְתֶּךָ.
וְיוֹם הַשְּׁבִיעִי שַׁבָּת לַה' אֱלֹקֶיךָ, לֹא תַעֲשֶׂה כָל מְלָאכָה, אַתָּה
וּבִנְךָ וּבִתֶּךָ עַבְדְּךָ וַאֲמָתְךָ וּבְהֶמְתֶּךָ וְגֵרְךָ אֲשֶׁר בִּשְׁעָרֶיךָ.

Remember the Sabbath day to sanctify it.

Six days you shall labor and perform all your work.

But the seventh day is a Sabbath to the Lord your God. On it you shall not do any work, neither you, nor your son or daughter, nor your male or female servant, nor your animals, nor any foreigner residing in your towns.

Text 2

LOUIS H. FELDMAN, *JEW AND GENTILE IN THE ANCIENT WORLD* (PRINCETON, NJ: PRINCETON UNIVERSITY PRESS, 1996), P. 166

Seneca (cited in Augustine, *De Civitate D-i* 6.11) derides the observance of the Sabbath as inexpedient because the Jews thus lose one-seventh of their lives in idleness and often, indeed, suffer loss through failure to act in time of urgency. The charge that Jews are lazy (Tacitus, *Histories* 5.4.3; Juvenal 14.105–6) may have originated in this idleness on the seventh day. . . . Indeed Philo (*De Specialibus Legibus* 2.15.60) seems to be answering such a charge when he says, "On this day [the Sabbath] we are commanded to abstain from all work, not because the law inculcates slackness; on the contrary, it always inures men to endure hardship and incites them to labor."

Philo was a (Hellenist) Jew and he was defending Judaism to his audience of Alexandrian Hellenist philosophers. The need for him to go out of his way to say that Shabbos is not about "slackness," and his proving this by saying that the Torah encourages people "to endure hardship and incites them to labor," goes to show what non-Jews of the time thought about the Jewish Shabbos. For whatever reason, it was by no means an intuitive idea back then, which leads us to the following question.

LOUIS H. FELDMAN
1926–2017

Literary scholar and historian. Louis Feldman received his degrees in classic literature from Trinity College and Harvard University, and was a long-serving professor of classics and literature at Yeshiva University. Feldman was recognized as a leading authority on the writings of Josephus Flavius and the Jewish interaction with Greco-Roman culture.

Question for Discussion

Imagine for a moment you were Moses. You come to the Jews and want them to take off one day of work each week. No other surrounding culture is doing this; on the contrary, they will mock this and label it as laziness. Convincing the Jews to adopt this practice would be no easy task. What will you tell them that might persuade them to accept this practice? How would you market this?

Learning Exercise 1

With a partner (*chavruta*), study Texts 3a–3d. Then, together with your partner, summarize in the chart below how you might use each quote to answer the aforementioned question.

	"What will you tell them that might persuade them to accept this practice?"
Text 3a	
Text 3b	
Text 3c	
Text 3d	

Text 3a

RABBI YONAH OF GERONA, *HOMILIES, PARASHAT* VAYAKHEL

בַּעֲשׂוֹתוֹ מְלָאכָה בִּשְׁאָר יְמֵי הַשָּׁבוּעַ, יִזְדָּרֵז בָּהּ, בְּהַעֲלוֹתוֹ עַל לִבּוֹ כִּי תִקְרַב אֵלָיו עֵת הַמְּנוּחָה. וְכֵן אַחַר עֲבוֹר יוֹם הַמְּנוּחָה, יֵצֵא לִמְלַאכְתּוֹ בִּזְרִיזוּת. כִּי הָרוֹאֶה שֶׁאֵין לוֹ מְנוּחָה יַעֲשֶׂה מְלַאכְתּוֹ בְּעַצְלָה וְעַל כָּרְחוֹ.

A person who considers that a period of rest is approaching will work with enthusiasm during the workweek. And after the day of rest passes, the person will return to work with zeal. But if a person sees no upcoming rest, the work will be done lethargically and begrudgingly.

RABBI YONAH OF GERONA
D. 1263

Spanish rabbi and Talmudist. Rabbeinu Yonah from Gerona, Catalonia, was a cousin of Nachmanides. He is renowned for his outspoken critique of Maimonides' works, and for later recanting his opposition and vowing to travel to Maimonides' grave in Israel to beg his forgiveness. He left France, but was detained in Toledo, Spain, where he stayed and became one of the greatest Talmudists of his time. He is best known for his moralistic works on repentance and asceticism.

Text 3b

MIDRASH, *SHEMOT RABAH* 1:28

"וַיַּרְא בְּסִבְלוֹתָם" (שְׁמוֹת ב, יא): רָאָה שֶׁאֵין לָהֶם מְנוּחָה. הָלַךְ וְאָמַר לְפַרְעֹה: מִי שֶׁיֵּשׁ לוֹ עֶבֶד אִם אֵינוֹ נָח יוֹם אֶחָד בַּשָּׁבוּעַ הוּא מֵת, וְאֵלּוּ עֲבָדֶיךָ, אִם אֵין אַתָּה מֵנִיחַ לָהֶם יוֹם אֶחָד בַּשָּׁבוּעַ הֵם מֵתִים.

אָמַר לוֹ: לֵךְ וַעֲשֵׂה לָהֵן כְּמוֹ שֶׁתֹּאמַר.

הָלַךְ מֹשֶׁה וְתִקֵּן לָהֶם אֶת יוֹם הַשַּׁבָּת לָנוּחַ.

"Moses [grew up and went out to his brothers and] saw their suffering" (Exodus 2:11). He saw that they had no respite. So he went to Pharaoh and said, "If someone does not allow his slaves to rest once a week, they will perish. The Jews are your slaves; if you do not give them respite once a week, they will die."

Pharaoh said, "Go and do with them as you have spoken."

And so Moses went and instituted the Shabbat so that the Jews would have rest.

SHEMOT RABAH

An early rabbinic commentary on the Book of Exodus. Midrash is the designation of a particular genre of rabbinic literature usually forming a running commentary on specific books of the Bible. *Shemot Rabah,* written mostly in Hebrew, provides textual exegeses, expounds upon the biblical narrative, and develops and illustrates moral principles. It was first printed in Constantinople in 1512 together with four other Midrashic works on the other four books of the Pentateuch.

Text 3c

MIDRASH, *ELIYAHU RABAH* 1

עוֹשֶׂה אָדָם מְלָאכָה כָּל שִׁשָּׁה יָמִים וְנָח בַּשְּׁבִיעִי, נִתְרַצֶּה עִם בָּנָיו וְעִם בְּנֵי בֵּיתוֹ.

שׁוּב עוֹשֶׂה אָדָם מְלָאכָה בִּפְנֵי אוֹיְבָיו כָּל שִׁשָּׁה יָמִים וְנָח בַּשְּׁבִיעִי, שָׁכַח כָּל צַעַר שֶׁהָיָה לוֹ.

כַּךְ הִיא מִדָּתוֹ שֶׁל אָדָם, יוֹם טוֹב מַשְׁכַּחַת רָעָה, וְיוֹם רָע מַשְׁכַּחַת טוֹבָה.

כַּךְ אָמַר לָהֶן הַקָּדוֹשׁ בָּרוּךְ הוּא לְיִשְׂרָאֵל, בָּנַיי לֹא כַּךְ כָּתַבְתִּי לָכֶם בְּתוֹרָתִי, "לֹא יָמוּשׁ סֵפֶר הַתּוֹרָה הַזֶּה מִפִּיךָ" (יְהוֹשֻׁעַ א, ח), אַף עַל פִּי שֶׁאַתֶּם עוֹשִׂים מְלָאכָה כָּל שִׁשָּׁה יָמִים, יוֹם הַשַּׁבָּת יַעֲשֶׂה כּוּלוֹ תּוֹרָה. מִיכַּן אָמְרוּ, לְעוֹלָם יַשְׁכִּים אָדָם וְיִשְׁנֶה בְּשַׁבָּת, וְיֵלֵךְ לְבֵית הַכְּנֶסֶת וּלְבֵית הַמִּדְרָשׁ, יִקְרָא בַּתּוֹרָה וְיִשְׁנֶה בִּנְבִיאִים.

וְאַחַר כַּךְ יֵלֵךְ לְבֵיתוֹ וְיֹאכַל וְיִשְׁתֶּה, לְקַיֵּים מַה שֶּׁנֶּאֱמַר (קֹהֶלֶת ט, ז) "לֵךְ אֱכֹל בְּשִׂמְחָה לַחְמֶךָ וּשְׁתֵה בְלֶב טוֹב יֵינֶךָ".

People work for six days, but when they rest on the seventh, there is a reconciliation with their children and families.

Similarly, people work for six days with their adversaries, and when they rest on the seventh, they forget all of the pain that they endured.

This is human nature: a good day dismisses a bad day, and a bad day dismisses a good day.

In a similar sense, God says to the Jewish people, "My children, it is true that I conveyed to you, 'Study the Torah continually' (Joshua 1:8) and that this is largely unfeasible because of the need to work for a living; so let Shabbat be dedicated completely to Torah." The sages therefore taught that one should arise early on Shabbat morning

TANA DEVEI ELIYAHU

A Midrashic work, sometimes referred to as *Seder Eliyahu*. Midrash is the designation of a particular genre of rabbinic literature usually forming a running commentary on specific books of the Bible. This work deals with the divine precepts, their rationales, and the importance of knowledge of Torah, prayer, and repentance. The work is divided into two sections *(Sedarim): Eliyahu Rabah* and *Eliyahu Zuta*.

in order to study, and one should visit the synagogue and study hall to study the Torah and the words of the prophets.

Subsequently, one should return home to eat and drink, to fulfill the verse (Ecclesiastes 9:7), "Go, eat your food with happiness, and drink your wine with a joyful heart."

Text 3d

MIDRASH TANCHUMA, VAYEIRA 1

אַתָּה מוֹצֵא י"ח מִתְפַּלְלִין בְּכָל יוֹם, וְאֵינָן כֻּלָּן לְשִׁבְחוֹ שֶׁל הַקָּדוֹשׁ בָּרוּךְ הוּא, אֶלָּא שָׁלֹשׁ רִאשׁוֹנוֹת וְשָׁלֹשׁ אַחֲרוֹנוֹת, וּשְׁתֵּים עֶשְׂרֵה בְּרָכוֹת כּוּלָּן לְצוֹרְכוֹ שֶׁל אָדָם.
וּלְפִיכָךְ, אֵין מִתְפַּלְלִין בְּשַׁבָּת שְׁמוֹנֶה עֶשְׂרֵה, שֶׁאִם יִהְיֶה לוֹ חוֹלֶה בְּתוֹךְ בֵּיתוֹ, נִזְכַּר בְּרוֹפֵא חוֹלֵי עַמּוֹ יִשְׂרָאֵל, וְהוּא מֵיצֵר. וְהַשַּׁבָּת נִתְּנָה לְיִשְׂרָאֵל לִקְדוּשָּׁה, לְעֹנֶג, וְלִמְנוּחָה, וְלֹא לְצַעַר. לְכָךְ מִתְפַּלֵּל ג' בְּרָכוֹת רִאשׁוֹנוֹת, וְג' אַחֲרוֹנוֹת, וְהַמְּנוּחָה בָּאֶמְצַע.

You will find that the daily *Amidah* prayer (a central prayer, prayed three times a day) does not exclusively consist of praise for the Almighty. Only the first and last three blessings are of this nature; the middle twelve blessings are requests concerning human needs.

However, on Shabbat, we do not recite this version of the *Amidah*. If people were to have a personal problem, they would take note of this while reciting the *Amidah* and they would be in a state of pain. Shabbat, however, was given to the Jews for sanctity, pleasure, and rest—not pain.

Hence, the Shabbat *Amidah* consists of the first and last three blessings [which convey God's praises] and one additional blessing recited between them on the theme of rest.

MIDRASH TANCHUMA

A Midrashic work bearing the name of Rabbi Tanchuma, a 4th-century Talmudic sage quoted often in this work. Midrash is the designation of a particular genre of rabbinic literature usually forming a running commentary on specific books of the Bible. *Midrash Tanchuma* provides textual exegeses, expounds upon the biblical narrative, and develops and illustrates moral principles. *Tanchuma* is unique in that many of its sections commence with a halachic discussion, which subsequently leads into non-halachic teachings.

THE BENEFITS

Learning Exercise 2

In his highly acclaimed book, *The Seven Habits of Highly Effective People,* Stephen Covey suggests a system that makes use of a four-quadrant time-managed grid.

Fill in a few areas of your life in each of the quadrants below—those that are important, not important, urgent, and not urgent.

	Urgent	Not Urgent
Important		
Not Important		

Text 4a

HERMAN WOUK, *THIS IS MY GOD* (BOSTON: LITTLE BROWN AND CO., 1987), PP. 45–46

The Sabbath has cut most sharply athwart my own life when one of my plays has been in rehearsal or in tryout. The crisis atmosphere of an attempt at Broadway is a legend of our time, and a true one; I have felt under less pressure going into battle at sea. Friday afternoon, during these rehearsals, inevitably seems to come when the project is tottering on the edge of ruin. . . .

Leaving the gloomy theatre, the littered coffee cups, the jumbled scarred-up scripts, the haggard actors, the shouting stagehands, the bedeviled director, the knuckle-gnawing producer, the clattering typewriter, and the dense tobacco smoke and backstage dust, I have come home. It has been a startling change, very like a brief return from the wars. My wife and my boys, whose existence I have almost forgotten in the anxious shoring up of the tottering ruin, are waiting for me, gay, dressed in holiday clothes, and looking to me marvelously attractive. We have sat down to a splendid dinner, at a table graced with flowers and the old Sabbath symbols: the burning candles, the twisted loaves, the stuffed fish and my grandfather's silver goblet brimming with wine. I have blessed my boys with the ancient blessing; we have sung the pleasantly syncopated Sabbath table hymns. The talk has had little to do with tottering ruins. My wife and I have caught up with our week's conversation. The boys, knowing that the Sabbath is the occasion for

HERMAN WOUK
1915–

American novelist and playwright. Wouk was born in New York City to a Jewish-Russian immigrant family. When the U.S. entered World War II, he joined the Navy, serving in the Pacific Theater for four years. Wouk's wartime experiences gave him the material and background for his bestseller and Pulitzer-Prize-winning *The Caine Mutiny*. *This Is My God* was his best-selling affirmation of faith in traditional Judaism, penned after much self-examination and exposure to many secular influences. His later works include the novel *Inside, Outside*, which discusses Judaism in private life and in politics, and *The Will to Live On: This Is Our Heritage*.

asking questions, have asked them. The Bible, the encyclopedia, the atlas, have piled up on the table. We talk of Judaism, and there are the usual impossible boys' queries about God, which my wife and I field clumsily but as well as we can. For me it is a retreat into restorative magic.

Saturday has passed in much the same manner. The boys are at home in the synagogue, and they like it. They like even more the assured presence of their parents. In the weekday press of schooling, household chores, and work—and especially in a play-producing time—it often happens that they see little of us. On the Sabbath we are always here, and they know it. They know too that I am not working, and that my wife is at her ease. It is their day. . . .

My producer one Saturday night said to me, "I don't envy you your religion, but I envy you your Sabbath."

Text 4b

KAREN BARROW, "WHEN THE SUN SETS EARLY, IT'S A RACE TO PREPARE FOR SHABBAT," *THE NEW YORK TIMES,* DECEMBER 23, 2016

Soon after I light the candles, we set the table with our fancy dishes, put out the wine glasses... Then, finally, we gather around the dining room table. My husband, Leron, and I look at each other and we take a collective breath and exhale.

Out with that breath goes the stress of a long week of work and the commotion of a busy family: the unrelenting weekly routine, the scheduling and preparing and endless to-dos. We have made it to another Friday night. For the next day the world around us will slow. We will stay in pajamas until after breakfast, linger over meals with neighbors, take naps, read books on our cozy couch, play games as a family or maybe take a walk outside if it's not too cold. But everything else will have to wait; if it wasn't already done, it won't be done today....

Saturday afternoon is the time I am most likely to pause to appreciate my family. I notice how mature my 4-year-old is becoming. She is so generous to the friends who come over for playdates, and she is always excited to take them on tours of her room. Our 2-year-old, too, is growing. I can see how hard she works to speak like her sister; her brain now holds more words then her mouth can handle.

In the winter, the Sabbath starts early enough for us to eat dinner together as a family, and still put the children to bed by 8 p.m. Then, Leron and I get to spend a few precious moments together in

KAREN BARROW

Senior staff editor for *The New York Times*. Barrow has published many articles on the topics of health and well-being.

the quiet of our house. We discuss replacing the worn couch in the living room, and then muster the energy to play a board game or read a book next to each other (trying our hardest not to fall asleep).

Observing the Sabbath requires a certain amount of discipline to take a break from our digital media and entertainment, but it also forces us to be disciplined about taking time for ourselves and our family.

One of the great blessings of Shabbos is that it connects us to others. It sustains an oasis of love and connections in the desert of lonely individualism. I can say for myself that there are weeks when I literally have little time for my family and friends because I'm so caught up in dealing with the urgencies of life. That's why I love Shabbos. It really is an anchor for my week, granting me the time and space to reconnect.

In fact, I cannot think of an institution in all of history that has more thoroughly supported and beautified the relationships between husband and wife, and parents and children, than Shabbos.

Text 5

HELEN KELLER, "THREE DAYS TO SEE,"
ATLANTIC MONTHLY, JANUARY 1933

Only the deaf appreciate hearing, only the blind realize the manifold blessings that lie in sight. Particularly does this observation apply to those who have lost sight and hearing in adult life. But those who have never suffered impairment of sight or hearing seldom make the fullest use of these blessed faculties. Their eyes and ears take in all sights and sounds hazily, without concentration and with little appreciation. It is the same old story of not being grateful for what we have until we lose it, of not being conscious of health until we are ill.

I have often thought it would be a blessing if each human being were stricken blind and deaf for a few days at some time during his early adult life. Darkness would make him more appreciative of sight; silence would teach him the joys of sound. . . .

Recently I was visited by a very good friend who had just returned from a long walk in the woods, and I asked her what she had observed. "Nothing in particular," she replied. I might have been incredulous had I not been accustomed to such responses, for long ago I became convinced that the seeing see little.

HELEN ADAMS KELLER
1880–1968

American author, political activist, and lecturer. Keller was the first deaf-blind person to earn a bachelor of arts degree. The story of how Keller's teacher, Anne Sullivan, taught her how to communicate has become widely known through the dramatic depictions of the play and film, *The Miracle Worker*. A prolific author, Keller was well-traveled and outspoken in her convictions. She campaigned for women's suffrage, labor rights, and socialism.

TETHERED TO TECHNOLOGY (OPTIONAL SECTION)

Learning Exercise 3

The Web, smartphones, and social media are phenomena that play a significant role in most of our lives. Please write three positives that these have brought to your life (or to those you know) as well as three challenges that these pose to your life (or to those you know).

Positives	Challenges

Question for Discussion

Do the points made in Texts 3a–3d relate to some of the downsides regarding the misuse of the internet, the smartphone, and social media? How so?

Text 3a (Rabbi Yonah) was about disengaging from work in order to produce better at work. Randi Zuckerberg talks about how this idea is relevant to her in terms of unplugging from her smartphone and social media:

Text 6

"RANDI ZUCKERBERG 'LIKES' UNPLUGGING FOR SHABBAT," SEPTEMBER 4, 2016, WWW.YNETNEWS.COM

Randi Zuckerberg, an entrepreneur, radio host and sister to Facebook co-founder Mark Zuckerberg, discussed and encouraged "unplugging" from electronic devices on Shabbat while at the One-to-One forum in New York this past June.

Zuckerberg, who currently has over 1.75 million Facebook followers, worked at the social media giant until 2011, when she founded Zuckerberg Media, a social media firm. Though she works in digital media, she still advocates taking a regular break and unplugging. . . .

Addressing the forum, Zuckerberg discussed the concept of unplugging from the perpetual connection to one's telephone.

She said, "I find that it's so important in my own life. Any big entrepreneur, any CEO you talk to—they're not coming up with the world-changing ideas by being constantly plugged in and constantly on text message, distracted, getting emails. You can only come up with those amazing world-changing ideas by giving yourself the time and space distraction-free to be creative. . . .

"I talk about unplugging a lot, and people are like, 'Wow, that's such a new concept—so exciting,' and I'm like, 'Well, it's not actually that new. This is like a multi-thousand-year-old concept of Shabbat and unplugging and taking time.'"

RANDI ZUCKERBERG

1982-

A native of New York, Randi Zuckerberg graduated from Harvard University with a degree in psychology. Her brother Mark founded Facebook in 2004, and Randi joined as as one of the first employees, serving as director of marketing and a spokesperson for the company. Randi later founded Zuckerberg Media, and among other pursuits, serves as editor-in-chief (EIC) of Dot Complicated, a digital lifestyle website.

DIVINE REST
THE TEN COMMANDMENTS

Learning Exercise 4

Underline the phrases or words of the Fourth Commandment that are different in the two passages below.

Exodus 20:8–11

זָכוֹר אֶת יוֹם הַשַּׁבָּת לְקַדְּשׁוֹ.
שֵׁשֶׁת יָמִים תַּעֲבֹד וְעָשִׂיתָ כָּל מְלַאכְתֶּךָ.
וְיוֹם הַשְּׁבִיעִי שַׁבָּת לַה' אֱלֹקֶיךָ,
לֹא תַעֲשֶׂה כָל מְלָאכָה אַתָּה וּבִנְךָ
וּבִתֶּךָ עַבְדְּךָ וַאֲמָתְךָ וּבְהֶמְתֶּךָ
וְגֵרְךָ אֲשֶׁר בִּשְׁעָרֶיךָ.
כִּי שֵׁשֶׁת יָמִים עָשָׂה ה' אֶת הַשָּׁמַיִם
וְאֶת הָאָרֶץ אֶת הַיָּם וְאֶת כָּל אֲשֶׁר
בָּם וַיָּנַח בַּיּוֹם הַשְּׁבִיעִי, עַל כֵּן בֵּרַךְ
ה' אֶת יוֹם הַשַּׁבָּת וַיְקַדְּשֵׁהוּ.

Deuteronomy 5:12–15

שָׁמוֹר אֶת יוֹם הַשַּׁבָּת לְקַדְּשׁוֹ
כַּאֲשֶׁר צִוְּךָ ה' אֱלֹקֶיךָ.
שֵׁשֶׁת יָמִים תַּעֲבֹד וְעָשִׂיתָ כָּל מְלַאכְתֶּךָ.
וְיוֹם הַשְּׁבִיעִי שַׁבָּת לַה' אֱלֹקֶיךָ,
לֹא תַעֲשֶׂה כָל מְלָאכָה, אַתָּה וּבִנְךָ
וּבִתֶּךָ וְעַבְדְּךָ וַאֲמָתֶךָ וְשׁוֹרְךָ וַחֲמֹרְךָ
וְכָל בְּהֶמְתֶּךָ וְגֵרְךָ אֲשֶׁר בִּשְׁעָרֶיךָ,
לְמַעַן יָנוּחַ עַבְדְּךָ וַאֲמָתְךָ כָּמוֹךָ.
וְזָכַרְתָּ כִּי עֶבֶד הָיִיתָ בְּאֶרֶץ מִצְרַיִם
וַיֹּצִאֲךָ ה' אֱלֹקֶיךָ מִשָּׁם בְּיָד חֲזָקָה
וּבִזְרֹעַ נְטוּיָה, עַל כֵּן צִוְּךָ ה' אֱלֹקֶיךָ
לַעֲשׂוֹת אֶת יוֹם הַשַּׁבָּת.

Exodus 20:8–11	Deuteronomy 5:12–15
Remember the Shabbat day to sanctify it.	Guard the Shabbat day to sanctify it, as God, your God commanded you.
Six days you shall labor and perform all your work.	Six days you shall labor and perform all your work.
But the seventh day is a Shabbat to the Lord your God. On it you shall not do any work, neither you, nor your son or daughter, nor your male or female servant, nor your animals, nor any foreigner residing in your towns.	But the seventh day is Shabbat for the Lord your God. You shall perform no work, neither you, your son, your daughter, your slave, your maid, your ox, your donkey, any of your livestock, and the foreigner in your gates, in order that your servant and your maid may rest like you.
Because for six days God made the heaven, the earth, the sea, and all that is in them, but He rested on Shabbat. God therefore blessed the day of Shabbat and made it holy.	You shall remember that you were a slave in the land of Egypt, and that God, your God, took you out from there with a strong hand and with an outstretched arm; therefore, God, your God, commanded you to observe the day of Shabbat.

Text 7

ECCLESIASTES 3:19–21

כְּמוֹת זֶה כֵּן מוֹת זֶה, וְרוּחַ אֶחָד לַכֹּל, וּמוֹתַר הָאָדָם מִן הַבְּהֵמָה אָיִן, כִּי הַכֹּל הָבֶל.

הַכֹּל הוֹלֵךְ אֶל מָקוֹם אֶחָד. הַכֹּל הָיָה מִן הֶעָפָר וְהַכֹּל שָׁב אֶל הֶעָפָר.

מִי יוֹדֵעַ, רוּחַ בְּנֵי הָאָדָם הָעֹלָה הִיא לְמָעְלָה, וְרוּחַ הַבְּהֵמָה הַיֹּרֶדֶת הִיא לְמַטָּה לָאָרֶץ.

As the death of a human, so is the death of an animal; each has a vivifying spirit, and the superiority of the human over beast is naught, for all is vanity.

All go to one place. All came from the dust, and all return to the dust.

How many understand, however, that the spirit of the human ascends on high, while the spirit of the beast descends to the earth?

Text 8

RABBI PINCHAS STOLPER, *LIVING BEYOND TIME: THE MYSTERY AND MEANING OF THE JEWISH FESTIVALS* (NEW YORK: SHAAR PRESS, 2003), P. 44

The essence of Shabbos is its ability to free us from the narrow straits of materialism and attach ourselves to the endless values of the spiritual. The prohibitions of "work" on Shabbos are designed to facilitate our ability to pursue this goal, to help us detach ourselves from the world of creativity so that we can enwrap ourselves in spiritual creativity. This is why in Hebrew we call the Sabbath "*Shabbos Kodesh,* the holy Shabbos."

RABBI PINCHAS STOLPER

Rabbinic leader and author. Rabbi Stolper is the founder and national director of the National Conference of Synagogue Youth (NCSY) of the Orthodox Union. He has written numerous books, including *Living Beyond Time: The Mystery and Meaning of the Jewish Festivals.*

LESSON CONCLUSION

Learning Exercise 5

1. In what way is Shabbat already a part of your life?
2. What would your life look like if you decided to integrate more of Shabbat into your routine?
3. What factors are getting in the way of integrating more of Shabbat into your life?
4. What is one piece of advice that you can give yourself that could enrich your Shabbat experience?

Text 9

RABBI ARYEH KAPLAN, *SABBATH: DAY OF ETERNITY* (NEW YORK: NCSY, 1982), P. 44

The Sabbath is more than a mere set of rules. It is another way of life completely, totally divorced from weekday life. When put in handbook form, a different life style may seem very difficult and complex. When lived, however, it is really very easy.

A good example is going off to college. Every university prints a catalog, telling of all its rules and regulations and including a list of courses. If your sole impression of campus life were to be based on this catalog, it would seem impossibly complicated. After all, it takes a 200-page book just to describe it! But once you get there, you learn to live it.

The same is true of Shabbat. You learn to keep the Sabbath by reading books, but that makes it seem impossibly difficult. It is almost like learning about love from a marriage manual. You have to live it to see its true dimensions of beauty.

RABBI ARYEH KAPLAN
1934–1983

American rabbi, author, and physicist. Rabbi Kaplan authored more than 50 volumes on Torah, Talmud, Jewish mysticism, and philosophy, many of which have become modern-day classics. He is best known for his popular translation and elucidation of the Bible, *The Living Torah,* and his translation of the Ladino biblical commentary, *Me'am Lo'ez.*

Key Points

1. The notion of a universal weekend—where an *entire* society would benefit from a day of rest *each week*—was nonexistent in the ancient world. The Torah introduced this concept to the world.
2. There are many observable benefits afforded by the Shabbat oasis. It can be beneficial for work and production. It provides a necessary breather not only to ensure that we don't overwork ourselves to our physical and emotional detriment, but also to ensure that we retain a sense of personal liberty. It helps us to focus on what is important—love and relationships—rather than on what is urgent. It helps us reorient our attention toward the plethora of good and blessings in our lives, which allows for added feelings of gratitude and joy.
3. Jewish mystical sources discuss how the seven-day week is not random but reflective of spiritual phenomena. During the week, the Creator's relationship with the world is somewhat distant, but on Shabbat it is more intimate. Shabbat, therefore, is a holy day and conducive for spiritual exploration.
4. Because Shabbat is a day for spiritual exploration, we revisit the most important ideas and questions about God on this day: His Creation of the world, His involvement in our lives, and the purpose He set out for us. This is why we recall the Creation and Exodus on Shabbat.
5. Everyone can find some element of Shabbat that is within her reach and use that to connect more deeply to her cherished heritage.

ADDITIONAL READINGS

THE SHABBAT EXPERIMENT: LIMITING OR LIBERATING?

By Lisa Sugarman

So consider this (and I mean really take a minute and think this through): No e-mails. No telephones (yes, that includes cells). No TV. No iPods or laptops. No driving. No radio. No electronics whatsoever. Period. For 24 hours.

Imagine giving up everything with an on-off switch. Could you do it? And why would you want to? Would it restrict or release you?

Well, a few months ago in this column I opened my big mouth and admitted to the entire town of Marblehead that every once in awhile I fantasize about chucking all the devices and gadgets in my life just so I could remember what real life feels like. Not permanently, just sort of a reboot for the soul.

Ever since I put it out there it's been on my mind. I wanted to make it happen, but the timing never seemed to be right. Plus, I'd be lying if I said I wasn't a little intimidated by the thought of giving everything up. It sounded great in theory, but when you think about the actual ramifications it ends up looking like a pretty outrageous idea, especially considering how most of us live our lives day to day. We're constantly either refreshing, updating or checking something, and if we're not doing that we're chauffeuring someone somewhere or making a call or using a gadget that's supposed to make the quality of our life better.

But does it?

LISA SUGARMAN

Lisa Sugarman is a wife and mother who writes about her take on parenting, marriage, and life in general in her nationally syndicated humor column, *It Is What It Is,* and in her book, *Untying Parent Anxiety* (2017).

So when the e-mail came in from my daughter's Hebrew school, Chabad, a few weeks ago inviting people to take The Shabbat Challenge I knew someone was sending me a sign that this was my shot. So I took it.

For anyone who doesn't know what's involved in "keeping Shabbat," it means that every week, from sundown on Friday to sundown on Saturday, Jews all over the world unplug. Fifty-two weeks a year. And for those 24 hours, they stay unplugged. They eat, they rest, they reflect, many pray, they spend time with family and friends, and they recover physically and spiritually from their week.

Chabad picked the weekend in late January, and they spelled out the rules: driving, not OK; board games, OK; power, not OK; walking, OK (it's a long list). So for one, full day my family would flip the master breaker and go completely dark. And we decided that if we were going to do it we were going to go all in, which for a Reformed family who practices the most liberal form of Judaism that was WAY in. The fact that it was temporary definitely took the edge off. But it was still intimidating no matter how you looked at it.

So we picked which lights would stay on for the full 24 hours; we unscrewed the light bulb in the fridge so it didn't go on when we opened the door; we cooked everything before sundown on Friday night; we unplugged every device; we picked out all our board games and books. And then it came.

And it was painless.

Without really even noticing, Shabbat settled in and the vibe of our whole house shifted. It was a quietude that was defined by the fact that we knew it would last, even for only a day. All the pressure was gone. The anticipation of rushing or fussing or preparing had disappeared. Once we committed to the challenge, everything was surprisingly easy. And it became shockingly obvious that we all carry around a very misplaced sense of urgency—when there's actually very little that we can't do without.

My brother-in-law gave me the best analogy right before sunset. He said, "There's a beauty created in the quietude of the Sabbath that's difficult to describe or capture otherwise. You need to focus on that quietude rather than on the things you might otherwise be doing."

Then he put it in terms that I could really understand. He said that my sister-in-law made some amazing salsa the other night and also some homemade tortilla chips with a hint of lime. He said he noticed the hint of lime when he ate the chips without the salsa but then forgot all about it once he started dipping into the fiery salsa. After the salsa was gone, he said he started eating the chips dry again and realized how much he liked that subtle hint of lime that was invisible in the context of the salsa. He said the same thing goes for the Sabbath. Enjoy removing the noise to find the quietude that's always there waiting to be revealed.

OK, so we may have bent the rules a little and taught our girls how to play Texas Hold'em to pass the time (gambling can't exactly be promoted on Shabbat, but it's a game, and games are OK). But since flexibility is the real root of Reformed Judaism we cut ourselves some slack.

We also stayed in our pajamas until 4 in the afternoon, getting dressed only to walk down to Preston Beach to see the sunset. And by that point, even the sound of the cars on the road seemed a little intrusive because we were used to such a comfortable quiet. It was a little surreal, at least for me, feeling so far away from home even though I was right there—probably because everything felt so different.

In the end, the 24 hours flew by and we all ended up with much more than we bargained for. It gave us a clarity and peace that would be tough to duplicate any other way. And it changed each one of us somehow, too. My girls said they were shocked at how fast the time went by and how "not boring" the experience was. And my husband, who would sleep with an earpiece in if he could, said he felt amazingly liberated to shut everything down and just walk away. And for him that's big.

Now this doesn't mean we're going all in and making this a weekly thing, but it definitely gave us all something to think about. It showed us that there's a place we can always go to get away—far away, like a "staycation" for the spirit. And those are in right now, aren't they?

So it's ironic: After all that, the real challenge was letting the Sabbath go. Who knew?

The Marblehead Reporter, Feb. 10, 2010
Reprinted with permission of the publisher

THE JEWISH SABBATH MOVEMENT IN THE EARLY TWENTIETH CENTURY

By Benjamin Kline Hunnicutt

During the first three decades of the twentieth century and especially the 1920s, Jewish groups and individuals paid an increasing amount of attention to questions of the Sabbath, how it should be observed and what its larger place was in American culture. The Sabbath also became an important cause for a number of Jews, combining religious purpose with social reform goals. The Sabbath had a practical social dimension since it directly involved the reduction of the work week and as such coincided with labor's demands for the five-day week. Spokesmen for the Sabbath movement supported labor's shorter-hour cause, reasoning that modern industrial developments made jobs harder, more stressful, specialized and unrewarding, and as such increased the practical need for more time off. But concerns about workers' health, safety, and social well-being were joined in the Sabbath movement by larger, more idealistic, and religious motives. Individuals and groups saw in the idea of the Sabbath some profound truths that transcended the workaday world and opened up a new kind of human reform and a new field for "genuine" progress. They came to believe that the Sabbath, as a special time set aside for real human needs and apart from material concerns, provided the model and rationale for the "progressive shortening of the hours of labor"—a labor clause that began to outrun practical reform goals with the beginning of the five-day week. They also saw values contained by the Sabbath that countered modern materialism, "spurious progress," mass, cheap culture, and the philistinism of the "gospel of consumption." Hence these people represented twentieth century's Sabbatarianism as combining a very real improvement of the worker's life (a shorter workweek), a general criticism of a culture and economy sunk in materialism, without a transcendent vision, and a new direction for a qualitatively different type of progress.

One of the main difficulties that Jews fac ed in America during the nineteenth and early twentieth centuries was the loss of Saturday as the historical Sabbath. By law and custom, Americans worked six days a week and, if possible, took Sunday off. Paradoxically, the reason why most Americans worked the six-day week was due in part to a social reform which was sparked by religious concerns, the nineteenth-century Christian Sabbatarian movement. This movement, in the 1820s and 1830s, had a strong social reform motive and a stronger result, although it was heavily sentimental and designed for the most part for religious purposes. But even though Jews and Christians alike shared its social benefits, Jews were denied its religious possibilities. Any deviation from the six-day–Sunday-off pattern was difficult, almost impossible unless one worked the full seven days (even though this was exceptional since blue laws augmented the Sabbatarian's reform). Although the Jewish concern for keeping the Sabbath was as keen as the Christian, Jews were practically prohibited this religious freedom and forced by society and their jobs to observe Sunday as what amounted to a national religious holiday.[1]

BENJAMIN KLINE HUNNICUT

As the professor of leisure studies in the University of Iowa, Hunnicut's focuses his research on our society's relationship with work and leisure time. He has published three books on the subject, most recently *Free Time: The Forgotten American Dream* (2013).

1 David Philipson, *The Reform Movement in Judaism* (New York: Macmillian, 1931), pp. 195-214, 373; *Historical Statistics*

Throughout the nineteenth and early twentieth centuries, Jews faced this problem but never resolved it. The problem also caused a rift among Jews between the Orthodox and Reform leadership. Orthodox spokesmen were afraid that the Sabbath as a unique part of their religion was dying out—being observed more in the breach than in the keeping. Often they would predict that the Sabbath was doomed because of the constraints of the American culture. They saw in the death of the Sabbath one more force that would speed up the assimilation and even the conversion of the Jewish people. For example, Rabbi Israel Herbert Levinthal argued that "if we see Jewish life crumbling before our very eyes in America it is mainly due to the fact that we have lost our Sabbath."[2] That this view was widely held was demonstrated by a joint statement issued by the Union of Orthodox Rabbis of the United States and Canada, the Rabbinical Assembly of America, the Union of Orthodox Jewish Congregations of America, and the United Synagogue of America: "... this violation of the Sabbath, if continued indefinitely, must inevitably lead to the gradual disintegration of our people."[3] For the Orthodox and a number of Conservatives, the preservation of the Sabbath was a precondition to the preservation of American Judaism. The Sabbath also contained ideals and values central to their religion. It was the special, holy time for ritual matters, for community, for family, for tradition, and for the individual and his God, set aside from the busy, materialistic and profane world. A strict observance of that day preserved the forms and institutions of Judaism to be sure, but it also contained central truths that were timeless.

The importance of the Sabbath cannot be overstated. Since prominent Jews were later to graft the traditional ideas associated with the Sabbath onto the larger social reform cause of the "progressive shortening of the hours of labor," some insight into how the Sabbath was viewed during this period is useful. A fine, poetic example may be found in Ben Eliezer's book, *Letters of a Jewish Father to his Son.* In the chapter, "Princess Sabbath," Ben Eliezer stated that "the Sabbath is probably the greatest cultural contribution that the Jews have made to the world," even surpassing "the gift of the idea of the unity of God." The Sabbath has acted both as "a national unifying and cementing influence" for Jews as well as a "universal humanizing factor." Its place in the tradition was assured in talmudic literature with such passages as: "The Sabbath outweighs the whole of the Torah and he who observes it properly has all his sins forgiven." Ben Eliezer, as did many Jews, believed that the observance of the Sabbath put man into contact with his real needs and his true nature, and put the material world into perspective.

What does ... give the Sabbath its sacred significance is the fact that during its 24 hours, there is an abandoning of all material interests, followed by complete retirement into a self-contained spiritual world, free from earthly cares and worries ... For it is only in such an environment, free from the thoughts of daily affairs, that the highest religious and ethical sentiments can come uppermost to mind ... By cultivating such an atmosphere ... [modern Jews] would also grow in knowledge possessed by their forefathers ... that our souls are capable of deriving more lasting pleasure from other joys which raise man beyond the level of mere animal enjoyment, drawing him nearer to the source of the great unknown from which he emanates.[4]

The Sabbath was, in fact, the goal of work and material concerns: the time "longed for ... with the same fervor as a prince awaiting his bride." Labor and "the thought of labor" were important chiefly because they led to the Sabbath and to "its self-contained spiritual world." In this Jews and Christians agreed. The Sabbath was a kind of "escathon" in this world, a taste of that

---

of the United States from Colonial Times to the Present (Washington, D.C.: Government Printing Office, 1975), pp. 155, 172; Robert Moats Miller, *American Protestantism and Social Issues 1919–1939* p. 172.

2 *New York Times,* January 10, 1925, p. 15:2.

3 *New York Times,* September 17, 1926, p. 9:2.

4 Ben Eliezer [pseudonym], *Letters of a Jewish Father to His Son* (London: J. Murray, 1928), pp. 214, 216-217.

eternal Sabbath described by St. Augustine at the end of his *Confessions.*

On the other hand, during the last half of the nineteenth and first quarter of the twentieth century, many progressive rabbis, in an attempt to "modernize" Judaism, held Sunday services and argued that all American congregations should permit Sunday observances. The rabbinical conference at Pittsburgh in 1885 unanimously agreed that:

Whereas we recognize the importance of maintaining the historical Sabbath as a bond with our great past and a symbol of the unity of Israel the world over; and,

Whereas, on the other hand, it cannot be denied that there is a very large number of Jews who, owing to economic and industrial conditions, are not able to attend services on our sacred day of rest; be it:

Resolved, that in the judgment of this conference there is nothing in the spirit of Judaism to prevent the holding of divine services on Sunday, or any other day of the week, where the necessity of such services is felt.[5]

This resolution was reaffirmed in 1902, 1905, 1906 and afterwards, periodically until the 1920s in the Committee on "Weekday Services," by the Central Conference of American Rabbis. The Central Conference also watered down the Orthodox notion of how the Sabbath should be kept, agreeing that activities like tramrides, work at necessary jobs, shaving, and secular amusements were permissible given the realities of the American environment.[6]

In addition, the more radical leadership pressed for the total transfer of the Sabbath to Sunday immediately following the Pittsburgh Conference. The center for this movement seems to have been the *Jewish Tidings*, a publication out of Rochester, New York, which espoused the cause.[7] This notion remained viable in Reform Judaism until 1902 when in New Orleans, after a long and heated debate, the Central Conference committed itself to a struggle for the Saturday Sabbath. The Conference resolved that it was "in favor of maintaining the historical Sabbath as a fundamental institution of Judaism and exerting every effort to enforce its observance."[8]

Despite their disagreement, Orthodox and Reform groups joined together in the struggle for the Saturday Sabbath as it developed from 1903 to 1920. The two most important groups engaged in this movement were the Central Conference of American Rabbis and the Orthodox Jewish Sabbath Alliance. On the one hand, the Central Conference did not vigorously pursue its 1902 commitment. It continued to promote Sunday services (rearranging rituals accordingly) and to interpret Sabbath laws in a more "liberal" manner and seems to have held little hope that Saturday observance and traditional rules could be revived in America. But the Sabbath Alliance took the initiative in the movement and was much more active, fully committing itself to the ideal of the traditional Sabbath.[9]

Nevertheless, during this early period, both groups used the same two techniques. Both endorsed the broader social reform of one day's rest out of seven (a cause supported originally by the Federal Council of Churches of Christ in 1908 and afterwards), but argued that industry and business should make special accommodations for their Jewish workers by allowing them to take Saturday instead of Sunday off. In contrast to the Central Conference's passive endorsement of the scheme (it never got far beyond Conference resolutions), the Sabbath Alliance actively promoted the staggered work week in New York, Boston, Philadelphia, and other major cities where Jews were employed by specific industries in large numbers. Both groups also joined together in opposition to Sunday blue laws. Again the Sabbath Alliance was more active, launching what the *New York*

5 Philipson, *op. cit.*, p. 375.

6 *Yearbook of the Central Conference of American Rabbis,* XV (1905), 60, 61, 72-74; XVI (1906), 87-113; XXIV (1914), 84-91.

7 Stuart E. Rosenberg, "The *Jewish Tidings* and the Sunday Services Question," *Publications of the American Jewish Historical Society,* XLII (June, 1952), 371-385.

8 *Yearbook of CCAR,* XIII (1902), 77, 102-122.

9 *Ibid.,* XVI (1906), 87-113; Frank T. DeVyver, "The Five-Day Week," *Current History,* XXXIII (November, 1930), 223-227.

Times called a national "campaign" against these laws. Hence Jewish Sabbatarianism faced two fronts at first: the rearranging of the work week to allow for free Saturdays and the defeating of blue laws to open up Sunday work. Both were necessary if the Sabbath was to be observed on Saturday in a country where the six-day week was standard.[10]

This original and narrowly focused struggle seemed doomed from the start. The Alliance had little success in promoting the staggered work week since industrial managers were unwilling or unable to administer the production and personnel problems that would have resulted from a reduced and changed work force for two days a week. Progressive businessmen, who supported the six-day work week, were not willing to extend its potential religious benefit to Jews by altering the work force and thereby the very means of production. Even Jewish employers, the target for most of the Sabbatarians' efforts, were not ready to disrupt their businesses for this cause. In addition, some members of the Sabbath Alliance conceded that even in the best of circumstances, the staggered work week could be instituted only by special industries in large cities and would not solve the Sabbath problem for the majority of Jews.[11] Consequently, during these early years, the Central Conference of the Sabbath Alliance devoted most of their efforts against enforcement of the nineteenth-century blue laws and the passing of new ones. But again, in this effort they faced great difficulty. Beginning around 1918 the Lord's Day Alliance, the Central Sabbath Crusade Committee, the International Reform Bureau, and several other Christian organizations were promoting a new and militant campaign for the strict observance of Sunday. The original social gospel concern with the six-day week as a constructive labor reform had by this time deteriorated into a new and repressive drive to eliminate by local and state ordinances and even federal laws all sorts of Sunday activities including movies, newspaper publications, sports, voluntary recreation pursuits, as well as most commerce and all manufacturing. As with Prohibition and immigrant restriction the dark side of modern reform was exhibited by the wave of blue laws passed in the 1920s. In many cases the campaign for strict Sunday observance had anti-Semitic overtones. For example, blue laws in Boston and New York were often enforced selectively against Jews. In addition, leaders of the Lord's Day Alliance such as H. L. Bowlby attacked the Jewish Sabbath Alliance, charging that its efforts were motivated by the desire to give Jews an unfair business advantage on Sunday or else were a front for the movie trade, which, according to Bowlby, was dominated by Jewish interests. The result of the new campaign for strict Sunday observance was a vigorous enforcement of existing blue laws and the passing of numerous new laws by city councils and state legislatures.[12]

In this situation supporters of the Jewish Sabbath could do little except fight a rearguard action. Nevertheless, beginning in 1920, the Jewish Sabbath Alliance began its national "campaign" against blue laws. Its major argument was that such legislation "forced Jews to observe a Christian holiday" and as such violated the Constitutional provision for the separation of church and state. Acting on this assumption, the Sabbath Alliance promoted the introduction of the Dickstein Bill in the New York legislature in 1920, a bill that would have allowed Jews to operate commercial concerns on Sunday (a law similar to statutes in New Jersey and Oklahoma). But because of the rising tide of public sentiment about Sunday reform, this bill was defeated in March, 1921. Several other such bills were introduced in state legislatures in the 1920s, including one proposed by Bernard Downing, senator from

10 John A. Hutchinson, *We Are Not Divided: A Critical and Historical Study of the Churches of Christ in America* (New York: Round Table Press, 1941), p. 104; *New York Times,* May 31, 1909, p. 16:1; December 1, 1920, p. 36:1.

11 *New York Times,* February 7, 1924, p. 20:4.

12 *New York Times,* December 11, 1920, p. 3:8; July 12, 1921, p. 27:2; June 13, 1922, p. 20:3; May 27, 1927, p. 16:2; January 7, 1921, p. 18:3; March 14, 1923, p. 3:5; January 21, 1925, p. 1:4; January 31, 1925, p, 17:1; January 21, p. 5:3; March 7, 1921, p. 28:2; April 3, 1921, p. 14:4; June 27, 1921, p. 15:3; January 17, 1921, p. 28:2; March 5, 1924, p. 17:3.

New York City, that would have prohibited on Saturday all activities prohibited on Sunday. Downing supported his bill by declaring, "if this bill becomes law, it will give 1,600,000 Jews . . . no further justification for saying that legislation designed to compel them to observe our Sunday laws involves discrimination, placing them at an economic disadvantage, . . . and a little more rest and leisure will do us no harm." But these bills had little chance in state legislatures that were passing new blue laws in record numbers.[13]

Moreover, in their fight against blue laws, the Jewish organizations had little help from the courts, although the Sabbath Alliance at first considered them to be a major hope for redress. By the 1920s, the Supreme Court of the United States had twice accepted the constitutionality of Sunday laws, with *Hennington vs. Georgia* (163, U.S. 299, 1896) and *Pettit vs. Minnesota* (177, U.S. 164, 1900), even though never ruling on the First Amendment issue of separation of church and state involved. However, lower courts were laying the foundations for the secular interpretation of these laws, ruling in over fifteen instances that the police power of localities permitted enforcement of Sunday laws, and that they were civil, not religious in purpose, since they permitted everyone to have one day of rest in the week, essential for public order, rest, recreation, health, and welfare. The New Jersey court, for example, held in *Kislingbury vs. Treasurer of Plainfield* (160A. 654, 10 NJ misc. 798) that the New Jersey law exempting Jews and others who observed Saturday from prosecution under the state's Sunday closing ordinance was unconstitutional in its exemption and that the First Amendment did not speak on the issue of Sunday laws.[14]

Hence in their first attempts to free American Jews to observe the traditional Sabbath, the Sabbath Alliance and Central Conference seemed blocked by the nature and requirements of industry, the wave of Christian Sunday reform, legislatures more interested in passing Sunday blue laws than exempting people from them, and courts not willing to apply the First Amendment to this issue. It was only when the Sabbath Alliance began to concentrate on larger labor reform matters that it was able to make headway in its first, primarily religious cause. In the five-day week its members found what seemed to be a natural vehicle for both their concern for the Sabbath and their hopes for more general social justice achievements. Again in support of the five-day week, the Orthodox Sabbath Alliance led the way. It is interesting to note that other more liberal groups were slow to recognize the coincidence of this labor reform and the religious cause. Historians have always supposed that the liberal, reform groups such as the Central Conference were those who advocated this program of social reform, but in the struggle for the Sabbath/five-day week, it was Orthodox Jewry which demonstrated its own brand of social consciousness.

As early as 1910, Rabbi Bernard Drachman, president of the Sabbath Alliance, told that group that the problem of the Sabbath was so interwoven with American conditions that the issue could be resolved only if both Saturday and Sunday were observed as days of rest by "Christians and Jews alike." As the efforts to exempt Jews from Saturday work failed and the attempts to open up Sunday work proved fruitless and generated hard feelings among Christian Sabbatarians, more people came to appreciate the wisdom of Drachman's original vision. Beginning in 1919, the Sabbath Alliance supported local unions in New York, Boston, Philadelphia, and other cities which were launching their campaigns

---

13 *New York Times*, February 9, 1921, p. 3:2; March 24, 1921, p. 3:2; March 24, p. 36:3; March 11, 1924, p. 21:8; *American Jewish Year Book*, XXVI (1924), 24-26.

14 *New York Times*, June 16, 1924, p. 16:3; John J. McGrath, *Church and State in American Law* (Milwaukee: Bruce Publishing Co., 1962), Code Virginia 1930 and 4570, Broad-Grace Arcade Corporation v. Bright, 48 F. 2d 348, affirmed 52 S. Ct. 137, 284 U.S. 588, 76 L. Ed. 507; Ky. St and 1321—Stand Amusement Co. v. Commonwealth, 43 S.W. 2d 321, 241 Ky. 48; Code Pub. Loc. Laws 1930, art. 4 and 6 (18); Const. art. 11A.—Ness V. Ennis, 160 A. 8, 162 Md. 529; Komen v. City of St. Louis, 289 S.W. 838, 316 Mo. 9; *New York Times*, October 12, 1924, Section VIII, p. 11:3, State v. Dean, 184 N.W. 275, 149 Minn. 410; Pirkey Bros. v. Commonwealth 114 S.E. 764, 134 Va. 713, 29, A.L.R. 1290.

for the five-and-a-half day week, a campaign that worked directly toward the institution of Saturday holidays.[15]

It is hard to judge religion's influence on this new labor cause. But since the unions that first pressed for the five-day week were composed mostly of Jews, the desire to revive Saturday observance was very prevalent in Jewish groups, and national Jewish organizations as well as local congregations endorsed the five-day week, a prima facie case has been made that religion was a motive of union members in this cause. But union leaders did not stress the five-day week's religious benefit. In fact, they seldom mentioned it. Instead, they represented their unions with economic and social arguments that were applicable to all workers. There is no way of telling whether economic and social consideration of the desire for the traditional Sabbath was more important for the Jewish union members who were beginning to demand and strike for the five-day week. But since the religious and the economic/social purposes coincided in a practical fashion, and the union's economic/social arguments were endorsed by religious groups and even given a theological dimension, the question of union members' motives may be left unanswered for the purpose of this essay.[16]

The first national union to propose the five-day week was the Amalgamated Clothing Workers Union of America, which passed resolutions for this goal in their biennial conventions, beginning in 1920. Led by Sidney Hillman, this national union worked with local unions, especially in New York, during the decade to incorporate 40-hour clauses in trade agreements, or a clause that committed manufacturers to institute this reform "as soon as possible." But for several local Jewish unions, progress through trade agreements and resolutions was too slow. Strikes were called by the needle trade, the New York City clothing workers, and the Patterson, New Jersey silk workers and several other local unions between 1920 and 1924, which included demands for either the five-and-a-half-day or five-day week. These early strikes were settled for the most part by compromise, the workers agreeing to give up the hours' benefit for higher wages. But beginning in 1924, a series of major successful strikes were called by 50,000 New York City Ladies' Garment Workers' Union members (the largest strike in the nation that year), 40,000 clothing workers in New York City in 1926, 5,000 fur workers in New York and 3,000 in Boston (both in 1926) and all members of the New York and Philadelphia Cloth Hat and Cap Workers' Union in 1927, as well as other smaller unions in children's dresses, bathrobes, and kimonos. In these strikes, the 40-hour/five-day week was a major issue. When coupled with demands for higher wages, the issue dominated. For example, observers of the 17-week strike of the New York furriers concluded that "the main difficulty [prolonging the strike] seems to have been what points the union should barter away in order to gain the forty-hour week." These strikes were successful, so much so that by 1927 the Bureau of Labor Statistics concluded that the five-day work week was "practically the rule in trade agreements in the clothing industry."[17] Together with the painters' and plasterers' unions, other building trades such as plumbers and carpenters, and printing and publishing unions, these unions in the clothing industry with large, Jewish memberships initiated the five-day week movement. That their efforts were productive was demonstrated by the fact that before the war, less than twenty manufacturing establishments nationally had adopted the five-day week. Nearly all of these were managed and staffed by Jews. But during

15 DeVyver, *loc. cit.*, p. 223.

16 Marion C. Cahill, *Shorter Hours: A Study of the Movement Since the Civil War* (New York: Columbia University Press, 1932), p. 253; National Industrial Conference Board, *The Five-Day Week in Manufacturing Industries* (New York: National Industrial Conference Board, 1929), p. 28; *American Jewish Year Book,* XXVI (1924), 24.

17 Matthew Josephson, *Sidney Hillman: Statesman of American Labor* (New York: Doubleday, 1952), pp. 177-180; *Monthly Labor Review,* XVI (August, 1923), 503; XVIII (June, 1924), 1366-1368; XXIII (December, 1926), 1153; XX (June, 1925), 1390-1391; Bureau of Labor Statistics *Bulletin #439* (June, 1924), 373, 374, 573-575; *Bulletin #435,* 20-21.

the 1920s, over 240 manufacturers adopted this plan. By 1929, approximately 400,000 to 500,000 employees were working on a five-day pay basis. The 1920s was truly the decade of the beginning of the five-day work week.[18]

Between 1920 and 1925, the American Federation of Labor had its hands full mopping up "pockets of long hour resistance." Even though the eight-hour day/six-day week had become the norm by the 1920s, enough unions were still struggling to catch up with this standard to occupy the AFL's attention. Although it had endorsed the Amalgamated Clothing Worker's five-day week drive in 1920, it was not until 1926 that the AFL was ready to turn its full attention to this cause as the next logical step in the century-long process of shorter hours. The AFL supported the five-day week as one of its primary goals. But enough options were before it—the six- or seven-hour day and the five-and-a-half-day week—that it chose to commit itself to the larger cause of "the progressive shortening of the hours of labor" during the 1926 Convention.[19]

Jewish organizations actively supported these labor developments. In February, 1924, the convention of Orthodox Rabbis of New York, New Jersey and Connecticut met in New York City and endorsed the five-day week. This convention's efforts to "further the establishment of the five-day-week system" was an outgrowth of the Sabbath Alliance and the local congregations' original support of clothing, fur, and needle trade unions and the joint efforts of several Jewish groups to combat blue laws. A new note of optimism and conciliation was present at the convention. Several speakers (among them Drachman) noted that since opposition of blue laws was failing and bringing "protests from Christians," the five-day week offered a compromise. The convention concluded "so, to please both Jews and Christians, the plan for two days of rest each week was adopted."[20]

The idea gained ground rapidly among Jews and others. In 1925, the Sabbath Alliance formed an interdenominational committee to promote the cause, composed of such men as Drachman, Carlyle B. Haynes, Cyrus Adler, and N. Taylor Phillips. Spokesmen for this group agreed that "this great public reform . . . will . . . tend to remove the greatest causes of friction and religious intolerances existing in America today." Also, in 1925, representatives of several rabbinic bodies (Orthodox, Reform, and Conservative) met in New York to "further the five-day week in American industry." They launched what they called "a vigorous campaign in publications, lobbying, and promotion." Included in these efforts as leaders were M. Z. Margolies, Chaim Block and A. B. Burak of the Union of Orthodox Rabbis, Samuel Schulman and Nathan Stern of the Central Conference of American Rabbis, and "lay organizations" such as the Union of Orthodox Jewish Congregations of America, the Sabbath Alliance, and Young Israel. In addition, beginning in 1924, the United Synagogue of America planned a series of conferences between employers and labor unions "with a view to the establishing of a five-day week in as many industries as possible." By 1927, the Union of Orthodox Jewish Congregations, the Central Conference of American Rabbis, the Rabbinic Assembly, the United Synagogue, and the Union of Orthodox Rabbis of the United States and Canada had endorsed this cause as a general labor reform and in several instances actually encouraged the efforts of local unions, such as the needles trade and the Ladies' Garment Workers'. However, it was the Orthodox groups that took the active leadership role while the Reform group, such

18 National Industrial Conference Board, *op. cit.* pp. 15-24. *Monthly Labor Review,* XXIII (December, 1926), 1153-1169; John P. Frey, "Labor's Movement for a Five-Day Week," *Current History Magazine,* XXV (December, 1926), 369-373.

19 Chester M. Wright, "Epoch-Weakening Decisions in the Great American Federation of Labor Convention at Detroit," *American Labor World,* (1926), 22-24; American Federation of Labor (AFL), *Report of the Proceedings of the 46th Annual Convention* (Washington, D.C.: AFL, 1926); see especially the Report of the Committee on the Shorter Workday, pp. 195-207; Sidney Hillman, "Attitude of Organized Labor Toward the Shorter Work Week," *Monthly Labor Review,* XXIII (December, 1926), 1167-1168.

20 *New York Times,* February 7, 1924, p. 20:4.

as the Central Conference, acted mostly as a cheering section.[21]

The primary concern of all the groups and individuals was, of course, the revitalization of the Sabbath observance on Saturday. The five-day week cause and its successes turned the original pessimism of Reform Jews into a new enthusiasm and proved to be a justification for the Orthodox leadership's holding onto the cause. But Jewish Sabbatarianism was altered and expanded by the five-day week issue. The issue led naturally to larger concerns: broad scale labor reforms and general questions about economic development and cultural progress. The five-day week served the practical cause of Jewish Sabbatarianism to be sure; but Jewish Sabbatarianism, as expanded by the issue, served in turn to justify the broader labor reform of the "progressive shortening of the hours of labor" and to inform the cultural, social, and economic debate about the decreasing importance of work and the increasing importance of free time.

Rabbi Israel Herbert Levinthal expressed the logical broadening of the argument for the Sabbath in this way:

I can see but one way to save the Sabbath for the Jew, and that is through the establishment of the five-day week.... I would favor the five-day week even if I were not interested in the preservation of the Jewish Sabbath. I would favor it because it would add health and strength to the American people. It would promote the home and home life, giving the father an added opportunity to become more intimately acquainted with ... his children.[22]

In a like manner, other prominent Jews who supported the five-day week agreed with the social and economic arguments of union leaders. During the struggle for the ten-hour day, the eight-hour day, and the six-day week, unions relied on fairly simple, common sense arguments. They had stressed safety factors, health benefits, moral considerations, and increased production in their defense of the earlier advances. But with the beginning of the 40-hour/five-day week drive and the commitment to "the progressive shortening of the hours of labor" these earlier, generally acceptable goals were less applicable. It was not clear at all that Saturdays off improved production, was necessary for rest, or made the work place safer. Union leaders found that they had to discover new arguments to justify this new reform.

To do this men such as William Green, president of the American Federation of Labor, Matthew Woll, vice-president of the AFL, A. O. Whorton, president of the International Association of Machinists, and Sidney Hillman, founder and president of the Amalgamated Clothing Workers of America turned their attention to the larger economy. They suggested that shorter hours were essential in order to deal with chronic unemployment and with general overproduction—new problems of the new era. These union leaders, and others, especially in the New York garment industry, firmly believed that with increasing mechanization, the economy was beginning to be overbuilt and the demand for goods such as textiles was being saturated. As production "outran the rate of natural consumption," general overproduction and chronic, acute unemployment would soon follow. In order to deal with these two new developments, they stressed two solutions—higher wages and shorter hours. Higher wages would allow workers to buy the necessities of life and as such increase the consumption of certain types of traditional products. Shorter hours, on the other hand, would create more jobs and would act to increase wages.[23] But they would also limit production that was beginning to outstrip demand. As A. O. Wharton put it:

---

21 *New York Times,* May 10, 1926, 21:4; January 14, 1925, 5:3; September 17, 1926, p. 9:2; *Yearbook of CCAR,* XXIV (1924), 51; *American Jewish Yearbook,"* (1925), 26-28.

22 *New York Times,* January 10, 1925, p. 15:2.

23 William Green, "The Five Day Week," *American Federationist,* XXXIII (November, 1926), 1299, 1300; for Green and Woll's attitudes see also American Federation of Labor, *op. cit.,* pp. 195-207; for Hillman's view see "Attitude of Organized Labor Toward the Shorter Work Week," *Monthly Labor Review,* XXIII (December, 1926), 1167-1168; William Green, "Leisure for Labor," *Magazine of Business,* LVI (August, 1929), 136-137; James M. Lynch, "Shorter Working Day Urged as Alleviation for Depression Cycles," *American Labor World* (November, 1926), 28, 29.

> Increased production accentuates the problem of overproduction or underconsumption. Increased wages and reduced hours go hand in hand with increased production. . . . Economic balance can be maintained only if . . . wages advance and leisure hours increase. If some sort of balance is not maintained, we are headed straight for disaster.[24]

Unions were perhaps the first major group in American history to suggest that economic growth had a limit, a limit being reached in the 1920s and as such made the limiting of production necessary to stabilize the new, mature economy.

Bernard Drachman echoed the arguments of the union officials. He pointed out "the only cure for overproduction is limitation of production" since "it is perfectly possible under modern methods of production, that commodities can be produced in quantities greater than can be consumed. . . ." He also suggested that as a result, technological unemployment, especially in the garment industry was increasing and would continue to increase as technology outran the "rate of natural consumption. . . . The machines invented in recent years . . . with uncanny, almost demoniacal super ability . . . accomplish . . . tasks formerly requiring the labor of thousands and for the . . . displaced multitudes no opportunities of employment present themselves." Drachman saw shorter hours as a way to improve the workers' bargaining position for higher wages (by making labor scarce and hence more valuable) and also to deal with unemployment caused by overproduction. Shorter hours would distribute fairly the available work which was diminishing and would limit production to "reasonable levels." He concluded that he supported "the idea of the shorter work week, not only on economic grounds, but also on social, cultural, and spiritual grounds." This reform would stabilize the economy and help deal with unemployment. But it would also provide a new kind of freedom from material concerns and a new opportunity for human achievements by the masses.[25]

Union leaders also stressed the fact that work had lost its ethical and human dimensions and was becoming increasingly hard and "dehumanizing." As such, it had increased the importance of leisure. Formerly, they believed, work had been a place for creativity, community, craftsmanship, the way for social mobility, and the vehicle for self expression, personal fulfillment, and individualism. But modern means of production had changed all that, creating jobs that were specialized, repetitive, boring and routine as well as establishing a permanent industrial labor force. As William Green put it,

> there must be a progressive reduction of the hours of labor, so that men and women may have time to rebuild their exhausted physical energies. This is more than ever important in the highly specialized process of modern industry, where speed and monotony tax physical existence to the utmost.

He saw the AFL policy as a "complement of labor's long struggle to prevent work from becoming deading toil." Sidney Hillman agreed that the "speed and strain of American industry was always greater."[26]

Green, Woll, and Hillman also defended the "leisured proletariat" by criticizing the "devitalized nature of modern work" and by renewing their support of traditional values that had been lost in modern occupations. Green, for example, insisted in order that ". . . our social and human values may not be merged with the machines until, they too, become mechanical, shorter hours [were] essential because they safeguard our human nature" and "lay the foundation for the higher development of spiritual and intellectual powers." He predicted "a dawn of a new era, leisure for all" and "a revolution in living" because of reduced hours.

24 James L. Wright, "Is the Machine Replacing Men?" *Nation's Business* (September, 1927), 79.

25 Bernard Drachman, *Looking at America* (New York: Books for Libraries Press: 1934), pp. 97-102.

26 William Green, "Leisure for Labor," *loc. cit.*, pp. 136-137; William Green, *The Five-Day Week: Inevitable* (New York: American Federation of Labor: 1932), pp. 1-6; Wright, "Is the Machine Replacing Man?" *loc. cit.*, p. 79.

He saw leisure as a new opportunity for craftsmanship, creativity, community development, for fellowship, the "finer things in life" such as "music, art, literature, and travel," as a way "to worker's education" and "increased knowledge of technological principles," and for "recreation and recuperation . . . necessary to sustain vigor." For Green, gradually increasing leisure could redeem traditional values that had been lost at work, as well as open up new democratic vistas for the masses.[27]

Matthew Woll, like other union leaders, criticized work in new forms and looked to leisure to compensate workers for human values that they had lost. But he also criticized that fact that "unfortunately, our industrial life is dominated by the materialistic spirit of production, of work and more work, giving little attention to the development of the human body, the human mind, or the spirit of life. . . . All the finer qualities of life are entirely ignored." The dehumanized nature of modern jobs was complicated by the "materialistic spirit" of the business community. For Woll, increasing leisure was both a "restraining influence" limiting production to basic needs as well as a hedge against the material values of the "New Era."[28]

Jews active in the Sabbath movement agreed with the idea that work was becoming less rewarding and meaningful and that leisure offered the opportunity to recover some of the old values that work once had. Felix Cohen, for example, offered a parable of the modern economy that was able to provide the necessities of life and still supported work as a prime virtue.

Adam's children inherited the [curse of work] and soon learned to make a virtue of necessity. Idleness came to be regarded as a sin rather than a source of love, art, inspiration, and wisdom. Offered a chance by "God's messenger" or by the machine to slip the bonds of toil, men chose instead to "sing new hymns in praise of the sweetness of chains" and hold onto work because "they had so long praised each other . . . for industriousness. . . . The message of the machine is that we shall work without end."

According to Cohen, much of that work was useless. It no longer had the firm, external sanction of necessity. Work was being channeled in absurd directions: the production of useless or shoddy articles, advertising and a new industry, war. If useless work were abolished, then the work week could be reduced to "thirty hours immediately" and a "general working week of ten hours is then a fairly immediate possibility," given the rate of increased productivity. For Cohen, work's new forms—specialization, mechanization, and impersonal organization—destroyed the old nineteenth-century ideals about work's value, such as creativity, craftsmanship, self-fulfillment. In this he agreed with the union leaders. But he also suggested that work's purpose—its product—had been undercut by the machine. Much of modern work was useless, was without a firm purpose because there was "no natural" use for its product. Consequently work had been made a demigod—a thing worshipped for its own sake. It mattered little if its products were useless. One consumed them out of respect for this supreme virtue, like it or not.[29]

Sabbatarians, such as Cohen, extended the union leaders' arguments and engaged in the larger economic debates about overproduction with a new breed of economic businessmen. In contrast to the union and some pessimistic businessmen who were stressing limited production, most businessmen and economists were entering, practically and ideologically, a new age of mass consumption. They did not accept the argument that human needs for industrial products were finite or set by some nineteenth-century idea of human nature. Instead they took a new view of economic growth. They promoted what Edward Cowdrick called

27 Green, "Leisure for Labor," *loc. cit.*, pp. 136-137; Green, "The Five-Day Week," *loc. cit.*, pp. 567-574.

28 Matthew Woll, "Labor and the New Leisure," *Recreation*, XXVII (1933), 418; Matthew Woll, "Leisure and Labor," *Playground*, XIX (1925), 322.

29 Felix Cohen, "The Blessing of Unemployment," *The American Scholar*, II (1933), 203-214.

the "new economic gospel of consumption." In their view, the best way to deal with unemployment and overproduction was not to limit production by reducing working hours, but by stimulating demand. For many businessmen, if supply exceeded demand, then the reasonable response was to increase and insure consumption of those goods in oversupply through new domestic and foreign markets, advertising and even higher wages. They were sure that Americans would naturally (or be convinced to) buy those things produced by industry which they had never needed before and consume goods and services, not in response to some set of economic motives, but according to a standard of living that constantly improved. They concluded that human needs were social and plastic, capable of being molded to fit the needs of a growing economy by the hard work of marketing experts, advertisers and business leaders.[30]

Businessmen's new interest in consumption had been well documented as well as their optimism that demand could be stimulated. Herbert Hoover's Committee on Recent Economic Changes, however, presented one of the first and finest examples of this documentation. The Committee pointed out that "economists have long declared that consumption, the satisfaction of wants, would expand with little evidence of satiation, if we could so adjust our economic processes as to make dormant demands effective." But businessmen had proven this assumption in the 1920s. This "almost insatiable appetite for goods and services, this abounding production of all things which almost any man could want, which is so striking a characteristic of the period covered by the survey" eliminated suspicion that the demand could be saturated and markets limited. The Committee found that people . . . have become steadily less concerned about the primary needs—food, clothing, shelter. . . . The slogan of the "full dinner pail" is obsolete. . . . Our wants have ranged more widely and we now demand a broad list of goods and services which come under the category of optional purchases.

It is in the area of "optional purchases" that the Committee saw the best hope for economic advance. Criticizing the pessimists' ideas about "remote saturation points" the Committee observed that

the survey has proved conclusively what was long held to be theoretically true, that our wants are almost insatiable, that one want satisfied makes way for another. The conclusion is that economically we have a boundless field before us; that there are new wants that will make way endlessly for newer wants as fast as they are satisfied. . . . As long as the appetite for goods and services is practically insatiable, as it appears to be, and as long as productivity can be consistently increased, it seems that we can go on with increasing activity.[31]

Union leaders did not meet this argument head on. But some Jewish supporters of the five-day week did. For example, Abba Hillel Silver, later president of the Central Conference of American Rabbis, saw in the Sabbath movement a direct counter argument—one that justified the "progressive shortening of the hours of labor" and opposed what he called the

30 Report of the 15th Annual Meeting of the Chamber of Commerce, "Prosperity and Production," *Nation's Business*, XV (May 20, 1927), 40, 41; William Foster and Waddill Catchings, "What is Business Without a Buyer?" *Nation's Business*, XIV (June, 1926), 27; William Craig, "Digest of the Business Press," *Nation's Business*, XIV (June, 1926), 14; Glen Buck, "This American Ascendancy," *Nation's Business*, XV (March, 1927), 15; "Business Views in Review," *Nation's Business*, XV (July, 1927), 117; (August, 1927), 95; Edward Cowdrick, "The New Economic Gospel of Consumption," *Industrial Management*, LXXIV (October, 1927), 208; Irvin S. Paull, "When is Industry's Job Complete?" *Nation's Business*, XV (December, 1927), 28, 29; James L. Wright, "Is the Machine Replacing Man?" *Nation's Business*, XV (September, 1927), 78-80, for views about increased consumption by James Maloney and Secretary of Labor David, who argued that "the luxuries of yesterday become the necessities of today"; Merle Thorpe, "The Amazing Decade," *Nation's Business*, XVI (September, 1928), 9; J. H. Collins, "Producer Goes Exploring for the Consumer," *Saturday Evening Post*, CXCV (April 7, 1923), 8; T. C. Sheehan, "Must We Limit Production?" *Magazine for Business*, LIII (February, 1928), 150-152.

31 Report of the President's Committee on Recent Economic Changes, *Recent Economic Changes* (New York: National Bureau of Economic Research, 1929), pp. xv, xviii, 52, 59, 80, 81, 574-578.

"philistine" gospel of consumption. He began by describing the Sabbath as representing "the day of rest, the consecrated covenant between God and man." As such it was "much more than mere relaxation from labor. It is a sign and symbol of man's higher destiny."[32] The five-day week could help solve the economic problem of overproduction and unemployment to be sure. But the progressive shortening of the hours of labor could open up a new field of human progress. Increased leisure could provide a time for culture, for learning, for individual creativity and freedom, for the appreciation of life and creation, for spiritual exercise, and for essential rituals, those things which Ben Eliezer ascribed to the Sabbath as the "universal humanizing factor." Silver suggested "we must say to ourselves . . . so far shall I go in my pursuit of the things of life and no further. Beyond that I am a free man, a child of God. Beyond that I have a soul and I must give to it time, energy, and interest." He saw in the gospel of consumption a new way in which "our population has been victimized." Just when the opportunity for real human development had been opened through technology and increased free time, it had been closed again by businessmen intent on selling the "golden fleece" of useless luxuries and "excessive wealth." For Silver, human needs for industrial products could still be defined—they were not infinite. Increased productivity and job specialization had created two potential avenues of progress, one spurious and one genuine. If Americans chose to pursue "success" defined in terms of the piling up of useless luxuries, they would turn their backs on the more human form of progress offered by reduced working hours. For Silver, the Sabbath was the pattern for a new form of progress, being cut in the American economy by shorter hours and increased leisure for human, non-material needs.[33]

The job preparing individuals for "worthy use of leisure" was great. But Silver saw the new wealth of free time as a force revitalizing the church, the family, and the school. As people who were able to spend more of their time and energy in these more human institutions, they would naturally learn how to use their time to develop their higher potentials and humane interests.

Moreover, according to Silver, it was no longer possible to assume that all work was valuable because of its extrinsic results. The relationship between work and the necessities of life was becoming increasingly tenuous. Businessmen and economists ignored this problem. Instead, they had begun to understand work and increased wealth as indeterminant values, relative to no set of given, basic or higher standards. Yet, they continued to support and value these things. As such, work, increased production and consumption were redefined as ends in themselves, values to be used to judge other economic and social needs. Losing extrinsic justification, these things took on intrinsic values during the decade. For Silver, these ideas were a corruption of that which was truly valuable in itself—that which Ben Eliezer describes as "the highest religious and ethical sentiments." For him, the Sabbath was the only true "telos" in its "self-contained spiritual world," the model for a qualitatively new kind of progress through increased leisure. Businessmen and economists had entered the realm of philosophy and theology in their "gospel of consumption," promoting the old virtue of work and economic growth by new, virtually existential arguments. Silver believed that work and increased productivity were still instrumental in that they could meet rational needs and then lead to real virtues through shorter hours of work—to human activities that were really worth doing for their own sake.[34]

The Jewish Sabbath movement, beginning as a narrowly focused attempt to allow Jewish workers to have free Saturdays and to work on

32 Abba Hillel Silver, "Leisure and the Church," *Playground*, XX (January, 1927), 539.

33 Abba Hillel Silver, *Religion in a Changing World* (New York: Richard R. Smith, Inc., 1930), pp. 63, 77, 143-146, 184-187, 190-194.

34 Samuel Strauss, "Things are in the Saddle," *Atlantic Monthly* (November, 1924), 577-588; *idem, American Opportunity* (Boston: 1935), pp. 182-193.

Sunday, broadened in two stages. Failing in the first limited attempt, the movement flourished in the second stage as a supportive part of the general labor movement for the five-day week. Finding practical success in this reform, individuals in the Sabbath movement then went on to engage in even larger economic and social debates about modern progress and work, using the Sabbath model as a philosophical base. Certainly many Jews were content with the five-day week's practical accomplishments. It did, after all, satisfy their original purpose and constitute a significant social reform. But others such as Drachman, Cohen, and Silver went on to support the "progressive shortening of the hours of labor," reasoning that as human needs for industry's products were met, increased technology and productivity should free the worker from his job for other, "higher" pursuits. They understood the economy as beginning to offer two avenues for progress—increased wealth and luxuries or increased leisure. Rejecting the first option as a philistine "chasing after the phantom of insatiable desires," they supported the second as the way to authentic progress, humanistic rather than materialistic, individualistic rather than collective. They saw in the Sabbath the "symbol of man's higher destiny" and in increased leisure the practical opportunity to broaden and spread the Sabbath's values and truths.

American Jewish History 79:2 (Dec. 1979), pp. 196–225

pause & AFFECT

LESSON 2

Glow of Peace

ROSHCHODESH society

SHABBAT IS COMING!

Text 1

ELIE WIESEL, *WISE MEN AND THEIR TALES* (NEW YORK: SCHOCKEN BOOKS, 2003), P. 328

One can never speak enough of what Shabbat was like in the shtetl—and what it did for its inhabitants. Shabbat helped people endure the other six days of the week, often gray and dark, heavy with sorrow and anxiety. Hence the waiting for Shabbat, which actually began much earlier. Thursday evening or early Friday morning, the housewife would already be busy preparing the hallah, gefilte fish, and cholent, the traditional elements of a Shabbat meal in the shtetl. The white tablecloth, the white shirt: everything had to be ready. . . . We couldn't wait for her arrival.

In the stores, business was conducted with haste. Sellers and customers were equally in a hurry to go home. Men would go to the *mikvah,* then dress and prepare to be worthy of welcoming the Shabbat, already on the horizon. The first to spot her would be the beadle, the shammash: he would go around stores and homes shouting "*Yiden, greit zicht tzu Shabbes!*"—Jews, ready yourselves for the Sabbath! Or a variation on the same theme: "*Yiden, s'is bald Shabbes oif der velt!*"—Jews, it's almost Shabbat in the world!"

ELIE WIESEL
1928–2016

Writer, professor, and political activist. Wiesel was born in Sighet, Romania, and was deported by the Nazis to Auschwitz when he was 15. He is the author of more than 40 books of fiction and non-fiction, including the acclaimed memoir *Night*, which has been published in more than 30 languages. In 1986, Wiesel won the Nobel Prize for Peace. He has received numerous awards, including the Presidential Medal of Freedom and the U.S. Congressional Gold Medal.

Text 2

BELLA CHAGALL, *BURNING LIGHTS: A UNIQUE DOUBLE PORTRAIT OF RUSSIA* (NEW YORK: SCHOCKEN BOOKS, 1988), PP. 48–49

With a match in her hands she lights one candle after another. All the seven candles begin to quiver. The flames blaze into mother's face. As though an enchantment were falling upon her, she lowers her eyes. Slowly, three times in succession, she encircles the candles with both her arms; she seems to be taking them into her heart. And with the candles, her weekday worries melt away.

She blesses the candles. She whispers quiet benedictions through her fingers and they add heat to the flames. Mother's hands over the candles shine like the tablets of the decalogue over the holy ark.

I push closer to her. I want to get behind her blessing hands myself. I seek her face. I want to look into her eyes. They are concealed behind her spread-out fingers.

I light my little candle by mother's candle. Like her, I raise my hands and through them, as through a gate, I murmur into my little candle flame the words of benediction that I catch from my mother.

My candle, just lighted, is already dripping. My hands circle it to stop its tears.

I hear mother in her benedictions mention now one name, now another. She names father, the children, her own father and mother. Now my

BELLA CHAGALL
1895-1944

Writer; wife of Marc Chagall. Born Bella Rosenfeld in Vitebsk, Russia to a Chasidic family, she married Chagall in 1915, and after living in Paris for a few years, they immigrated to the US following the outbreak of World War II. Her major work, *Burning Lights,* was written in Yiddish and published posthumously by her husband.

name too has fallen into the flame of the candles. My throat becomes hot.

"May the Highest One give them his blessing!" concludes mother, dropping her hands at last.

"Amen," I say in a choking voice behind my fingers.

"Good Shabbes!" mother calls out loudly. Her face, all opened, looks purified, I think that it has absorbed the illumination of the Sabbath candles.

A GUIDE TO CANDLE LIGHTING

WHEN DO WE LIGHT?

Shabbat candles must be lit before sunset because that is when Shabbat begins, and it is forbidden to kindle a fire on Shabbat itself. Conversely, one shouldn't light the candles too early on a Friday—not more than roughly 1¼ hours before sundown—so that it will be clear that you are lighting in honor of Shabbat. In many communities, the custom is to light the candles eighteen minutes before sunset (and some communities have other customs in this regard). This is the candle-lighting time that we see on our calendars. If candles were not lit before the eighteen minutes, they should be lit during the eighteen minutes, but not after sunset.

For the proper candle-lighting time for any date and location, go to: www.chabad.org/candlelighting.

WHO SHOULD LIGHT?

The mitzvah of lighting Shabbat candles applies to men and women. However, if there is a woman (over the age of bat mitzvah) in a home, she lights the candles for the entire household.

In prewar Europe, there was a custom in some circles for girls to kindle Shabbat candles in addition to those kindled by their mothers. However due to war, candle shortages, and other logistical issues, this custom was discontinued in these communities. The Lubavitcher Rebbe initiated a campaign to reinstate this practice, encouraging every Jewish girl to light her own candle. Girls can start lighting Shabbat candles as soon as they start speaking and can recite the candle-lighting blessing, around the age of three.

Because by lighting Shabbat candles a person marks personal acceptance of Shabbat and may no longer do any of the forbidden Shabbat activities, including striking a match or lighting a candle, young girls light before their mothers so that she may assist them.

WHAT TYPE OF CANDLE AND HOW MANY?

We may use wax candles or oil of any color or shape for this mitzvah; the main consideration is that the flames emit a clear continuous light, which prevents us from needing to adjust the flame to make it burn brighter, an act prohibited on Shabbat. All candles manufactured today emit a clean stable flame and are kosher for lighting. The candles should be long enough to burn until nightfall, and ideally, until after the meal.

The mitzvah can technically be fulfilled by lighting only one candle. However, there are various customs with regards to the number of candles women light. The established custom is for single girls and women to light one candle, and married women to light (at least) two. Many women have the additional custom of lighting one additional candle upon the birth of each child, increasing the light as the family grows.

WHAT IS THE PROCEDURE FOR LIGHTING?

1. Set the candles on a metal tray in a location that is out of the reach of young children and clear of flammable objects.
2. The candles should ideally be visible from the table on which the Shabbat meal will be eaten.
3. It is customary to light the Shabbat candles while dressed in Shabbat clothing.
4. It is appropriate to place some money in a charity box before lighting the Shabbat candles.
5. Light the candle(s).
6. Do not extinguish the match, but let it burn down on the metal tray upon which the candles are standing.
7. Circle your hands over the flames and toward yourself three times. Cover your eyes with your hands, and recite the following blessing:

בָּרוּךְ אַתָּה יְיָ אֱלֹהֵינוּ	Baruch ata Ado-noy
מֶלֶךְ הָעוֹלָם אֲשֶׁר	Elo-hai-nu Melech
קִדְּשָׁנוּ בְּמִצְוֹתָיו	ha'olam asher kid-
וְצִוָּנוּ לְהַדְלִיק נֵר	sha-nu b'mits-vo-tav
שֶׁל שַׁבַּת קוֹדֶשׁ.	v'tsi-vanu li-had-leek ner
	shel Shabbat Kodesh.

Blessed are you, Lord our God, King of the universe, Who has sanctified us with His commandments, and commanded us to kindle the light of the Holy Shabbat.

8. While your eyes are still covered, take a moment to silently pray for whatever your heart desires, as these moments—while one is immersed in the mitzvah of lighting the Shabbat candles—are an auspicious time for prayer. It is customary to use this special time to beseech God for children who will be illuminated by the radiance of the Torah, and to ask God to illuminate the world with the light of redemption.

9. Open your eyes and say "Shabbat Shalom," or "Good Shabbos" to all who are present.

THE FUNCTION OF SHABBAT CANDLES
IN A TIME OF DARKNESS

Text 3

RABBI EPHRAIM OSHRY, *SHA'ALOT UTESHUVOT MIMA'AMAKIM* 1:11

I was asked in 1942 by fellow inmates in the Kovno Ghetto whcther they might fulfill the mitzvah of lighting Shabbat candles by using electric lights, and whether they might recite the blessing *lehadlik ner shel Shabbat* on those lights. These were people who all their lives had been careful to fulfill this mitzvah, but now they were unable to obtain candles because they had no money, and it was anyway impossible to find candles because we were locked up in the ghetto. But the wicked ones did allow electricity to flow into the ghetto.

RABBI EPHRAIM OSHRY
1914–2003

Halachist. Rabbi Oshry was a young rabbinical scholar in Kovno, the second-largest city in Lithuania, when the Nazis invaded in June 1941. He carefully recorded the halachic questions that Lithuanian Jews asked him during the war, as well as his responses—writing them on bits of paper torn from cement sacks he carried on forced labor—and buried them in tin cans. He dug up the cans after the war and used these notes as the basis for his collection of Holocaust responsa, the five-volume *She'elot Uteshuvot Mima'amakim.*

PEACE THROUGH LIGHT

Text 4a

TALMUD, SHABBAT 23B

אָמַר רָבָא, פְּשִׁיטָא לִי: נֵר בֵּיתוֹ וְנֵר חֲנוּכָּה - נֵר בֵּיתוֹ עָדִיף, מִשּׁוּם שְׁלוֹם בֵּיתוֹ. נֵר בֵּיתוֹ וְקִידּוּשׁ הַיּוֹם - נֵר בֵּיתוֹ עָדִיף, מִשּׁוּם שְׁלוֹם בֵּיתוֹ.

Rava said: It is obvious to me that if [one cannot afford both and must choose between] the Shabbat candle and the Chanukah candle—the Shabbat candle is preferable on account of the peace in the home. And [if one must choose between] the Shabbat candle and wine for *kiddush,* the Shabbat candle is preferable on account of the peace in the home.

BABYLONIAN TALMUD

A literary work of monumental proportions that draws upon the legal, spiritual, intellectual, ethical, and historical traditions of Judaism. The 37 tractates of the Babylonian Talmud contain the teachings of the Jewish sages from the period after the destruction of the 2nd Temple through the 5th century CE. It has served as the primary vehicle for the transmission of the Oral Law and the education of Jews over the centuries; it is the entry point for all subsequent legal, ethical, and theological Jewish scholarship.

Text 4b

RASHI, SHABBAT 25B

וּבְמָקוֹם שֶׁאֵין נֵר, אֵין שָׁלוֹם, שֶׁהוֹלֵךְ וְנִכְשָׁל וְהוֹלֵךְ בַּאֲפֵילָה.

In a place where there is no lamp, there is no peace, for a person stumbles about and gropes in darkness.

RABBI SHLOMO YITSCHAKI (RASHI)

1040–1105

Most noted biblical and Talmudic commentator. Born in Troyes, France, Rashi studied in the famed *yeshivot* of Mainz and Worms. His commentaries on the Pentateuch and the Talmud, which focus on the straightforward meaning of the text, appear in virtually every edition of the Talmud and Bible.

Learning Exercise 1

"We are all the same."

Where on the continuum below would you place this attitude? Is it more conducive to peace or discord?

Peace — Discord

"We are all different."

Where on the continuum below would you place this attitude? Is it more conducive to peace or discord?

Peace — Discord

Text 5

RABBI YEHUDAH LOEW, *CHIDUSHEI AGADOT*, SHABBAT 25B

וְיֵשׁ לְךָ לָדַעַת, כִּי אֵין נִקְרָא שָׁלוֹם רַק הָאוֹר בִּלְבַד, מִפְּנֵי שֶׁהוּא נוֹתֵן הֶבְדֵּל בֵּין הַדְּבָרִים, וְזֶהוּ הַשָּׁלוֹם כַּאֲשֶׁר יֵשׁ הֶבְדֵּל בֵּין הַדְּבָרִים.

כִּי כַּאֲשֶׁר נִקְרָא הַחוֹשֶׁךְ עֶרֶב, מִפְּנֵי שֶׁבְּחוֹשֶׁךְ הַדְּבָרִים הֵם מְעוּרָבִים, וְאֵין נִכָּר זֶה בִּפְנֵי זֶה . . . וְהָאוֹר נִקְרָא בּוֹקֶר שֶׁעַל יְדֵי הָאוֹר יֵשׁ בִּיקּוּר בֵּין הַדְּבָרִים בֵּין זֶה לָזֶה.

וְכַאֲשֶׁר יֵשׁ בִּקּוּר בֵּין דָּבָר לְדָבָר הוּא הַשָּׁלוֹם אֲשֶׁר הוּא בֵּין הַדְּבָרִים, וְאֵין אֶחָד נִכְנַס וּמִתְעָרֵב בַּחֲבֵירוֹ רַק כָּל אֶחָד בִּפְנֵי עַצְמוֹ.

וּלְפִיכָךְ נִקְרָא נֵר שַׁבָּת שָׁלוֹם.

Know that only light is referred to as "peace" because it provides distinction between different things. Peace requires distinction between things.

Darkness is called *erev*—mixture—because in darkness all items are jumbled together and we cannot distinguish one from the other. . . . Light is called *boker*—examination—because in light we can examine things and distinguish between them.

When we can examine differences, this brings peace between things, for one thing does not invade or mix into the domain of the other thing, rather each remains within its own place.

This is why Shabbat light is called peace.

RABBI YEHUDAH LOEW (MAHARAL OF PRAGUE)
1525–1609

Talmudist and philosopher. Maharal rose to prominence as leader of the famed Jewish community of Prague. He is the author of more than a dozen works of original philosophic thought, including *Tiferet Yisrael* and *Netsach Yisrael*. He also authored *Gur Aryeh,* a supercommentary to Rashi's biblical commentary, and a commentary on the non-legal passages of the Talmud. He is buried in the Old Jewish Cemetery of Prague.

Learning Exercise 2

List three differences between you and a family member or coworker. Describe how those differences can make you a more efficient team.

EATING WITH EYES

Text 6a

NUMBERS 11:5–6

זָכַרְנוּ אֶת הַדָּגָה אֲשֶׁר נֹאכַל בְּמִצְרַיִם חִנָּם, אֵת הַקִּשֻּׁאִים וְאֵת הָאֲבַטִּחִים וְאֶת הֶחָצִיר וְאֶת הַבְּצָלִים וְאֶת הַשּׁוּמִים. וְעַתָּה נַפְשֵׁנוּ יְבֵשָׁה אֵין כֹּל, בִּלְתִּי אֶל הַמָּן עֵינֵינוּ.

We remember the fish that we ate in Egypt free of charge, the cucumbers, the watermelons, the leeks, the onions, and the garlic. But now, our spirits are parched, for there is nothing at all; we have nothing but manna to look at.

Text 6b

MIDRASH PELI'AH, BINAT NEVONIM 81

זָכַרְנוּ אֶת הַדָּגָה: מִכָּאן שֶׁמַּדְלִיקִין נֵרוֹת בְּשַׁבָּת.

"We remember the fish"—from here we learn that we light Shabbat candles.

MIDRASH PELI'AH

Midrash Peli'ah (literally, mysterious Midrash) consists of ingenious riddles. Typically, these riddles link a verse in the Torah with a seemingly unrelated concept, and the answer usually relies on a third concept from elsewhere that explains the connection. Most of these riddles were composed by rabbinic figures in Poland in recent centuries, though the ideas they convey are usually from the Talmud or Midrash. There are numerous collections of *Midrash Peli'ah*. Rabbi Yitzchak Lipietz of Shedlitz published one such volume with his commentary, *Binat Nevonim,* in Warsaw in 1895.

Question for Discussion

Can you solve this riddle? What is the connection between the fish in Egypt (or the lack thereof in the desert) and Shabbat candles?

Text 7

AMY BRIGGS, "WHAT YOU SEE IS WHAT YOU TASTE, SAYS SCIENTIST," *NATIONAL GEOGRAPHIC VOICES*, APRIL 12, 2013; HTTP://VOICES.NATIONALGEOGRAPHIC.COM

Speaking at the National Meeting of the American Chemical Society, Terry E. Acree, PhD, announced his findings that the appearance of foods and drinks can make people "see" flavors before they actually taste anything, a phenomenon that can influence their flavor experiences, food likes, and dislikes. . . .

Traditionally, scientists have thought the tongue, nose, and brain dominated how people experience the flavors of the food, but Acree's work reveals how the visual can forcefully come into play. "Years ago, taste was a table with two legs—taste and odor," said Acree, who is with Cornell University's Department of Food Science.

"Now we are beginning to understand that flavor depends on parts of the brain that involve taste, odor, touch and vision. The sum total of these signals, plus our emotions and past experiences,

AMY BRIGGS

Freelance writer and author. Amy Briggs is the former senior editor with National Geographic Books. She has authored *National Geographic Angry Birds Space* and regularly contributes to *National Geographic* on a plethora of topics.

result in perception of flavors, and determine whether we like or dislike specific foods." . . .

Acree described how people's eyes can deceive them when it comes to different foods and beverages. In his talk, he described how looking at a glass of wine before smelling or tasting it affects how people experience the wine's flavors.

Sauvignon Blanc, a popular white wine, has lots of flavors derived from natural chemicals. When people drink it, they may taste banana, passion fruit, bell pepper, and even a flinty, mineral taste. But if a flavorless food coloring is added to the Sauvignon Blanc to turn it a deep red, people's taste perceptions change. They taste flavors associated with merlots or cabernets, wines known for their deep red colors.

Text 8

RABBI MENACHEM MEIRI, *BEIT HABECHIRAH*, SHABBAT 25B

הַדְלָקַת נֵר בְּשַׁבָּת חוֹבָה מִדִּבְרֵי סוֹפְרִים מִפְּנֵי שֶׁהִיא רֹאשׁ לְכָל עוֹנֶג, שֶׁאֵין עוֹנֶג בְּלֹא אוֹרָה.

Lighting Shabbat candles is a rabbinic obligation because light is a prerequisite for all pleasure. There can be no pleasure where there is no light.

RABBI MENACHEM ME'IRI
1249–1310

Talmudist and author. Me'iri was born in Provence, France. His monumental work, *Beit Habechirah,* summarizes in a lucid style the discussions of the Talmud along with the commentaries of the major subsequent rabbis. Despite its stature, the work was largely unknown for many generations, and thus has had less influence on subsequent halachic development.

HONOR BEFITTING A QUEEN

Text 9a

RABBI SHLOMO GANZFRIED, *KITSUR SHULCHAN ARUCH* 72:7

וִיתַקֵּן אֶת הַבַּיִת, וְיַצִּיעַ אֶת הַמִּטּוֹת, וְיִפְרוֹס מַפָּה עַל הַשֻּׁלְחָן . . . וְיִשְׂמַח בְּבִיאַת הַשַּׁבָּת. וְיַחְשׁוֹב בְּדַעְתּוֹ אִלּוּ הָיָה מְצַפֶּה שֶׁיָּבוֹא אֵלָיו אֵיזֶה אָדָם יָקָר וְחָשׁוּב אֵיךְ הָיָה מְתַקֵּן אֶת הַבַּיִת לִכְבוֹדוֹ, וּמִכָּל שֶׁכֵּן לִכְבוֹד שַׁבָּת מַלְכְּתָא.

One should clean the house, make the beds, and spread a tablecloth over the table to remain there the entire Shabbat. . . . One should rejoice at the arrival of Shabbat, thinking to oneself, "If I were expecting an important guest imagine how I would prepare! All the more so in honor of the Shabbat queen."

RABBI SHLOMO GANZFRIED
1804–1886

Rabbi and halachic authority. Rabbi Ganzfried was born in Uzhhorod (today part of Ukraine), and after being orphaned at a very young age, he was adopted by Uzhhorod's chief rabbi, Rabbi Tzvi Hirsh Heller. Rabbi Ganzfried is best known for his *Kitsur Shulchan Aruch*, a user-friendly summary of the Shulchan Aruch and the observations of subsequent halachic commentators. This highly acclaimed work quickly became a classic, a mainstay in every Jewish home.

Text 9b

RABBI SHLOMO GANZFRIED, IBID., 72:16

יִשְׁתַּדֵּל שֶׁיִּהְיוּ לוֹ בְּגָדִים נָאִים . . . שֶׁלֹּא יְהֵא מַלְבּוּשׁךְ שֶׁל שַׁבָּת כְּמַלְבּוּשׁךְ שֶׁל חוֹל. וַאֲפִילוּ אִם הוּא בַּדֶּרֶךְ בֵּין הַנָּכְרִים יִלְבַּשׁ בִּגְדֵי שַׁבָּת, כִּי אֵין הַמַּלְבּוּשִׁים לִכְבוֹד הָרוֹאִים אֶלָּא לִכְבוֹד הַשַּׁבָּת.

One should try to have elegant clothes . . . so that the Shabbat garments should not be like the weekday garments. Even if one is on the road amongst those who are not celebrating Shabbat, one should wear one's Shabbat clothes, because the clothing is not for the honor of one's company, but rather in honor of Shabbat.

Text 9c

MAIMONIDES, *MISHNEH TORAH*, LAWS OF SHABBAT 30:5

וְצָרִיךְ לְתַקֵּן בֵּיתוֹ מִבְּעוֹד יוֹם מִפְּנֵי כְּבוֹד הַשַּׁבָּת, וְיִהְיֶה נֵר דָּלוּק וְשׁוּלְחָן עָרוּךְ וּמִטָּה מוּצַעַת שֶׁכָּל אֵלּוּ לִכְבוֹד שַׁבָּת הֵן.

One must clean the home before sunset in honor of Shabbat. A candle should be lit, a table set, and a bed prepared, all in honor of Shabbat.

RABBI MOSHE BEN MAIMON (MAIMONIDES, RAMBAM)
1135–1204

Halachist, philosopher, author, and physician. Maimonides was born in Cordoba, Spain. After the conquest of Cordoba by the Almohads, he fled Spain and eventually settled in Cairo, Egypt. There, he became the leader of the Jewish community and served as court physician to the vizier of Egypt. He is most noted for authoring the *Mishneh Torah,* an encyclopedic arrangement of Jewish law, and for his philosophical work, *Guide for the Perplexed.* His rulings on Jewish law are integral to the formation of halachic consensus.

THE RULING

Question for Discussion

Knowing what you do regarding the objectives meant to be achieved through candle lighting, what do you think Rabbi Oshri's response should have been: Are electrical lights permitted to be used as Shabbat lights, and may one recite the blessing recited over them?

SHARING THE LIGHT

Text 10a

MIDRASH, *BEREISHIT RABAH* 60:16

כָּל יָמִים שֶׁהָיְתָה שָׂרָה קַיֶּמֶת, הָיָה נֵר דוֹלֵק מִלֵּילֵי שַׁבָּת וְעַד לֵילֵי שַׁבָּת. וְכֵיוָן שֶׁמֵּתָה, פָּסַק אוֹתוֹ הַנֵּר. וְכֵיוָן שֶׁבָּאת רִבְקָה, חָזַר.

During Sarah's lifetime, a lamp burned from Shabbat eve to Shabbat eve. When she died, this lamp ceased. When Rebecca came, the lamp returned.

BEREISHIT RABAH

An early rabbinic commentary on the Book of Genesis. This Midrash bears the name of Rabbi Oshiya Rabah (Rabbi Oshiya "the Great") whose teaching opens this work. This Midrash provides textual exegeses and stories, expounds upon the biblical narrative, and develops and illustrates moral principles. Produced by the sages of the Talmud in the Land of Israel, its use of Aramaic closely resembles that of the Jerusalem Talmud. It was first printed in Constantinople in 1512 together with four other Midrashic works on the other four books of the Pentateuch.

Text 10b

RABBI SHMUEL BORNSTEIN, *SHEM MISHMUEL*, CHAYEI SARAH 5671

וְעִנְיָן נֵר דוֹלֵק מֵעֶרֶב שַׁבָּת לְעֶרֶב שַׁבָּת, הַיְינוּ שֶׁיְּמֵי הַחוֹל לֹא קִלְקְלוּ אֶת הָאוֹר שֶׁהִשִּׂיגוּ בְּשַׁבָּת קוֹדֶשׁ. וְאִם כֵּן כְּשֶׁבָּאָה שַׁבָּת שְׁנִיָּה, נִיתּוֹסַף אוֹר עַל אוֹר.

The light that burned from Shabbat eve to Shabbat eve displayed that the weekday did not tarnish the holiness that they achieved on the sacred Shabbat. Accordingly, when the following Shabbat would arrive, it brought [not a return to a previous state but] an added influx of light to what they had already achieved.

RABBI SHMUEL BORENSTEIN
1855–1926

Chasidic Rebbe. Rabbi Borenstein was born in Poland into a distinguished rabbinic family. His father and primary teacher, Rabbi Avraham—known by the title of his halachic responsa *Avnei Nezer*—was the first Rebbe of Sochatchov, and his maternal grandfather was Rabbi Menachem Mendel Morgenstern, the Rebbe of Kotzk. In 1910, Rabbi Shmuel succeeded his father as Rebbe of Sochatchov and established a yeshivah there. He is best known for the collection of his Chasidic sermons, *Shem MiShmuel*, which has gained wide popularity.

Text 10c

THE LUBAVITCHER REBBE, RABBI MENACHEM MENDEL SCHNEERSON, *LIKUTEI SICHOT* 15:171

בִּפְנִימִיּוּת הָעִנְיָנִים אִיז דָאס אַזוֹי בַּיי יֶעדֶערֶער וָואס בֶּענְטְשְׁט לִיכְט. הֲגַם אַז בְּעֵינֵי בָּשָׂר זֶעט מֶען דָאס נִיט, וָוארוּם – וויבַּאלְד אַז "מַעֲשֵׂה אָבוֹת" אִיז אַ "סִימָן" אוּן אַ נְתִינַת כֹּחַ לַ"בָּנִים" – הָאט יֶעדֶערֶע, וָואס אִיז בַּת שָׂרָה וְרִבְקָה וְכוּ' דֶעם כֹּחַ אַז דִי מִצְוָה לִיכְטִיקַיְיט פוּן אִיר שַׁבָּת-לִיכְט זָאל פּוֹעֵל זַיין אוֹיף דֶער גַאנְצֶער וָואךְ.

Everything that occurred in the lives of our patriarchs and matriarchs is both a lesson and an empowerment for their progeny. Therefore, on some level, what occurred with the matriarchs occurs to anyone who kindles the lights of Shabbat, even if we cannot readily observe this. When a descendant of Sarah and Rebecca kindles the Shabbat candle, she has the power to extend the light of this mitzvah in a way that affects her home for the entire week.

RABBI MENACHEM MENDEL SCHNEERSON
1902–1994

The towering Jewish leader of the 20th century, known as "the Lubavitcher Rebbe," or simply as "the Rebbe." Born in southern Ukraine, the Rebbe escaped Nazi-occupied Europe, arriving in the U.S. in June 1941. The Rebbe inspired and guided the revival of traditional Judaism after the European devastation, impacting virtually every Jewish community the world over. The Rebbe often emphasized that the performance of just one additional good deed could usher in the era of Mashiach. The Rebbe's scholarly talks and writings have been printed in more than 200 volumes.

Learning Exercise 3

Candle-lighting time presents a special opportunity to pray for our lives and homes to be filled with peace and light and to meditate upon the various symbolic aspects of this mitzvah. Based on what you have learned, write a short prayer/meditation for yourself for when you light Shabbat candles (in addition to the ritual blessing that you will recite).

Key Points

1. The precious moments of candle lighting transport us from the peak of the weekly grind to the deep inner peace of Shabbat. It is a ritual that leaves a potent impression on our children.
2. As with all areas of Jewish law, there are specific regulations for how and when the Shabbat candles are to be lit.
3. The Lubavitcher Rebbe initiated a campaign encouraging every Jewish woman and girl to light her own Shabbat candle(s).
4. In 1942, Rabbi Efraim Oshri was asked by fellow inmates in the Kovno Ghetto whether they might fulfill the mitzvah of lighting Shabbat candles by using electric lights. That they even asked such a question indicates that their devotion to Judaism exceeded the Nazi efforts to demoralize and dehumanize them.
5. There are three reasons why the sages instructed that we kindle lights before Shabbat: (a) for peace—so that the darkness in the home not lead to impatience, flaring tempers, and discord; (b) for pleasure—we cannot really enjoy the lavish foods of Shabbat without light; and (c) for honor—having candles lit in the home as Shabbat makes its entry honors this sacred day.
6. The ideal way of honoring Shabbat is realized when we use a form of light not generally used during the weekday. It is for this reason that Jewish women have for centuries designated a special candelabra to be used exclusively for Shabbat candles. This is also one of the reasons why we kindle flames for this mitzvah, as opposed to using electricity.
7. When one has no access to candles or oil, one may fulfill this mitzvah with electric lights.

8. In a deeper sense, Shabbat candles promote peace in a symbolic way. Light allows us to notice differences, whereas darkness conceals them. When we recognize peoples' differences, we will notice how each person offers something unique that complements everyone else. This realization generates respect and harmony.
9. When we kindle the special lights for Shabbat, we provide our homes with a sacred energy that remains with us all week.

ADDITIONAL READINGS

SHABBAT CANDLES

By Carrol Kasser

"The dimly burning wick shall he not quench." (Isaiah 42:3)

It was Friday afternoon, and the Jewish nursing home residents filled the activity room for Shabbat services. I lit the Shabbat candles—two tapers of the same size, lit from the same match. Yet one candle burned with a large orange flame and the other produced a minute, barely visible flicker of blue. "That one isn't lit," called out several of the residents. I looked again and saw that the blue flicker was still barely visible. I said the blessings, and as always I felt the spirit of Shabbat fill the room as the residents joined me in singing *Shalom Aleichem, Peace to You*. But my eyes kept going back to those two candles, the one blazing; the other just flickering. When it came time for my sermon, I threw out what I had prepared, and talked instead about those candles. It occurred to me that those candles were a metaphor for humanity. All of us were given the same spark of Divinity from the same Source. Yet some let that spark shine forth and brighten the world; others squelch the soul-light until it is almost extinguished. They show nothing of their soul-light to the world.

After flickering through most of the service, the little light suddenly burst into full flame. And that too was a metaphor for humanity. No matter how dark our lives have been, no matter how hard we have tried to extinguish our soul-light, it never goes out completely. And with repentance and change of heart, it is never too late to let G-d's light within us shine and brighten the world.

I think the metaphor of the candles is particularly appropriate for the nursing home residents. For some of them, in pain, frail, forgetful, life must seem like that flickering blue candle, but for a moment, during Shabbat, when they join in prayer, the life and the soul blaze forth brightly again.

I think again of Dr. Fishman, the silent man in the end state of Alzheimer's, who broke his silence to say, "Good Shabbos." I realize that for that one brief moment, I had seen a flicker again become a flame. And that is why life, even when it is reduced to a flicker, is so precious. . . . I am sometimes given the blessing of seeing the Divine spark shine forth from "the dimly burning wick."

CAROL KASSER

Carol Kasser is a children's book writer. Also known as "Bubbie, the Book Lady," she offers interactive book-writing workshops for children of all ages. Kasser received her doctorate in English education from Temple University.

Cast Me Not Off When I Am Old: A Sourcebook for the Aging, Their Families, and Caretakers. (Lincoln, NE: iUniverse, 2004), p. 39
Reprinted with permission of the publisher

SHABBAT POEMS

By Zelda Schneersohn Mishkovsky

MY MOTHER'S ROOM WAS LIT

The pale painter mixed in the wet paint
the faintest of pinks
the glory of apple blossom, a babe's smile.
Silver clusters he put, and brass crowns
engraved
in the candlesticks of inheritance,
glittering on the chest,
reflected in a round mirror,
(orchards of love from generation
to generation and the crowns of
lineage and tears).
And on the table, through the tales of the
righteous, the golden tales,
(that Rabbi Zevin gathered, collected),
a mountain breeze leafs slowly slowly,
mixing snowy landscapes with an arid
landscape.
My mother is praying—on her head, silken
checkers.
The big inner room is as dark
as Rabbi Shim'on bar Yochai's cave.
In it, a sea's silence—
in it, Sabbath, as if it were the world to come.
The entire flat is still.
My husband went to his office.
My mother is in the palace of her
prayers.
I'm in the kitchen.
And in the tin can, a geranium overflows
like blood.
In the paved courtyard, by the plants,
a cat is pacing like a landlady from the old
generation.
Slowly slowly
the door opens
to milk, to bread, to candles,
to taxes, to a letter.
Friday is the day of a laughing eye painted blue,
and the day of the sad mouth.
Friday is the day of the poor.
So pass the days,
so pass the years.
Faint light shall cover pain, helplessness,
mistakes.
So pass the days and the roaring life,
abounding with desires, buds, babes, seas and
forests,
stealthily deserting my limbs, spilling
like blood.
When I die,
God shall unravel my embroidery
thread by thread,
and to the sea throw my paints,
to His warehouses in the abyss.
And perhaps He shall turn them to a flower and
perhaps He shall turn
them to a butterfly,
dark-nocturnal-soft; dark-nocturnal-alive.

ZELDA SCHNEERSOHN MISHKOVSKY
1914–1984

Born in Slupsk, Poland, Zelda's family immigrated to Jerusalem when she was twelve years old. She worked as a school teacher before marrying and dedicating herself to writing. Known simply as Zelda, her poetry was awarded the Bialik, Brenner, and Wertheim Prizes. It is considered emotive and alive, drawing from the world of Jewish mysticism and Russian folklore. She was a first cousin of the Lubavitcher Rebbe, and some of their correspondence has been published.

THE SILVER CANDLESTICKS

The silver candlesticks, the radiance of
inheritance,
turned my room to an ancient castle,
to a heavenly castle, to a lofty abode on a starry
nothingness.
The silver candlesticks are songs of glory,
crowns scoured by tears,
which gladden the heart
with their engravings,
brighten the darkness
with wreaths of forged roses.

They are vessels of sensitive
greatness, which absorbed
bitter pain,
a weeping uprooting
the voice of praise and hope.
To silver flowers I likened them,
to ancient silver flowers,
whose calyxes hold the light of peace,
the joy of babes
and a candle of blessing to the Eternal One.
Their living flames
kissed my soul,
and my thoughts became a river of rose-colored flowers,
became fowls from the wild forests,
became lightning.

And all of me is a burning being
free, happy in God,
who has thrown off herself the tatters of conventions,
and my heart is again wide as a white cascade.
Where is the winsome one who fashioned
this diadem to rest,
who cast rejoicing and trembling like ornaments
for the Sabbath?
In metal he set down yearning for ancient holiness,
his desire for a living God,
I will hold in my hand.
These silver stems
are a prayer, a confession.

Bring forth wine, pour to the hidden!
I will beseech him, I will atone,
for I've forgotten that he is a silent crescent
in Death's forests,
that his name is buried in snow and his memory,
the storm blotted out,
only his tear is still warm,
and from my eye is spilling
at night, this evening,
with the flickering of the candles.

A SABBATH CANDLE

My heart asked the evening,
my deep and compassionate companion:
How can fire
sprout golden wings
and embark on a magical flight.
What is its secret?
A lonely flower replied to the heart:
Love is the root of fire.
The sea breeze
answered my thoughts:
The lily of all freedom in the universe,
this is the fire of wondrous light.

My blood hearkens—
and weeps bitterly.
Woe, a flame—even an auto-da-fe.
It was also said—
fire is a wondrous mockery of dust.

Is it proper for a mortal woman,
soft of heart,
to roam and wander
in the garden of fire?
How dare she
in the smoke of waste conjure
the ember of peace,
an ember with which Sarah Bat Tovim
would light
a Sabbath candle in the gloom of pain.
Between the walls of nightmare
it would bloom, burning slowly
in the crumbling house, in the pit.
Facing it, the woman of sorrowful depths
shut her eyes,
to worry, to mourning, to shame, to the mundane.

The candle's sparks are palaces,
and in the midst of the palaces
mothers sing to the heavens
to endless generations.
And she wanders in their midst
toward God, with a barefoot baby
and with the murdered.
Hurrah!
The soft of heart comes in dance
in the golden Holy of Holies, inside a spark.

SABBATH AND WEEKDAYS

To light candles in all the worlds
this is Sabbath.

To light Sabbath candles
is the leap of a soul pregnant with secrets,
mysterious with the fire of sunset,
to a magnificent sea.
As I light the candles, my room
turns to a River of Fire,
my heart sinks in emerald waterfalls.

But on the first day of the week
my soul is thrown
from the ocean's heart to a land's shore
long, narrow, and desolate.
When I come to the store
the grocer immediately senses
that I've come from another planet, and
with dismay
surveys my looks, foreign to him, the
remnant of the abyss—
and in his cold pupils, as if in a black mirror,
I see my crumpled scarf, my embarrassed smile.
And in the store stands another woman, a
round lady,
slowly selecting golden fruit,
a creature of a distant world.
I wake up from a daydream
when the tone of the air, the rhythm of
voices change, for the short one discovered
that her money was gone . . . Woe to me!
The dark grocer pours dung of suspicion
on my disheveled, neglected looks. Before
his gaze
my future wilts like a flower, my past withers.
My dreams are dying.
Woe to me for I'm alone in the thick of the
forest,
in the darkness, a roaring lion answers
my weeping, and mute trees
set on me from all sides . . .
The door is open, but I cannot get out
from the store's trap.
Now I see with cruel clarity
how little a person knows about one's fellows—
even your household
members, even your dear ones, may
in a moment of eclipse
find in you any wicked fault.
I drown in the darkness . . .

Suddenly, in the very heart of blindness,
I heard a voice:
Truth will not die with the grocer,
Truth will not die with the short lady,
Truth will not die with your death.
My soul awakened, and trembling
sensed that the King of Glory was with her
in the foul store.

I always said:
The voice of God is over the mighty waters,
The voice of God is in the song of the morn-
ing stars,
The voice of God is in the whirlwind.
And here
in the heart of the tumult, the Lord
of Winds gathered me,
on the waves of hatred as on a viscous stone
I came in dance before Him,
I raised my voice in song
to truth, whose footstool are sun, moon,
and stars.
I almost kissed the grocer,
for behind his worried back was revealed to me
the view of shining freedom,
the freedom of the lands of the Sabbath
which burns in the songs of the palace dwellers.

I did not lose favor with the butterfly
in paradise and with the winds
that roar above the sea.
I did not bow before the glance that sees
in my cheeks the wrinkles of defeat
but doesn't see my soul that roams
in the fullness of the universe, doesn't know
that my soul is a ray of the sun
and will not be caught in the palm.

Selected poems from "Seven Poems by Zelda," Trans. Varda Koch Ocker, Judaism, 54:1–2 (2005)

SHABBAT IN THE SHTETL

By Dr. Elie Wiesel

On Shabbat, if poverty did not vanish altogether, it was attenuated. One can never speak enough of what Shabbat was like in the shtetl—and what it did for its inhabitants. Shabbat helped people endure the other six days of the week, often gray and dark, heavy with sorrow and anxiety. Hence the waiting for Shabbat, which actually began much earlier. Thursday evening or early Friday morning, the housewife would already be busy preparing the hallah, gefilte fish, and cholent, the traditional elements of a Shabbat meal in the shtetl. The white tablecloth, the white shirt: everything had to be ready, and everything was the housewife's responsibility. One easily forgets that we owe the gift of Shabbat to the queen of the home, *Shabbat malka,* the Shabbat queen. We couldn't wait for her arrival.

In the stores, business was conducted with haste. Sellers and customers were equally in a hurry to go home. Men would go to the *mikvah,* then dress and prepare to be worthy of welcoming the Shabbat, already on the horizon. The first to spot her would be the beadle, the shammash: he would go around stores and homes shouting "*Yiden, greit zicht tzu Shabbes!*"—Jews, ready yourselves for the Sabbath! Or a variation on the same theme: "*Yiden, s'is bald Shabbes oif der velt!*"—Jews, it's almost Shabbat in the world! At home, one did not need these reminders: the mother, mine too, lit the candles honoring Shabbat, one for each member of the family, and blessed them silently, with gestures of grace and tenderness. Suddenly, her face would be illuminated by a light coming from another world, from another time, a light at once frail and eternal. And her beauty was multiplied sevenfold. So that even now as I am writing these words, the tears well up in my throat.

In the shul also, everything was different. More luminous, the candelabras. More serene, the faces. More melodious, the prayers. The Talmud is right: on Shabbat, one gains an added soul, the *neshama yeteira.*

Then, at the end of the service, many worshipers began running toward the visitors in shul. If there were none the shammash would yell aloud, "Are there strangers here?" It was forbidden, absolutely forbidden, to allow anyone to be without an invitation to partake with some family in a Shabbat meal. Frequently people would fight over a visitor. It was an honor to invite him or her to their table. I myself can hardly remember a Shabbat without an honored guest in our home.

Whenever my maternal grandfather, Reb Dodye, was with us, we would feel double honored. And I was three times as happy. I have sworn never to forget him, nor his return from the Shabbat-eve office. He would stop on the threshold, kiss the mezuzah, and, his face burning with delight, start the Wizsnitzer "*Sholem aleikhem malakhei ha'shareit*"—Be blessed, angels in the service of peace. And it was as if peace now reigned over the heaven and earth, a peace that brought together men and women of all nations, of all ages, a dream of which Shabbat remains the uplifting and inspiring symbol.

The end of Shabbat was signaled by mother and grandmother. Shortly before the Havdalah ceremony, which separates light from darkness

---

ELIE WIESEL

1928–2016

Writer, professor and political activist. Wiesel was born in Sighet, Romania, and was deported by the Nazis to Auschwitz when he was 15. He is the author of more than 40 books of fiction and non-fiction, including the acclaimed memoir *Night,* which has been published in more than 30 languages. In 1986, Wiesel won the Nobel Prize for Peace. He has received numerous awards, including the Presidential Medal of Freedom and the U.S. Congressional Gold Medal.

and the sacred from the profane, the Shabbat from the weekdays, both women, like all mothers, would recite the special prayer attributed to the great Rebbe Levi-Yitzhak of Berditchev: *"Gott fun Avrohom, Yitzhok un Yankev . . ."* God of Abraham, Isaac, and Jacob, extend your protection over Thy children and ours . . . When the prayer ends, the Havdalah begins. Whereupon another song takes hold of my memory: *"Bobeshi, zog nokh nit Gott fun Avrohom . . ."* It's a little child pleading with his grandmother not to recite her prayers, not yet, let her wait a bit longer, the sun hasn't set yet in the west, let Shabbat last a while longer . . . The little child loves the Shabbat and refuses to leave it behind—to be left behind.

Which, of course, recalls an old Hasid or rebbe who, during the mystical Third Meal, is doing in his way what the grandmother could have done in hers. He sings a song: *"Ven ich volt ge'hat koi'ekh,"* if I had the strength, *"volt ich in di gassen gelofen,"* I would run through the streets, *"un ich volt geshere'in hoikh,"* and I would yell with all my might, *"Shabbess, heiliger shabbess,"* Holy, holy Sabbath . . . And legend has it that as long as he sang, the Shabbat would remain with him and his followers. So he sang and sang . . .

Wise Men and Their Tales (New York: Schocken Books, 2003), pp. 328–330
Reprinted with permission of the publisher

THE MEANING BEHIND THE FLAMES

By Rhona Lewis

My mother bought me a gift: a glass cube in the center of which is carved the image of a woman lighting candles. This gift stands sparkling next to my Shabbat candlesticks. Every week, when I hurry to kindle my Shabbat lights, I feel the warmth of my mother's love.

Sometimes, I marvel at the powerful simplicity of the image engraved within my gift. Over centuries the image of a woman lighting Shabbat candles has been captured in every medium—canvas, glass, silk, clay, silver. What makes this image so evocative, so powerful and eternal?

To try and understand this, let's go to where the mitzvah, the commandment of lighting Shabbat candles, is first mentioned. In Parshat Yitro, G-d gives us the Ten Commandments and tells us to remember *(zachor)* Shabbat. In Parshat Va'etchanan, Moshe repeats the commandments and tells us to safeguard *(shamor)* Shabbat. This is a warning not to violate the sanctity of the day. Our sages tell us that at the time the Torah was given, G-d uttered the words *shamor* and *zachor* simultaneously, to teach us that both are equal parts of the Shabbat commandment. To commemorate this, the sages instructed us to kindle lights. The minimum mitzvah, as they instituted, is to kindle one light. Nevertheless, the universally accepted custom is to kindle two lights, thus hinting at both dimensions of *shamor* and *zachor*.

The commentary Ohr Hachayim explains why the first mitzvah of Shabbat is the kindling of lights. Why don't we make kiddush first? Shabbat is actually a celebration of the Creator and His Creation. G-d's creation of the world follows a seven-day cycle, which peaks each Shabbat and begins anew. At Creation, the first thing that was brought into being was light. Therefore, it is appropriate to kindle lights at the start of Shabbat in commemoration of the first light that was created.

Now let us look a little more deeply into what this light was. The light was not sunlight, for the sun and the other luminaries were created on the fourth day of creation. The Gemara tells us that the light created on the first day enabled a person to see from one end of the world to the other. Then, when G-d saw that corrupt generations would arise, He took this light, hid it away, and saved it for the righteous people to come.

Now, while most of us cannot see this light, the spiritual glow that comes into the home upon kindling Shabbat lights is certainly available to us all. As my six-year-old daughter observed one Friday night when we were all seated around the table eating the freshly baked challah, "Mummy, why is the light in the house different on Shabbat?" I looked around the living room. The cream and beige room was bathed in a soft, golden light. How could I have thought it was simply a glow cast by my candles?

Now that we know why kindling lights is the first mitzvah we do as Shabbat approaches, let us look for the meaning behind the flames.

We kindle Shabbat candles for *kavod Shabbat* and *oneg Shabbat*: to honor and to enjoy Shabbat. Candles are lit to lend an air of dignity to the gathering and to brighten the meal, which cannot be enjoyed in the dark. Rashi explains that "... without light there can be no peace, because [people] will constantly stumble and be compelled to eat in the dark."

Rashi's words tell us something else too. As a result of bringing light into the home and helping us practically, light also brings peace. Does this mean only that because people can see they won't bump into each other, they will eat with ease, and therefore everyone will be at peace? What is the deeper meaning?

Light is referred to as peace, because it gives us the ability to distinguish between different

---

RHONA LEWIS

Born and raised in Kenya, Lewis lives in Jerusalem with her family. She contributes to a number of Jewish magazines.

things, and thus to perceive the uniqueness of every person. When we have light, we can recognize the sublime qualities inherent in each other, and in this way we have peace. Peace, *shalom*, comes from the word *shalem*, which means completeness. When people relate to each other in a way that they see the whole person and are not caught up in the differences between them, the externalities that so often irk and irritate, then they can get along with each other peacefully. Peace is unity: it is the joining of separate parts that leads to completeness. Peace is what I feel when, at the end of a day of frenzied preparations, I kindle the lights and then sit down with my daughters, each one so very different from the other, and sing *Lecha Dodi*, the song that welcomes in Shabbat.

There is another way in which kindling lights increases peace. The Talmud tells us that a woman who regularly kindles Shabbat lights is rewarded with children who are Torah scholars. Rashi expounds on this idea using the verse, "For a candle is a mitzvah and the Torah is light." This means that through the mitzvah of lighting candles, she will merit the light of Torah. The Gemara also tells us that Torah scholars increase peace in the world. Hence the connection between the Shabbat candles and peace.

Let us now look at some of the more practical applications of kindling Shabbat lights. Shabbat lights are usually kindled by lighting wax candles or wicks floating in oil. Why not simply switch on an electric light? After all, technically, switching on an electric light ought to be sufficient.

But a candle is special because it is similar to a soul. First, just as the flame depends on the material candle, the soul depends on the body to express its potential in this world. Second, a flame gives light, which is in essence intangible, like the soul which is intangible. Finally, just as a flame is always reaching upwards, a soul is always striving to reach upwards to higher levels and to its source.

The Shulchan Aruch states that it is preferable to light with olive oil, for it burns with a particularly bright and steady flame. Today there are candles that burn as well as olive oil, so many consider them to be as good as olive oil. Even so, many people continue to light with olive oil. Why? The Gemara compares Torah scholars to olives and olive oil. It has been posited, therefore, that those who light particularly with olive oil will be rewarded with sons who are Torah scholars.

Another reason for using olive oil is that only pure olive oil was used to light the menorah in the Beit Hamikdash. Since our candles recall the menorah, many people like to use olive oil. One more reason is also mentioned in the Talmud. Just like an olive tree never loses its leaves, the nation of Israel will never be destroyed.

We have looked at the origins of the mitzvah, the meaning behind it and the practical aspects. Now let's try to understand why this mitzvah was given to women in particular. Practically, the woman is the hostess who ushers in Shabbat, because she is usually more often present in the home than the husband and generally looks after household matters. But we can go deeper. Bearing in mind that light helps us to see the beauty within each other, we can understand why this mitzvah is particularly suited to women: a woman has a very strong ability to see the good in others. Just as a candle lights up the tiniest crevices, a woman is willing to peek into the darkest cracks of the souls of her husband and children to find the good. In fact, when searching for leaven on the eve of Passover, we use a candle at night, because this way we are able to peer into the tiniest cracks and check that they are free of leaven.

Furthermore, candle-lighting is the perfect opportunity for a woman to focus on enhancing her relationship with her husband. Although a woman lights two flames, the light created is unified into one. This reminds her that while she and her husband are two distinct bodies, they are one soul. Our sages tell us that a husband and wife were a single united soul under G-d's throne before they came down to earth. It is the work of a lifetime for the couple to unite the two halves, and after 120 years to return the soul whole to G-d. Kindling lights thus reminds a woman of one of her key roles.

So much for women on an individual level. What about women on a national level? Our sages teach us that in the merit of the righteous women we were redeemed from Egypt. What did they do? Pharaoh was intent on destroying the Jewish people. To achieve this, he disrupted family life by separating the men from their wives and sending them into the fields to do backbreaking labor. At the end of the day, their wives would draw pails of water, which G-d miraculously filled with fish, and go to their husbands in the fields. The women would wash their husbands' feet, serve them the fish and revive them. At a time when they were being methodically decimated, the women were willing to perpetuate the Jewish nation. Their belief and hope in the future, despite the horror around them, was the impetus that transformed the darkness of the exile into the light of the Exodus. Today, when we continue the work of these women and light Shabbat candles, we are helping to transform the darkness of exile into an eternal light of deliverance.

In conclusion, let us see how especially beloved the mitzvah of kindling lights for Shabbat is to both G-d and Jewish women. The Midrash tells us that G-d says: "If you kindle the Shabbat lights, I will show you the marvelous radiance that will shine upon Jerusalem." Why are we promised such extraordinary merit? To teach us how dear the Shabbat lights are to G-d. Similarly, Shabbat candles are beloved to Jewish women. History is replete with stories of the sacrifices that women made to light candles during the Inquisition and in the ghettos.

Let us see to what extent candle-lighting has become associated with our nation. On January 1, 2000, the *New York Times* ran a Millennium Edition. It was a special issue that featured three front pages. One had the news from January 1, 1900. The second was the actual news of the day, January 1, 2000. And then they had a third front page—projecting envisioned future events of January 1, 2100. This fictional page included things like a welcome to the fifty-first state: Cuba; a discussion as to whether robots should be allowed to vote; and so on. And in addition to the fascinating articles, there was one more thing. Down on the bottom of the Year 2100 front page was the candle-lighting time in New York for January 1, 2100. Reportedly, the production manager of the New York Times—an Irish Catholic—was asked about it. His answer was right on the mark. It speaks to the eternity of our people, and to the power of Jewish ritual. He said, "We don't know what will happen in the year 2100. It is impossible to predict the future. But of one thing you can be certain—that in the year 2100 Jewish women will be lighting Shabbat candles."

Since this mitzvah is so beloved to G-d, and since women have upheld it with strength and devotion, it is no wonder that every medium of art has tried to capture this spark of eternity. May we merit to perform this eternal mitzvah and to reap its rewards.

www.chabad.org
Reprinted with permission of the publisher

pause
& AFFECT

LESSON 3

The Feminine Shabbat

ROSH CHODESH
society

CELEBRATING THE FEMININE
SHABBAT GREETINGS

Text 1
TALMUD, SHABBAT 119A

רַבִּי חֲנִינָא מִיעֲטַף וְקָאֵי אַפַּנְיָא דְמַעֲלֵי שַׁבְּתָא, אָמַר: בּוֹאוּ וְנֵצֵא לִקְרַאת שַׁבָּת הַמַלְכָּה. רַבִּי יַנַאי לָבִישׁ מָאנֵיה בְּמַעֲלֵי שַׁבָּת, וְאָמַר: בּוֹאִי כַלָּה בּוֹאִי כַלָּה.

Toward sunset on Friday, Rabbi Chanina would robe himself and stand. He exclaimed, "Come and let us go forth to greet the Shabbat queen."

Rabbi Yanai donned his robes on Friday and exclaimed, "Come in, O bride; come in, O bride!"

BABYLONIAN TALMUD

A literary work of monumental proportions that draws upon the legal, spiritual, intellectual, ethical, and historical traditions of Judaism. The 37 tractates of the Babylonian Talmud contain the teachings of the Jewish sages from the period after the destruction of the 2nd Temple through the 5th century CE. It has served as the primary vehicle for the transmission of the Oral Law and the education of Jews over the centuries; it is the entry point for all subsequent legal, ethical, and theological Jewish scholarship.

Text 2

LECHAH DODI, FRIDAY NIGHT LITURGY

לְכָה דוֹדִי לִקְרַאת כַּלָּה
פְּנֵי שַׁבָּת נְקַבְּלָה . . .

לִקְרַאת שַׁבָּת לְכוּ וְנֵלְכָה
כִּי הִיא מְקוֹר הַבְּרָכָה
מֵראשׁ מִקֶּדֶם נְסוּכָה
סוֹף מַעֲשֶׂה בְּמַחֲשָׁבָה תְּחִלָּה . . .

בּוֹאִי בְשָׁלוֹם עֲטֶרֶת בַּעְלָהּ
גַּם בְּרִנָּה וּבְצָהֳלָה
תּוֹךְ אֱמוּנֵי עַם סְגֻלָּה
בּוֹאִי כַלָּה בּוֹאִי כַלָּה
בּוֹאִי כַלָּה שַׁבָּת מַלְכְּתָא.

Come my beloved, to meet the bride,
Let us welcome the Shabbat. . . .

Come, let us go to welcome the Shabbat,
For it is the source of blessing;
From aforetime it was chosen;
Last in creation, first in [God's] thought. . . .

Come in peace, O crown of her husband,
Both with song and gladness;
Among the faithful, the beloved people,
Come, O bride, come O bride,
Come, O bride, O Shabbat queen.

RABBI SHLOMO ALKABETS
CA 1500–1580

Born in Salonica, Greece. Kabbalist and poet; best known for his composition of the Shabbat hymn, *Lechah Dodi*. He eventually moved to Safed, Israel, where he was accepted into the circle of Rabbi Moshe Alshich, Rabbi Yosef Caro, and Rabbi Moshe Cordovero.

WOMAN OF VALOR

Text 3

PROVERBS 31:10—31

אֵשֶׁת חַיִל מִי יִמְצָא וְרָחֹק מִפְּנִינִים מִכְרָהּ.
בָּטַח בָּהּ לֵב בַּעְלָהּ וְשָׁלָל לֹא יֶחְסָר . . .
קָמוּ בָנֶיהָ וַיְאַשְּׁרוּהָ בַּעְלָהּ וַיְהַלְלָהּ.
רַבּוֹת בָּנוֹת עָשׂוּ חָיִל וְאַתְּ עָלִית עַל כֻּלָּנָה.
שֶׁקֶר הַחֵן וְהֶבֶל הַיֹּפִי אִשָּׁה יִרְאַת ה׳ הִיא תִתְהַלָּל.
תְּנוּ לָהּ מִפְּרִי יָדֶיהָ וִיהַלְלוּהָ בַשְּׁעָרִים מַעֲשֶׂיהָ.

A woman of valor, who can find, for her price is beyond that of gems?

The heart of her husband trusts in her, and he will lack no gain. . . .

Her children rise and acclaim her; her husband, and he praises her.

Many daughters have done worthily, but you surpass them all.

Charm is deceptive and beauty is naught, a God-fearing woman is the one to be praised.

Give her the fruit of her handiwork, and let her deeds laud her at the gate.

Text 4a

MIDRASH HAGADOL, CHAYEI SARAH 23:1

"שֶׁקֶר הַחֵן וְהֶבֶל הַיֹּפִי": זוֹ וַשְׁתִּי. "אִשָּׁה יִרְאַת ה' הִיא תִתְהַלָּל": זוֹ אֶסְתֵּר, "וַיָּשֶׂם כֶּתֶר מַלְכוּת בְּרֹאשָׁהּ וַיַּמְלִיכֶהָ תַּחַת וַשְׁתִּי" (אֶסְתֵּר ב, יז).

"Charm is deceptive and beauty is naught": this refers to Vashti. "A God-fearing woman is the one to be praised": this refers to Esther. Indeed, it is written, "And [Ahasuerus] placed the royal crown upon her head and appointed her in place of Vashti" (Esther 2:17).

MIDRASH HAGADOL

A midrashic work on the five books of the Pentateuch. Midrash is the designation of a particular genre of rabbinic literature usually forming a running commentary on specific books of the Bible. *Midrash Hagadol* quotes widely from Talmud and other earlier midrashic works, serving as a valuable resource to reconstruct lost sections of Midrash. A traveler, Yaakov Sapir, first discovered the anonymous Midrash in Yemen in the middle of the 19th century. Some ascribe it to Rabbi Avraham, son of Maimonides.

Text 4b

MIDRASH HAGADOL, IBID.

"תְּנוּ לָהּ מִפְּרִי יָדֶיהָ", לְרַבּוֹת שְׁאָר כָּל הַנָּשִׁים הַצַּדִּיקוֹת וְהַכְּשֵׁירוֹת שֶׁבָּעוֹלָם.

"Give her the fruit of her handiwork." This includes all the righteous and upstanding women in the world.

MASCULINE AND FEMININE

THE FLOOD: A TIME OF TRANSITION

Text 5a

GENESIS 9:15

וְזָכַרְתִּי אֶת בְּרִיתִי אֲשֶׁר בֵּינִי וּבֵינֵיכֶם וּבֵין כָּל נֶפֶשׁ חַיָּה בְּכָל בָּשָׂר וְלֹא יִהְיֶה עוֹד הַמַּיִם לְמַבּוּל לְשַׁחֵת כָּל בָּשָׂר.

And I will remember My covenant, which is between Me and you and every living creature among all flesh, and the water will never again be a flood to destroy all flesh.

Text 5b

RABBI SHNE'UR ZALMAN OF LIADI, *TORAH OR* 8C

הַמַּבּוּל בָּא לְטַהֵר אֶת הָאָרֶץ, שֶׁנֶּאֱמַר "כִּי מָלְאָה הָאָרֶץ חָמָס" (בְּרֵאשִׁית ו, יא) וְנִתְקַלְקְלָה מְאֹד, וְהָיָה נִצְרָךְ לְטָהֳרָה. וּלְזֹאת בָּא הַמַּבּוּל דַּוְקָא שֶׁהִיא בְּחִינַת מַיִם, בִּכְדֵי לְטַהֵר אֶת הַטְמֵאִים. שֶׁהוּא כְּדוּגְמַת הַמִּקְוֶה מ' סְאָה, שֶׁהִיא מְטַהֶרֶת אֶת הַטָּמֵא, כְּמוֹ כֵּן הָיָה הַמַּבּוּל בָּא בִּכְדֵי לְטַהֵר אֶת כָּל הָאָרֶץ, וּכְמוֹ שֶׁכָּתוּב "וְזָרַקְתִּי עֲלֵיכֶם מַיִם טְהוֹרִים וּטְהַרְתֶּם" כוּ' (יְחֶזְקֵאל לו, כה).

The flood came [not only to punish, but also] to purify the world. The world had become exceedingly corrupt, as the Torah says (Genesis 6:11), "the earth filled with violence," and required purification. God therefore released a flood so that the waters would purify the impure. The flood, which fell for forty days, acted like a *mikveh,* (which must be, at minimum, forty *se'ah*). Just as the *mikveh* purifies the impure, so did the flood purify the entire world. As the Torah states (Ezekiel 36:25), "I shall sprinkle upon you pure waters, and you shall become pure."

RABBI SHNE'UR ZALMAN OF LIADI (ALTER REBBE)
1745–1812

Chasidic rebbe, halachic authority, and founder of the Chabad movement. The Alter Rebbe was born in Liozna, Belarus, and was among the principal students of the Magid of Mezeritch. His numerous works include the *Tanya,* an early classic containing the fundamentals of Chabad Chasidism, and *Shulchan Aruch HaRav,* an expanded and reworked code of Jewish law.

DISCIPLINE VS. NURTURE

Learning Exercise 1

Were there two parenting approaches in your home when you were growing up, one more nurturing, the other more disciplinarian?

If you are/were married with children, does/did your parenting style differ from that of your spouse?

Text 6

TALMUD, BERACHOT 10A

הַנְהוּ בִּרְיוֹנֵי דַהֲווּ בְּשִׁבָבוּתֵיהּ דְרַבִּי מֵאִיר וַהֲווּ קָא מְצַעֲרוּ לֵיהּ טוּבָא, הֲוָה קָא בָעֵי רַבִּי מֵאִיר רַחֲמֵי עֲלָוַיְהוּ כִּי הֵיכִי דְלֵימוּתוּ.
אָמְרָה לֵיהּ בְּרוּרְיָא דְבֵיתְהוּ: מַאי דַעְתָּךְ? - מִשּׁוּם דִּכְתִיב (תְּהִלִּים קד, לה): "יִתַּמּוּ חַטָּאִים", מִי כְּתִיב חוֹטְאִים? חַטָּאִים כְּתִיב.
וְעוֹד, שְׁפִיל לְסֵיפֵיהּ דִקְרָא: "וּרְשָׁעִים עוֹד אֵינָם", כֵּיוָן דְיִתַּמּוּ חַטָּאִים - וּרְשָׁעִים עוֹד אֵינָם?
אֶלָא בָּעֵי רַחֲמֵי עֲלָוַיְהוּ דִלַהֲדְרוּ בִּתְשׁוּבָה - וּרְשָׁעִים עוֹד אֵינָם.
בְּעָא רַחֲמֵי עֲלָוַיְהוּ וְהָדְרוּ בִּתְשׁוּבָה.

Some bandits who lived in Rabbi Meir's neighborhood were a great nuisance to him. Rabbi Meir prayed that they should die. His wife, Beruriah, remarked: "Where do you find precedent for your prayer? Is it because King David prayed (Psalms 104:35), 'May sins cease'? He didn't pray that *sinners* should cease, only that *sins* should cease.

"Furthermore, consider the end of the verse: 'And let wicked men be no more.' If they stop sinning, they will no longer be wicked.

"Rather, pray for them that they should repent, and they will no longer be wicked."

He did pray for them, and they repented.

GRADUATING TO FEMININITY

Question for Discussion

Which approach, masculine or feminine, is more effective?

Figure 3.1

Who	**Masculine**	**Feminine**
Approach	Asserts will forcefully.	Talks pleasantly and respectfully.
Impact	Causes change in behavior.	Influences change in thinking.
Result	Imposes change from outside.	Change is accepted internally.
Effect	Change is only short-term.	Change is long-term.

Text 7

THE LUBAVITCHER REBBE, RABBI MENACHEM MENDEL SCHNEERSON, *TORAT MENACHEM* 5751, 1:243

לֹא זוּ בִּלְבַד שֶׁאֵצֶל הָאִשָּׁה אֵין שׁוּם חִסָּרוֹן לְגַבֵּי הָאִישׁ, אֶלָּא אַדְּרַבָּה: בְּאוֹפֶן פְּעוּלָּתָהּ יֵשׁ מַעֲלָה לְגַבֵּי פְּעוּלַּת הָאִישׁ: מִכֵּיוָן שֶׁ"אִישׁ דַּרְכּוֹ לִכְבּוֹשׁ" הֲרֵי זֶה מוֹרֶה שֶׁעִיקַּר הָאוֹפֶן שֶׁיָּכוֹל לִפְעוֹל הוּא עַל יְדֵי כִּיבּוּשׁ וּמֶמְשָׁלָה . . . מַה שֶּׁאֵין כֵּן הָאִשָּׁה, שֶׁ"אֵין דַּרְכָּהּ לִכְבּוֹשׁ", פּוֹעֶלֶת בְּאוֹפֶן "פְּנִימָה" וּבְאוֹפֶן דֶּרֶךְ אֶרֶץ (בְּאוֹפֶן שֶׁל נַיְיחָא) הַשְׁפָּעָה פְּנִימִית – כַּךְ שֶׁהַמּוּשְׁפָּע מְקַבֵּל בִּרְצוֹן עַצְמוֹ הַהַשְׁפָּעָה. כְּפִי שֶׁרוֹאִים בְּפוֹעַל, שֶׁכְּשֶׁמְּדַבְּרִים עִם הַזּוּלַת עִם כָּבוֹד וְדֶרֶךְ אֶרֶץ, בְּדַרְכֵי נוֹעַם וּבְדַרְכֵי שָׁלוֹם, הֲרֵי זֶה פּוֹעֵל עָלָיו שֶׁלֹּא בְּעֶרֶךְ יוֹתֵר מֵאֲשֶׁר אִם צוֹעֲקִים עָלָיו וּמַפְחִידִים אוֹתוֹ וְרוֹצִים לִכְפּוֹת עָלָיו "כַּךְ וְלֹא אַחֶרֶת".

עַד שֶׁדֶּרֶךְ הָעֲבוֹדָה דִּנְשֵׁי וּבְנוֹת יִשְׂרָאֵל נַעֲשָׂה גַּם לִימוּד וּמוֹרֶה-דֶּרֶךְ לַאֲנָשִׁים וּבָנִים אֵיךְ שֶׁהֵם צְרִיכִים לַעֲשׂוֹת עֲבוֹדָתָם, דַּוְקָא בְּדֶרֶךְ כָּבוֹד וּבְדֶרֶךְ פְּנִימָה.

In many respects, the feminine approach is the more advanced approach. The masculine approach is to impose and control. . . . However, the feminine approach is not to conquer, but to touch others from within in a pleasant and respectful way. The feminine influence, born of internal bonding, inspires the other to accept willingly. Experience shows that respectful, pleasant, and peaceful discussion is much more effective than harsh talk of intimidation and imposition.

In this way, the feminine approach of the Jewish woman becomes an example to men on how to soften their masculine approach—to speak with respect and to establish an internal bond.

RABBI MENACHEM MENDEL SCHNEERSON
1902–1994

The towering Jewish leader of the 20th century, known as "the Lubavitcher Rebbe," or simply as "the Rebbe." Born in southern Ukraine, the Rebbe escaped Nazi-occupied Europe, arriving in the U.S. in June 1941. The Rebbe inspired and guided the revival of traditional Judaism after the European devastation, impacting virtually every Jewish community the world over. The Rebbe often emphasized that the performance of just one additional good deed could usher in the era of Mashiach. The Rebbe's scholarly talks and writings have been printed in more than 200 volumes.

THE FEMININE SHABBAT
SHABBAT AND THE WEEK

Learning Exercise 2

Choose a partner and take two minutes to review what we just learned about masculine and feminine, Shabbat and weekday.

Question for Discussion

In light of what we have learned, why do you think the mitzvah of lighting Shabbat candles is allocated to women and girls?

THE PROGRESSIVE SHABBAT

Text 8a

RABBI YESHAYAH HALEVI HOROWITZ, *SHENEI LUCHOT HABERIT, MASECHET SHABBAT*, 29

הִנֵה שַׁבָּת נִקְרֵאת כַּלָה וְנִקְרֵאת מַלְכָּה. נִקְרֵאת כַּלָה בְּעֵת שֶׁמִתְקַדֶשֶׁת וְאַחַר כָּךְ נִקְרֵאת מַלְכָּה בְּיִחוּד הָעַצְמִי עִם הַמֶלֶךְ הָעֶלְיוֹן . . .

וְזֶה מַעֲשֶׂה מִתְעַטֵף וְאָמַר "בּוֹאִי כַלָה בּוֹאִי כַלָה", זֶהוּ בְּהַכְנָסַת הַשַׁבָּת שֶׁהַכַּלָה בָּאָה לְהַסְעוּדָה. וּמֵאַחַר שֶׁאֵינָהּ רַק כַּלָה, כִּי בְּחִינַת מַלְכָּה הִיא בְּיוֹם סוֹד הַנִישׂוּאִין עַל כֵּן בְּהַכְנָסַת שַׁבָּת קְרָאָהּ כַּלָה.

עַל כֵּן בְּהַכְנָסַת הַשַׁבָּת קְרָאָהּ כַּלָה וְאָמַר "בּוֹאִי כַלָה בּוֹאִי כַלָה". וְאַחַר כַּךְ הָיָה דָשׁ בָּהּ וּמַגְדִיל בִּכְבוֹדָהּ, וְכָבוֹד יוֹם עָדִיף מִכָּבוֹד לַיְלָה לְכַבֵּד אֶת הַמַלְכָּה.

Shabbat is called a bride and it is also called a queen. She is called a bride at the time of betrothal, but afterward, when she forms an intrinsic bond with the Supernal King, she is called a queen. . . .

Rabbi Yanai would don his robes at the beginning of Shabbat, when the bride makes her initial entry, and exclaim, "Come in, O bride; come in, O bride!" Rabbi Yanai would call her a bride. Rabbi Yanai would call her a bride because at this point she is still a bride, inasmuch as she does not become a queen until the day of Shabbat, after her marriage to the Supernal King.

But as the day unfolded, he would increase his honor for Shabbat and respect it as a queen.

RABBI YESHAYAH HALEVI HOROWITZ (*SHELAH*)
1565–1630

Kabbalist and author. Rabbi Horowitz was born in Prague and served as rabbi in several prominent Jewish communities, including Frankfurt am Main and his native Prague. After the passing of his wife in 1620, he moved to Israel. In Tiberias, he completed his *Shenei Luchot Haberit*, an encyclopedic compilation of Kabbalistic ideas. He is buried in Tiberias, next to Maimonides.

Text 8b

RABBI DAVID ABUDRAHAM, *MA'ARIV SHEL SHABBAT*

מָה רָאוּ חֲכָמִים לְתַקֵּן ג' תְּפִילוֹת בְּשַׁבָּת מְשׁוּנוֹת זוּ מִזּוּ, "אַתָּה קִדַּשְׁתָּ", "יִשְׂמַח מֹשֶׁה", "אַתָּה אֶחָד"?...
מִפְּנֵי שֶׁשַּׁבָּת נִקְרָא כַּלָּה וְהַקָּדוֹשׁ בָּרוּךְ הוּא נִקְרָא חָתָן, תִּקְּנוּ "אַתָּה קִדַּשְׁתָּ" עַל שֵׁם הַקִּידוּשִׁין שֶׁהֶחָתָן נוֹתֵן לַכַּלָּה, וְאַחַר כַּךְ "יִשְׂמַח מֹשֶׁה" עַל שֵׁם שִׂמְחַת הֶחָתָן בַּכַּלָּה . . . וְאַחַר כַּךְ "אַתָּה אֶחָד" עַל שֵׁם שֶׁמִּתְיַיחֵד הֶחָתָן עִם הַכַּלָּה.

Why did the sages ordain three different texts for the prayers of Shabbat? On Friday night we say, "You betrothed us," and on Shabbat morning we say, "Moses rejoices," and on Shabbat afternoon, we say, "You are one"?...

Because Shabbat is called the bride and God is called the groom, our sages ordained that we say, "You betrothed us" on Friday night, when Shabbat is first betrothed. On Shabbat morning, we say "Moses rejoices" [with the Torah] because this is when the groom rejoices with the bride.... On Shabbat afternoon, we say "You are one" because the groom bonds with the bride, and they merge into a single unit.

RABBI DAVID BEN YOSEF ABUDRAHAM
14TH CENTURY

Resided in Seville, Spain, and is famous for his work on Jewish prayers and blessings. The work—completed around the year 1340—is a commentary on the daily, Shabbat, and festival prayers and collects many customs and laws relating to them. He is believed to have been a disciple of Rabbi Ya'akov ben Asher, author of *Arba'ah Turim*.

Key Points

1. In our Shabbat liturgy, as well as in the melodies that we sing at our Shabbat table, Shabbat is described as a feminine presence.
2. Before the flood, the world was beyond redemption. The flood purified the world and made it possible for people to repent no matter how far they had strayed.
3. There are two possible approaches to any relationship: The assertive approach and the nurturing approach. Historically, the assertive approach has been associated with masculinity, and the nurturing approach has been associated with femininity. Both are valuable. When we encounter resistance, we opt for the masculine approach. When we encounter responsiveness, we graduate to the feminine approach.
4. During the week, when we are immersed in worldliness, we take a strict masculine approach to our relationship with God. On Shabbat, when we are more amenable to holiness, we take a nurturing feminine approach to our relationship with God.
5. As Shabbat unfolds, our relationship with God progresses. This is why Shabbat is called a bride on Friday night, and by the time Shabbat day arrives, it is called a queen.

APPENDIX

Text 9

MIDRASH HAGADOL, CHAYEI SARAH, 23:1

"אֵשֶׁת חַיִל מִי יִמְצָא": זוֹ אֵשֶׁת נֹחַ . . . "וְרָחוֹק מִפְּנִינִים מִכְרָהּ":
שֶׁהָיְתָה הִיא וְכַלּוֹתֶיהָ רְחוֹקִין מִמַּעֲשֵׂה דוֹר הַמַּבּוּל.

"A woman of valor, who can find?" This refers to the wife of Noah. . . . "Her value exceeds that of gems," for her behavior and the behavior of her daughters-in-law [who were rescued with her in the ark] was far superior to that of their generation.

Text 10

MIDRASH HAGADOL, IBID.

"וַתָּקָם בְּעוֹד לַיְלָה" (מִשְׁלֵי לא, טו): זוֹ בַּתְיָה בַּת פַּרְעֹה שֶׁרָאֲתָה בְּרוּחַ הַקֹּדֶשׁ שֶׁעָתִיד מוֹשִׁיעָן שֶׁל יִשְׂרָאֵל לְהִתְגַּדֵּל עַל יָדֶיהָ, וְהָיְתָה מַשְׁכֶּמֶת וּמַעֲרֶבֶת, הִיא וְנַעֲרוֹתֶיהָ, לְהִטַּיֵּיל עַל הַיְאוֹר. וְכֵיוָן שֶׁבָּא מֹשֶׁה לְיָדָהּ, נָתַן לָהּ הַקָּדוֹשׁ בָּרוּךְ הוּא מַה שֶּׁבִּקְשָׁה וְשָׂמְחָה הַרְבֵּה, שֶׁנֶּאֱמַר "וַתִּפְתַּח וַתִּרְאֵהוּ אֶת הַיֶּלֶד" (שְׁמוֹת ב, ו).

"And she rose while it was still night," (Proverbs 31:15) this refers to Batyah (Bithiah), the daughter of Pharaoh. She and her maidens would stroll along the Nile from early morning to late evening, for she perceived prophetically that she would rear the savior of Israel. When Moses appeared, she knew that God had fulfilled her request, and she was exceedingly joyful, as it is written, "And she opened [the basket] and beheld the child." (Exodus 2:6)

Question for Discussion

Which positive character traits do you perceive in Batyah?

Text 11

MIDRASH HAGADOL, IBID.

"חָגְרָה בְעֹז מָתְנֶיהָ" (מִשְׁלֵי לא, יז): זוֹ מִרְיָם שֶׁאָמְרָה לְאָבִיהָ כְּשֶׁגֵּרֵשׁ אֶת אִמָּהּ, קָשִׁים גְזֵירוֹתֶיךָ מִשֶּׁל פַּרְעֹה. הוּא גָּזַר עַל הַזְּכָרִים, וְאַתָּה גָזַרְתָּ עַל הַזְּכָרִים וְעַל הַנְּקֵיבוֹת . . . וְלֹא עוֹד, אֶלָּא שֶׁרָאִיתִי שֶׁעָתִיד לָצֵאת מִמְּךָ מִי שֶׁעָתִיד לְהוֹשִׁיעַ אֶת יִשְׂרָאֵל. מִיַּד הֶחְזִיר אֶת אִשְׁתּוֹ, וְכֵיוָן שֶׁיָּלְדָה מֹשֶׁה וְהִשְׁלִיכַתּוּ לַיְאוֹר, טָפְחָה לָהּ אִמָּהּ עַל פָּנֶיהָ וְאָמְרָה לָהּ, הֵיכָן נְבוּאָתֵיךְ? מִיַּד "וַתֵּתַצַּב אֲחֹתוֹ מֵרָחֹק" (שְׁמוֹת ב, ד) שֶׁעָמְדָה בִּנְבוּאָתָהּ.

"She girds her loins with strength" (Proverbs 31:17): This refers to Miriam who told her father when he divorced her mother, "Your decree is worse than Pharaoh's decree. Pharaoh only decreed that male Jewish children shall be put to death, but by divorcing your wife, you ensure that neither male nor female will be born. . . . Not only that, [but] I foresee that the child destined to be born from you will be the savior of the Jewish people." Her father immediately remarried her mother. When Moses was born and placed in a basket upon the Nile River, her mother tapped her on the head and asked, "Where is your prophecy?" Miriam immediately followed the basket to ensure the fulfillment of her prophecy, as it says, "and his sister stood from a distance". (Exodus 2:4)

Question for Discussion

Which positive character traits do you perceive in Miriam?

Text 12

MIDRASH HAGADOL, IBID.

"רַבּוֹת בָּנוֹת עָשׂוּ חָיִל" (מִשְׁלֵי לא, כט): זוֹ רוּת שֶׁזָּכְתָה וְיָצָא מִמֶּנָּה דָּוִד וּבָנָיו הַיְשָׁרִים.

"Many daughters have done worthily [but you surpass them all]" (Proverbs 31:29): This refers to Ruth, who merited to count King David and his righteous offspring among her descendants.

Question for Discussion

Which positive character traits do you perceive in Ruth?

ADDITIONAL READINGS

FINDING OURSELVES

By Sara Esther Crispe

> *"When we take the time and make the effort we will find within ourselves that woman of valor waiting to be revealed."*

"Who can find a woman of valor? For her value is far above pearls."

What is a woman of valor? And why is she being compared to pearls?

The text of Eishet Chayil is very specific. While many English translations often misinterpret certain words, randomly choosing one gem for another, every single word, every single description, is carefully describing something unique about the power of the Jewish woman.

The word in Hebrew for "valor" is "chayil" which also means "soldier." When one thinks of a Jewish woman, a soldier is not necessarily the term that comes to mind. And yet a soldier is most definitely valorous and most aptly describes her role. A soldier is one who dedicates her life to fight and defend what is most precious and beloved. A soldier likewise must always be thinking not only of her own safety but of her comrades as well. The underlying principle of armies around the world, and most definitely of our Jewish army in Israel, is no soldier left behind. Every single person is indispensable and must be protected and cared for. Likewise, the Jewish woman protects her loved ones, constantly thinking about the balance of their needs and ensuring each one receives what is necessary at the right time. Every decision requires forethought for not only the immediate situation but the ultimate goal. And we all know that no one should get in the way of mama bear. A Jewish mother will go to the end of the world to make sure her babies are safe and sound.

But then the verse continues, comparing a Jewish woman to a pearl—yet even that is not as precious as she is. But why a pearl? There are many precious jewels. Why not the diamond or ruby (as the word is often mistakenly translated). Unlike these other gems, the process of the creation and formation of the pearl most brilliantly describes the development of a Jewish woman.

Just as one must seek to find the woman of valor, so too must one seek to find the pearl. The pearl is hidden within an oyster and rests at the bottom of the ocean. The external of the oyster however is ugly, hiding the beauty within. And yet the name in Hebrew for the pearl, *pnimim,* relates to the word for both *panim,* meaning "face" as well as *"pnimiyut"* which means "internal." While the pearl has a harsh and rough external casing but is beautiful within, the Jewish woman's true beauty lies within but shines and can be seen through the outside as well. Just as our face is the portal to our internal selves, our faces represent the beauty of our souls and should reflect what lies within, not hide it.

The Jewish woman of valor is not one who has it all, but one who works and betters all that she has. The pearl is the result of a process, and not an easy one at that. The pearl is formed inside the shell of certain mollusks as a defense mechanism against a potentially threatening irritant such as a parasite inside its shell, or

---

SARA ESTHER CRISPE

Sara Esther Crispe, a writer, inspirational speaker, and mother of four, is the co-director of www.Interinclusion.org, a multi-layered educational initiative celebrating the convergence between contemporary arts and sciences and timeless Jewish wisdom. She is currently working on a full-length novel about the power of the Jewish woman and the text of Eshet Chayil.

an attack from outside that could injure the mantle tissue. The mollusk therefore creates a pearl sac to seal off the irritation.

What this means is that our beauty, our strength, our accomplishments, take work, often very hard work. We might have a lot of barriers in our way, but with the right mentality, and keeping focused on our goal, we will become stronger and better *because* of the adversity. If anything, those tests and challenges will allow our true beauty to shine forth and will show us and those around us the strength we have within that otherwise may not have been revealed.

We are soldiers, valorous soldiers, fighting for our families, fighting for our beliefs, fighting for our values. We know challenge and we have faced it head on and we have overcome it. The woman of valor is not someone else. Each and every one of us has that potential within us. We just need to look. We just need to find her.

Perhaps this is why there are 150 words in the text of Eishet Chayil. This number, when represented by Hebrew letters, is *nun kuf*. The word for "female" is *nekeiva* which is spelled *nun kuf beit hei*. Since *nun kuf* = 150 and *beit hei* spell the Hebrew word "bah" which means "within her" the word for female, *nekeiva,* can be read as "150 within her." All the words, all the meaning, all the potential and all the beauty of the 150 words of Eishet Chayil are within her. Within each and every Jewish woman. Within us.

So who can find a woman of valor? As our Sages teach (Megila 6b), "If one looks and hasn't found, don't believe him. If one has found and didn't look, don't believe him. But if one has looked and one has found, believe him" When we take the time and make the effort we will find within ourselves that woman of valor waiting to be revealed. And once she is, then all those around us will recognize her as well.

Originally published in More Precious than Pearls, *edited by Mark Pearlman, Sinai Live Books, 2012.*
Reprinted with permission of the author

EXCHANGING SUPERMOM FOR EVERYWOMAN

By Shimona Tzukernik

"Doesn't it make sense that Eishet Chayil *alludes not to one woman's all-encompassing virtues (Supermom) but to our collective identity (Everywoman)?"*

About a year ago I spoke to a group of women in Pittsburgh. The topic was, "Will the Real Jewish Woman Please Stand Up?" The energy was already upbeat and intimate by the time I made reference to the famous text, "Woman of Strength" which Jews customarily sing at the Friday night meal. Before I could work my way into the point I intended to make, a woman blurted out something to the effect of, "I hate that song." I turned to her, inviting her to elaborate.

"Well . . . She's just so . . . perfect! I feel like a complete failure every Friday night. I mean, do you know anyone like her?" Laughter all round. I love when that happens–a real, visceral response to the topic at hand (especially when it resonates with my own inner passion, hesitancy or conflict around a particular idea). How many times had I balked at the words?!

Using the Hebrew letters as a springboard, it is a veritable Alphabet Soup of Perfection. I won't overwhelm you with all the details but how's this for starters?

- *Alef*–She's an *Eishet Chayil,* a "strong" woman. The word chayil connotes the power of war. She's a warrior. And a spiritual one too, with all the attributes needed to carry out any task at hand. Friday night rolls round; we haven't even gotten past verse one and I'm up against "Jewish Tiger Mom!"
- *Beit—Batach bah lev ba'alah,* her husband's heart trusts in her. Hmm. I can count on one hand (okay, two fingers) the number of girlfriends whose husbands are at peace with their wives' take on life and what's best for them. Verse two and I'm dealing with not only a powerhouse but someone who's wise and gentle enough to inspire confidence in her mate!
- *Gimmel—Gemalthu tov,* she imparts goodness and kindness to him, never evil. Who is this gal?

In short, a brief read-through of the song reveals that Kosher Tiger Mom has a loving, trusting husband; she's an entrepreneur and successful business woman; she's industrious, charitable, wise, empathic and intuitive. To boot she's well groomed (read: manicures, facials and Saks Fifth Avenue if not Vera Wang) and even has the time and cash to buy gorgeous bedroom linens in mindful attention to her sex life.

Is it any wonder the second phrase, in breathless pursuit of the words *Eishet Chayil,* asks "Who can find (her)?" She is not me! Which leaves me with the question of how to read and apply King Solomon's song to my life—along with the implications it has for my role not only as wife but as daughter to my mother and mother to my own children.

It seems to me that *Eishet Chayil* is "Everywoman," an archetype of us all. No, I'm not just looking for a backdoor escape from my perfectionism, a way to avoid the reflections of my flaws I encounter on a daily basis. I ask myself whether she represents an attainable goal. Certainly in a utopian era we may each come to embody the *Eishet Chayil* described by King Solomon, but in the here-and-now of life-as-we-know-it, I've yet to meet the woman who lives up to the persona he portrays. Rather than take the text as a description of Supermom,

---

SHIMONA TZUKERNIK

A native of South Africa, Tzukernik is the creator of The Method, a therapeutic application of Kabbalah, designed to help people achieve maximum performance by disrupting conventional thinking. Known as "The Kabbalah Coach," she is the founder and director of Omek, a center devoted to in-depth transformational learning for women.

it seems to me, the song serves to connect us with the universal image of wife and mother. After all, the passage has been interpreted as a metaphor for the *Shechina*, the Sabbath, the Torah and the soul. Doesn't it make sense that the acrostic, spanning all twenty-two letters of the Hebrew alphabet, alludes not to one woman's all-encompassing virtues (Supermom) but to our collective identity (Everywoman)?

Just before my marriage, a spiritual midwife told me, "King Solomon says, 'The wisdom of a woman builds her home.' The literal translation though states, 'The wisdom of women (plural) builds her home (singular).' You will build your home on the wisdom of many women. Pay attention to how they live and what they have to say." How right she was. I have enriched myself and my home through the collective wisdom and experience of the thousands of women I've merited connecting with. I carry them within me and am personally empowered by who they are. As *Eishet Chayil* is sung each Friday night, it affords me some brief moments of contemplation to rejoin with them and also to be eased by the knowledge that our physical and spiritual interconnectedness mitigates my own flaws, enabling me to bring their lights into my home.

By extension, I have access to the larger, cosmic Everywoman, namely the energies and insights of the women who have come before me all the way back to Sarah. (In fact, one reading of *Eishet Chayil* is as the eulogy Abraham said for Sarah before he buried her.) It may be a span of thousands of years between me and my first mother but it's not more than around 175 generations. That's not an impossible divide. I want some of the wisdom and joy of the women between the two of us. I now know how far from the truth my youthful stereotype of the *shtetel Bubby*—naïve, somewhat simple, lacking emotional subtlety–is. Today I'd love to have her over for brunch and glean her insights and tools on how to handle my life.

The same goes for all the women throughout those interceding generations, each of whom has her own shining letter from the Alphabet Soup of Perfection to impart to me. As their daughter and granddaughter I am bound with their point of perfection. Thereby, at some level, despite the fact that I'm no Supermom, *Eishet Chayil* is in my home each Friday night. More so I even carry her, the collective "Everywoman," within my own being.

In this way, I gain access to a dimension of myself that is way beyond my highest personal aspirations: For if the totality of who I can be is purely a result of my own endeavors, I will be very small indeed. Rather, it is in surrendering to my imperfections and humbly admitting the bigness of *Eishet Chayil* that I open the window to the full expanse of who I am.

But to me, the collective gestalt of Jewish womanhood embodied by *Eishet Chayil* allows us even more than access to this larger, truer self. In addition to this priceless gift, she affords us the possibility to reconfigure our relationship with our mothers. I know, easier said than done. The most potent reaction I ever got to a presentation was a lecture called, "Moms, the Magic and the Madness." The audience—and yours truly—wasn't quite sure whether to laugh or weep. Our relationship with our mothers is incomparably multi-dimensional, complex, overlaid with love and with hatred. It's a real big one to navigate but one that we are nonetheless expected to manage and even heal.

It's not that we can disregard that relationship if it's uncomfortable for us. "Honor your father and mother" even made it to fifth on the list of the Big Ten. Yet for many this instruction on how we ought to relate to our parents is something they find absurd. I can hear the disdain: "My Mom hangs out at the gym all day and gossips non-stop. She's dishonest in business, self-centered–nay narcissistic—and materialistic. She never had the courage to face her wounds so I get to be the beneficiary of her dysfunctional inheritance! Yadda, yadda . . ." Alright, this is Everymom we're talking about. But you get the idea. How are we to honor and respect our Moms despite their often startling imperfections?

Ultimately the reason we honor them has nothing to do with their personal or moral stature. G-d's directive is rooted in the fact that at the moment of conception, our parents take on something of the Divine. They become co-creators with G-d in bringing us into being. That's why honor of our parents is immutable.

It's not about the gym or manicures, how they do or don't pay taxes and show up in life. It's about the fact that in relation to us they are G-dlike in a certain respect. That's the ground-zero of honoring our parents, and until we get it, mostly nothing else we say or hear will be of use to us in moving the relationship forward.

But this immutable point of greatness aside, each Friday night *Eishet Chayil* reminds us of two key ideas that can change the way we negotiate our very first relationship. The first is that, as mentioned, none of us is perfect—and that's okay! The second is that in some mysterious way we can, if we choose to, receive what we need through the collective Everywoman.

In this way, we learn to lower the bar on our mothers. Whew! We don't have to hold her to an impossible standard. In fact (surprise) we can begin to accept her for who she is and learn to get our needs met elsewhere if she is not able to do so. We can stop blaming our unhappiness on someone who would not—or more accurately could not—come to the table in the way we needed her to. *Eishet Chayil,* Everywoman, becomes a reservoir of healing and nourishment for our being.

Through this forgiving of her for her imperfections, we can put down the aspects of our emotional and mental inheritance we'd rather do without. One of the first things we learn about our father Abraham is that he smashed his parents' idols! I am embarrassed to admit it but it was only well into my thirties that I realized I had to do the same. I'd spent decades bowing to my folks' false beliefs, accepting it as fact that I was doomed for time everlasting to live with the limitations those beliefs generated. Then one day the teaching about Abraham took hold in my mind with a vigorous vitality.

I took an inventory of what I'd inherited. In addition to the abundant goodness and wonder, it included beliefs about how much I was likely to earn, how to respond when angered, what the appropriate response to suffering is and a whole lot more. I trust you get what I'm talking about. How liberating to realize that I could systematically smash those idols—without betraying my parents!! I was not being faithless to them in subscribing to different truths and happiness.

The catch in doing so is to disown the false beliefs yet remain in the relationship. Abraham smashed Terach's idols but he continued to live with him—for another seventy-two years. Granted Terach came round to Abraham's way of thinking but our first father would have managed to negotiate the relationship regardless.

I believe that is because connection with G-d was the singular driving force in his life and as such he was able to a) see his father's flaws, b) not take them personally, c) not feel limited by them, and d) detach with love so that he could e) actually help Terach. He was able to not own another's dysfunction and yet remaining connected to the one he loved.

To accomplish this mode of conduct, we must discover a new mental set and learn to shift our reading of the events and relationships in our lives. Most of our pain in relation to our parents (and pretty much everything else) has to do with our own perception. We interpret things to mean what they are not. As such, we tend to live in the rather unhappy space between the way things are and the way we think they should be. We walk around confessing the sins of G-d and others in our life. And of course, we know our mothers' sins best of all! To be whole with her, we must find that new mental set that allows us to let go of the expectations we have of her and of our interpretation of the interactions between us. For me, *Eishet Chayil* enables me to begin to navigate this. It teaches me that I am not perfect but that that's okay—and the same goes for my Mom; that I no longer have to hold her to an impossible standard and that I can be enriched by my universal family of sisters and mothered by generations of women whose sterling qualities are inestimable. In other words, although I'm not Supermom, I have access to the superlative perfection of Everywoman. It turns out that Jewish Tiger Mom liberates me through the abundant truth that although none of us is perfect, we have access to a flawlessness that is way beyond pearls.

Reprinted with permission from TheJewishWoman.org, a project of the Judaism website, Chabad.org.

MEN ARE FROM WEEKDAY, WOMEN ARE FROM SHABBAT

By Miriam Kosman

(This blog was written for the Shabbat Project website. Apparently, with all the beauty of the Challah-baking aspect of that project, the organizers wanted to emphasize other aspects of the female connection to Shabbat and asked me to write an article on that. The article was subsequently published on aish.com.)

Is a pregnant woman one person or two? It's hard to be sure. True, the baby's heart beats beneath hers, but the pregnant woman continues to live her own life, think her own thoughts, and do her own thing. Baby flips and flops inside her, likes or dislikes the music she listens to and remains distinctly separate, even as his very being is nourished by her. Mother and baby remain two, even as they are one.

Birth becomes the act of separation in order to come together again. Mother and baby cuddle once more into a cocoon of brief but intense togetherness within the nursing relationship. And even though that nursing baby will soon toddle off into independence, some mothers would maintain that that change in identity—that widening of the boundaries of self—never really goes away; a mother entering the delivery room discovers it's a one-way journey. Biologically, women embody a blurring of boundaries between two discrete entities. Instead of clear demarcations where I am I and you are you, femininity flows over those borders in an undulating fluidity.

BODY AND SOUL, MIRROR IMAGES

From a Kabbalistic perspective which sees the physical world as paralleling the spiritual with exquisite exactitude, biological woman becomes a metaphor for relationship, connection, and bonding. Woman—created opposite Man because it "wasn't good for man to be alone"—experienced life as a dialogue from day one.

Maleness, on the other hand, in which relationship is externalized, represents separation and individuation. This drive for autonomy and independence can easily segue into a focus on competition, acquisitiveness, and hierarchy, in the determined attempt to keep the boundaries between people rigid.

Despite this biological metaphor, of course not all women are relationship oriented. Many women never gave birth to or nursed a baby, and others, even if they did, do not resonate with the concept of fluidic boundaries. And it goes without saying that there are many men who live their lives centered on relationships. Gender, here, is used to delineate two different pulses that animate the human soul; clearly both of them can be manifested by both men and by women.

Interestingly, of the two models, Judaism resonates most strongly with the feminine. Relationships with others, with God, and with ourselves—bridging the chasms which separate us—are the defining characteristics of Jewish life. Success in Judaism is measured by our relationships: the emotional, spiritual, and

---

MIRIAM KOSMAN

Miriam Kosman is an international lecturer for Nefesh Yehudi, a program that offers classes on Jewish thought and philosophy to Israeli university students. In that capacity, she teaches a few hundred students a week, who study at Tel Aviv University, Haifa University, Ben-Gurion University, the Technion, and others. She also runs a year-long course on Jewish thought that has been attended by hundreds of women. She is a doctoral candidate at Bar Ilan University; her dissertation topic touches on both Jewish philosophy and gender. She lives in Bnei Brak, Israel, with her family.

moral well-being of ourselves and the people in our orbit and how much room our relationship with G-d has in our lives.

It's hard to remember this truth in real life because Western philosophy valorizes the masculine and so sees people as intrinsically egotistical. The best we can hope for, Western philosophy maintains, is to convince people of the benefit of social contracts. Win friends and influence people because you never know when you will need those people in your determined rush up Mt. Success.

In this context, the feminine voice which realizes that not only I am I and you are you, but also I am you and you are I—gets trampled on, ridiculed, and all but drowned out. But that feminine voice (which can, of course, be articulated by men as well) gets one critical reprieve: Shabbat.

HAPPY RELATIONSHIP DAY!

Shabbat is relationship day—which is why it's referred to in Kabbalist sources as feminine—think Shabbat Queen, and Shabbat Bride. Shabbat is the day on which we place our to-do list firmly in the drawer, jump off the treadmill, and wriggle out from under the suffocating blindfold which our technological toys place over our eyes. On Shabbat we take a deep breath and look around at the family and friends who were at the periphery of our vision all week, at God who was waiting all this time for us to notice Him, and at our very own souls, malnourished and neglected, eagerly looking forward to some attention.

Shabbat is a strangely vulnerable day. Without our car keys dangling from our hands, with our technological digits gone, with no work to escape into, we enter into a scary, unfamiliar world in which we become human beings instead of human doings. We inhabit a world where what is important is not what you accomplish but who you are. As we light the candles that illuminate our journey into the magic world of Shabbat, our family and friends seek a guide to help them over the threshold, into that mysterious place.

Women metaphorically represent the concept of relationship, and in real life are often the guardians and nurturers of family ties (there is a reason why it takes so much longer to get off the phone when Mom calls then when Dad does). As such, women bring a unique gift to the Shabbat experience. Way beyond chicken soup, and even freshly baked challah, is the gift of having someone who speaks the language of Shabbat.

Being born into a feminine body does not guarantee an immediate affinity to placing relationships first, but since our bodies are the medium through which our souls interact with the world, God has gifted women with a readily accessible metaphor to help them help their families and friends—and themselves—to sing the song of Shabbat.

On Friday before dusk, women light two candles—two separate entities—shining beacons that lead us into the world of Shabbat. Saturday night, we recite the havdala service using one candle, which—Jewish law tells us—must have at least two wicks. After a weekend in the feminine world of Shabbat, those two separate candles we lit on Friday night merge into one candle with two wicks—two who are really one, one who is really two—shining the gift of femininity out into the week.

For more articles by this author, or to read an excerpt of her book, visit miriamkosman.com. Reprinted with permission of the author

pause
& AFFECT

LESSON 4

Divine Delights

ROSHCHODESH society

THE PARADOX
SURROUNDED BY ANGELS

Text 1

REBBETZIN ESTHER JUNGREIS, "THE THIRD MEAL," WWW.HINENI.ORG

In Bergen-Belsen, my revered father . . . would hide a portion of his meager daily ration of bread. And even as he did so, he would tell us children to count the days . . . 6 more days, 5 more days, 4 more days, 3 more days, and soon it will be Shabbos.

When Shabbos night actually came, he would gather us in that hell hole on earth and whisper in Yiddish, "*Meine lichtige kinderlech*—my precious lights, my children, *mach tzee dee oigelech*—close your eyes and imagine that we are at home. Mama just baked delicious challah . . ." And even as he spoke, he would bring forth those precious crumbs that he had saved at great sacrifice throughout the entire week and in his sweet beautiful voice, my father would sing, "*Shalom aleichem* . . . welcome angels of Shabbos . . ."

On one occasion, my younger brother, tugged at my father's hand and said, "*Tatie,* I don't see any *malachim,* angels here. Where are the *malachim* of Shabbos?"

My father's eyes filled with tears and in a trembling voice, he answered, "*Etz, lichtige kinderlech*"—"You, my precious lights, you are the angels of Shabbos."

REBBETZIN ESTHER JUNGREIS
1936–2016

Born in Szeged, Hungary. She came to the U.S. after surviving the Bergen-Belsen concentration camp. Determined to devote her life to strengthening Judaism in the U.S. and around the world, she founded Hineni, an organization that provides Torah classes and other programs for the Jewish community. She was a noted lecturer and author of numerous books, including *The Jewish Soul on Fire* and *The Committed Marriage.*

Text 2

SHALOM ALEICHEM

שָׁלוֹם עֲלֵיכֶם מַלְאֲכֵי הַשָּׁרֵת מַלְאֲכֵי עֶלְיוֹן מִמֶּלֶךְ מַלְכֵי הַמְּלָכִים הַקָּדוֹשׁ בָּרוּךְ הוּא.
בּוֹאֲכֶם לְשָׁלוֹם מַלְאֲכֵי הַשָּׁלוֹם מַלְאֲכֵי עֶלְיוֹן מִמֶּלֶךְ מַלְכֵי הַמְּלָכִים הַקָּדוֹשׁ בָּרוּךְ הוּא.
בָּרְכוּנִי לְשָׁלוֹם מַלְאֲכֵי הַשָּׁלוֹם מַלְאֲכֵי עֶלְיוֹן מִמֶּלֶךְ מַלְכֵי הַמְּלָכִים הַקָּדוֹשׁ בָּרוּךְ הוּא.
צֵאתְכֶם לְשָׁלוֹם מַלְאֲכֵי הַשָּׁלוֹם מַלְאֲכֵי עֶלְיוֹן מִמֶּלֶךְ מַלְכֵי הַמְּלָכִים הַקָּדוֹשׁ בָּרוּךְ הוּא.

Peace unto you, ministering angels, messengers of the Most High—of the supreme King of kings, the Holy One, blessed be He.

May your coming be in peace, angels of peace, messengers of the Most High—of the supreme King of kings, the Holy One, blessed be He.

Bless me with peace, angels of peace, messengers of the Most High—of the supreme King of kings, the Holy One, blessed be He.

May your departure be in peace, angels of peace, messengers of the Most High—of the supreme King of kings, the Holy One, blessed be He.

Text 3

ZOHAR CHADASH, ACHAREI MOT 80B

כַּד אָתֵי בַּר נַשׁ מִבֵּי כְּנִישְׁתָּא, יְהָכוּן עִמֵּיהּ מַלְאָכִין קַדִּישִׁין
מֵהַאי גִּיסָא וּמַלְאָכִין מֵהַאי גִּיסָא, וּשְׁכִינְתָּא עַל כֻּלְּהוֹן . . . אִם
אִינִישׁ יָעֵיל לְבֵיתֵיהּ בְּחֶדְוָוא, וִיקַבֵּל אוּשְׁפִּיזִין בְּחֶדְוָוא, וְכַד
אָתֵי שְׁכִינְתָּא וּמַלְאָכִין וְיֶחֱזוּ שְׁרַגָּא נַהֲרָא, וּפְתוֹרָא מִתְתַּקְנָא,
וְאִינִישׁ וְאִתְּתֵיהּ בְּחֶדְוָה, הַאי שַׁעְתָּא שְׁכִינְתָּא אָמְרַת: זֶה
שֶׁלִּי הוּא - "יִשְׂרָאֵל אֲשֶׁר בְּךָ אֶתְפָּאֵר" (יְשַׁעְיָהוּ מט, ג).

When we return from the synagogue, angels accompany us on each side while the divine presence hovers above us and the angels. . . . If we enter our homes with joy and receive guests with joy; and if upon arrival, the angels and the divine presence see the candles lit, the table set, and the husband and wife both joyous, at that moment, the divine presence says, "This is mine—'Israel in which I take pride'" (Isaiah 49:3).

ZOHAR

The seminal work of Kabbalah, Jewish mysticism. The *Zohar* is a mystical commentary on the Torah, written in Aramaic and Hebrew. According to Arizal, the *Zohar* contains the teachings of Rabbi Shimon bar Yocha'i who lived in the Land of Israel during the 2nd century. The *Zohar* has become one of the indispensable texts of traditional Judaism, alongside and nearly equal in stature to the Mishnah and Talmud.

Text 4a

RABBI SHMUEL BORNSTEIN, *SHEM MISHMUEL*, SHEMOT 5673

וּלְעוּמַּת שֶׁהָאָדָם נִרְתַּע לַאֲחוֹרָיו, זוֹכֶה שֶׁבָּאִין מַלְאָכִים וּמְדַדִין וּמְקַרְבִין אוֹתוֹ לְשַׁבָּת.

וּכְעֵין שֶׁהָיָה בְּסִינַי "וַיַּרְא הָעָם וַיָּנוּעוּ וַיַּעַמְדוּ מֵרָחוֹק" (שְׁמוֹת כ, טו) מִפְּנֵי יִרְאַת הַכָּבוֹד, הָיוּ בָּאִין מַלְאֲכֵי הַשָּׁרֵת וּמְדַדִין אוֹתָן . . .

וְזֶה שֶׁאָנוּ אוֹמְרִים שָׁלוֹם עֲלֵיכֶם בְּלֵיל שַׁבָּת.

When we shrink back from the awesomeness of Shabbat, the angels come and ease us toward the sanctity of this day.

This is similar to what occurred at Sinai, where the verse says (Exodus 20:15), "The people saw and they trembled and stood from afar," due to their awe of God's glory; but then the angels came and walked them back. . . .

This is why we recite *Shalom Aleichem* on Friday night.

RABBI SHMUEL BORNSTEIN
(1855–1926)

Second rebbe of Sochatchov; Chasidic thinker and author. Rabbi Bornstein was the son of Rabbi Avraham Bornstein, the first rebbe of Sochatchov, author of the halachic work *Avnei Nezer*. His mother, Sara Tsina, was the daughter of Rabbi Menachem Mendel Morgenstern, the rebbe of Kotzk. Rabbi Shmuel Bornstein is widely known for his *Shem MiShmuel*, his collection of Chasidic insights.

Text 4b

RABBI SHMUEL BORNSTEIN, IBID., BEHAR 5673

וְזֶהוּ הָעִנְיָן מַה שֶּׁאָנוּ אוֹמְרִים "שָׁלוֹם עֲלֵיכֶם" לַמַּלְאָכִים הַמְלַוִּין אֶת הָאָדָם, שֶׁהַמַּלְאָכִים מַעֲלִין אֶת הַנְּשָׁמוֹת וּמְנַקִּין אוֹתָן מֵעֲפְרוּרִיּוּת דִּימֵי הַחוֹל.

We recite *Shalom Aleichem* to the angels who escort us. They elevate our souls and cleanse our souls from the earthliness of the weekday.

Text 5

RABBI TSADOK HAKOHEN RABINOWITZ, *PERI TSADIK*, METSORA 9

[שֶׁ]נִּקְרָא סְעוּדָתָא דְּמַלְכָּא . . . דְּשַׁבָּת בִּזְמַן כְּמוֹ הַמִּקְדָּשׁ בְּמָקוֹם . . . וְאִיתָא בְּגְמָרָא (חֲגִיגָה יד, ב) "וְהָיוּ מַלְאֲכֵי הַשָּׁרֵת מִתְקַבְּצִין וּבָאִין לִרְאוֹת בְּמִזּוּמוּטֵי חָתָן וְכַלָּה כוּ'", שֶׁדֶּרֶךְ לְהִתְקַבֵּץ שָׁם בְּנֵי אָדָם.

אַךְ אַחַר כַּךְ כְּשֶׁאוֹכְלִין חָתָן כַּלָּה וּמִתְיַחֲדִין הוֹלְכִין לָהֶם.

וְכֵן כַּאן בָּאִים הַמַּלְאָכִים לִרְאוֹת בְּמִזְמוּטֵי חָתָן וְכַלָּה, וְקוֹדֶם הַסְּעוּדָה פּוֹטְרִין אוֹתָם וְאוֹמְרִים "צֵאתְכֶם לְשָׁלוֹם".

The Shabbat meal is called "the meal of the divine King." . . . Indeed, Shabbat in time is akin to the Holy Temple in place. . . . [Because of the immense spirituality of this day, the angels come to partake in it.] This is similar to what the Talmud says (Chagigah 14b) occurred when the rabbinic sages discussed esoteric teachings: "The angels gathered the way people gather to

RABBI TSADOK HAKOHEN RABINOWITZ
1823–1900

Chasidic master and thinker. Rabbi Tsadok was born into a Lithuanian rabbinic family and later joined the Chasidic movement. He was a follower of the Chasidic leaders Rabbi Mordechai Yosef Leiner of Izbica and Rabbi Leibel Eiger. He succeeded Rabbi Eiger after his passing and became a rebbe in Lublin, Poland. He authored many works on Jewish law, Chasidism, kabbalah, and ethics, as well as scholarly essays on astronomy, geometry, and algebra.

see the merrymaking performed before the bride and groom."

However, afterward, the bride and groom seclude themselves, and everyone else departs.

Likewise, the angels come to observe the intimate bond with God we experience at the Shabbat meal. But before the meal, we send them on their way saying, "May your departure be in peace."

SHABBAT FEAST

Text 6a

MAIMONIDES, *MISHNEH TORAH*, LAWS OF SHABBAT 30:9

חַיָּיב אָדָם לֶאֱכוֹל שָׁלֹשׁ סְעוּדוֹת בְּשַׁבָּת אַחַת עַרְבִית וְאַחַת שַׁחֲרִית וְאַחַת בְּמִנְחָה, וְצָרִיךְ לְהִזָּהֵר בְּשָׁלֹשׁ סְעוּדוֹת אֵלוּ שֶׁלֹּא יִפְחוֹת מֵהֶן כְּלַל, וַאֲפִילוּ עָנִי הַמִּתְפַּרְנֵס מִן הַצְדָקָה סוֹעֵד שָׁלֹשׁ סְעוּדוֹת . . . וְצָרִיךְ לִקְבּוֹעַ כָּל סְעוּדָה מִשְּׁלָשְׁתָּן עַל הַיַּיִן וְלִבְצוֹעַ עַל שְׁתֵּי כִּכָּרוֹת.

A person is obligated to eat three meals on Shabbat: one [Friday] evening, one [Shabbat] morning, and one [Shabbat] afternoon. One should be extremely careful not to skip any of these three meals. Even a poor person who derives his livelihood from charity should eat these three meals. . . . All three meals must be significant ones at which wine is served; and at each, one must break bread on two complete loaves.

RABBI MOSHE BEN MAIMON (MAIMONIDES, RAMBAM)
1135–1204

Halachist, philosopher, author, and physician. Maimonides was born in Cordoba, Spain. After the conquest of Cordoba by the Almohads, he fled Spain and eventually settled in Cairo, Egypt. There, he became the leader of the Jewish community and served as court physician to the vizier of Egypt. He is most noted for authoring the *Mishneh Torah,* an encyclopedic arrangement of Jewish law, and for his philosophical work, *Guide for the Perplexed.* His rulings on Jewish law are integral to the formation of halachic consensus.

Text 6b

MAIMONIDES, IBID., 30:7

אֵיזֶהוּ עוֹנֶג . . . שֶׁצָּרִיךְ לְתַקֵּן תַּבְשִׁיל שָׁמֵן בְּיוֹתֵר וּמַשְׁקֶה מְבוּשָּׂם לְשַׁבָּת הַכֹּל לְפִי מָמוֹנוֹ שֶׁל אָדָם. וְכָל הַמַּרְבֶּה בְּהוֹצָאַת שַׁבָּת וּבְתִיקּוּן מַאֲכָלִים רַבִּים וְטוֹבִים הֲרֵי זֶה מְשׁוּבָּח.

What does the obligation of delight on Shabbat entail? . . . A person must prepare a particularly sumptuous dish and a pleasantly flavored beverage for Shabbat—commensurate with one's financial ability. The more one spends for Shabbat and the more one prepares lavish and delicious dishes, the more praiseworthy it is.

Text 6c

TALMUD, BEITSAH 16A

אָמְרוּ עָלָיו עַל שַׁמַּאי הַזָּקֵן, כָּל יָמָיו הָיָה אוֹכֵל לִכְבוֹד שַׁבָּת. מָצָא בְּהֵמָה נָאָה אוֹמֵר: זוֹ לְשַׁבָּת. מָצָא אַחֶרֶת נָאָה הֵימֶנָּה מַנִּיחַ אֶת הַשְּׁנִיָּה וְאוֹכֵל אֶת הָרִאשׁוֹנָה.

It was said about Shamai the Elder that he ate Shabbat food all week. That is, if he found a robust animal he would say, "Let this be for Shabbat." If later in the week he found a superior one, he would reserve the second animal for Shabbat and eat the first during the week.

BABYLONIAN TALMUD

A literary work of monumental proportions that draws upon the legal, spiritual, intellectual, ethical, and historical traditions of Judaism. The 37 tractates of the Babylonian Talmud contain the teachings of the Jewish sages from the period after the destruction of the 2nd Temple through the 5th century CE. It has served as the primary vehicle for the transmission of the Oral Law and the education of Jews over the centuries; it is the entry point for all subsequent legal, ethical, and theological Jewish scholarship.

Text 7a

TALMUD, BEITSAH 16A

נְשָׁמָה יְתֵירָה נוֹתֵן הַקָּדוֹשׁ בָּרוּךְ הוּא בָּאָדָם עֶרֶב שַׁבָּת,
וּלְמוֹצָאֵי שַׁבָּת נוֹטְלִין אוֹתָהּ הֵימֶנּוּ.

On the eve of Shabbat, God gives a person extra soul; at the close of Shabbat it is withdrawn from the person.

Text 7b

RASHI, AD LOC.

רוֹחַב לֵב לִמְנוּחָה וּלְשִׂמְחָה, וְלִהְיוֹת פָּתוּחַ לִרְוָחָה, וְיֹאכַל
וְיִשְׁתֶּה וְאֵין נַפְשׁוֹ קָצָה עָלָיו.

An expanded and opened heart for rest and joy, and one can eat and drink without feeling disgusted.

RABBI SHLOMO YITSCHAKI (RASHI)
1040–1105

Most noted biblical and Talmudic commentator. Born in Troyes, France, Rashi studied in the famed *yeshivot* of Mainz and Worms. His commentaries on the Pentateuch and the Talmud, which focus on the straightforward meaning of the text, appear in virtually every edition of the Talmud and Bible.

Question for Discussion

If Shabbat is characterized as a day of coming closer to God and a day of transcendence, why is so much emphasis placed on eating and physical pleasure?

OF SOUL AND BODY

FOR THE SOUL'S SAKE

Text 8

RABBI YA'AKOV YOSEF OF POLNOYE,
TOLADOT YA'AKOV YOSEF, KEDOSHIM 1

וּבִיאֵר עַל פִּי מָשָׁל לְמֶלֶךְ שֶׁנִּשְׁבָּה בְּנוֹ יְחִידוֹ בַּשֶּׁבִי הַקָּשֶׁה מִכּוּלָם, וְעָבְרוּ זְמַנֵּי זְמַנִּים וְתוֹחַלְתּוֹ נִמְשְׁכָה מִלִּפְדוֹתוֹ וּלְהָשִׁיבוֹ אֶל אָבִיו.

וּבְרוֹב עִתִּים וְשָׁנִים הִגִּיעוּהוּ מִכְתָּב אָבִיו הַמֶּלֶךְ, לְבַל יִתְיָיאֵשׁ שָׁמָּה וְשֶׁלֹּא לִשְׁכּוֹחַ נִמּוּסֵי הַמַּלְכוּת בֵּין זְאֵבֵי עֶרֶב, כִּי עוֹד יָדוֹ נְטוּיָה לְהַחֲזִירוֹ אֶל אָבִיו, עַל יְדֵי כַּמָּה וְכַמָּה טַצְדְּקָאוֹת בְּמִלְחָמָה אוֹ בְּשָׁלוֹם וְכוּ'.

וּמִיַּד שָׂמַח בֶּן הַמֶּלֶךְ שִׂמְחָה גְּדוֹלָה, אֶפֶס שֶׁהָיָה מְגִילַּת סְתָרִים, וְאִי אֶפְשָׁר הָיָה לוֹ לִשְׂמוֹחַ בְּגָלוּי. מַה עָשָׂה, הָלַךְ עִם בְּנֵי עִירוֹ אֶל בֵּית הַיַּיִן אוֹ שְׁאָר דָּבָר הַמְשַׁכֵּר, וְהֵם שָׂמְחוּ בְּיַיִן שִׂמְחָה גַּשְׁמִיּוּת, וְהוּא שָׂמַח בְּאִגֶּרֶת אָבִיו וְכוּ'.

וּכְכֹל הַחִזָּיוֹן הַזֶּה הוּא מַמָּשׁ מִצְוַת עוֹנֶג שַׁבָּת אֶל הַגּוּף שֶׁהוּא הַחוֹמֶר, בְּמַאֲכָל וּמִשְׁתֶּה, כְּדֵי שֶׁיִּהְיֶה פְּנַאי לְהַצַּדִּיק לִשְׂמוֹחַ שִׂמְחָה ב' שֶׁהוּא שִׂמְחַת הַנְּשָׁמָה בִּדְבֵיקוּת הַשֵּׁם יִתְבָּרַךְ כָּל הַיּוֹם.

Rabbi Menachem Mendel of Baer explained this with a parable of a king whose only son was trapped in harsh captivity. Much time passed, yet there was longing that one day the prince might be redeemed and returned to his father.

After many years, the prince received a letter from his father exhorting him not to lose hope nor to forget the court etiquette while among the savages, for his father was still actively pursuing

RABBI YA'AKOV YOSEF OF POLNOYE
CA. 1710–1784

Chasidic pioneer and author. Rabbi Ya'akov Yosef was a dedicated disciple of the Ba'al Shem Tov, the founder of the Chasidic movement, and is credited with taking a leading role in the dissemination of the philosophy of Chasidism in its nascent years. He authored *Toladot Ya'akov Yosef*, the first printed work of Chasidic philosophy. This work is cherished in Chasidic circles.

the possibility of his rescue, whether through battle or peaceful means.

Upon receipt of this letter the prince was overjoyed but could not celebrate openly since the matter was secret. He took the townspeople to a tavern. They were joyous due to the wine, while he was joyous because of his father's letter.

This parable explains why we have a mitzvah to eat lavishly on Shabbat. The body eats and drinks so that the Jew[1] can be free to rejoice on another level: namely, the joy of the soul as it clings to God throughout Shabbat.

---

1. Literally: the *tsadik*. We are applying the principle of ועמך כולם צדיקים in our translation.
2. Talmud, Berachos 57b.

Learning Exercise 1

In the left-hand column are the elements of the parable. Together with a partner, think about what these elements represent with respect to the mitzvah of taking pleasure on Shabbat. Write your answers in the right-hand column.

Elements of the Parable	Symbolism
King	
Prince	
Trapped in a harsh captivity	
The prince longs to be redeemed.	
The prince receives a letter.	

The prince is given hope that his father will yet come to rescue him.	
The prince is happy but cannot openly celebrate this secret matter.	
The prince takes the townspeople to a tavern.	
The townspeople are joyous due to the wine.	
The prince is joyous because of his father's letter.	
The peasants rejoice, thereby allowing the prince to celebrate undisturbed.	

FOR THE BODY'S SAKE

Text 9

RABBI CHAIM VITAL, *ETS CHAIM, SHA'AR* 26, 1:42

וְאָמְנָם יָדַעְתָּ גַּם כֵּן כִּי כָּל הַמִּצְוֹת אֵינָם אֶלָּא לְצָרֵף וּלְבָרֵר הַצֶּלֶם וְהַחוֹמֶר. אַךְ הַצּוּרָה אֵינָהּ צְרִיכָה תִּיקּוּן כְּלַל. וְלֹא הוּצְרְכָה לְהִתְלַבֵּשׁ בְּצֶלֶם וְחוֹמֶר רַק לְהַמְשִׁיךְ בָּהֶם אוֹר לְתַקְּנָם. וְהָבֵן זֶה מְאֹד. כִּי זֶה טַעַם יְרִידַת הַנְּשָׁמָה בָּעוֹלָם הַזֶּה לְתַקֵּן וּלְבָרֵר.

Know as well that all of the *mitsvot* are only geared to purify the physical [body], but the spiritual [soul] does not require rectification. It did not need to be vested in the body for any reason other than to illuminate and sublimate the body. Understand this well: The reason the soul descends to this world is to rectify [not to be rectified].

RABBI CHAIM VITAL
CA. 1542–1620

Lurianic Kabbalist. Rabbi Vital was born in Israel, lived in Safed and Jerusalem, and later in Damascus. He was authorized by his teacher, Rabbi Yitschak Luria, the Arizal, to record his teachings. Acting on this mandate, Vital began arranging his master's teachings in written form, and his many works constitute the foundation of the Lurianic school of Jewish mysticism. His most famous work is *Ets Chaim*.

Text 10

THE LUBAVITCHER REBBE, RABBI MENACHEM MENDEL SCHNEERSON, *LIKUTEI SICHOT* 23:29

דָאס וואָס תּוֹרָה זאָגְט אָן, אַז שַׁבָּת (אָדער יוֹם טוֹב) דאַרְף זַיין אַ זְמַן פוּן עוֹנֶג בַּיי אִידְן ("**לָכֶם**"), מֵיינְט עֶס נִיט, אַז (נאָר) דִי נְשָׁמָה זאָל הָאבְּן תַּעֲנוּג (רוּחָנִי) פוּן יוֹם הַשַּׁבָּת (וְיוֹם טוֹב), נאָר אַז (אוֹיךְ) דער **גוּף** זאָל פִילְן אַן עוֹנֶג דערְפוּן וואָס דאָס אִיז יוֹם הַשַּׁבָּת (יוֹם טוֹב). וְאַדְרַבָּה: דער עִיקָר הַמְכוּוָן פוּן דער מִצְוָה אִיז דַוְקָא דער (לְצַרֵף דעם) גוּף.

אוּן וְוִיבַאלְד אַז דער תַּעֲנוּג **טִבְעִי** פוּן גוּף אִיז פוּן אֲכִילָה וּשְׁתִיָה, דעריבּער, זאָגְט תּוֹרָה אַז חִיוּב הָעוֹנֶג אִיז דוּרְךְ אֲכִילָה דַוְקָא; וַוייל דַוְקָא בְּאוֹפֶן זֶה ווערְט אוֹיפְגעטאָן אַז דער עוֹנֶג שַׁבָּת אִיז מְצַרֵף, נעמְט דוּרְךְ דעם גוּף מַמָּשׁ.

מַה שֶּׁאֵין כֵּן אַ תַּעֲנִית שֶׁל תְּשׁוּבָה (וְכַיוֹצֵא בָּזֶה) אִיז דאָךְ דאָס נִיט קֵיין (הַנָאָה) עוֹנֶג פאַרְן גוּף (נאָר אַ תַּעֲנוּג (רוּחָנִי) פאַר דער נְשָׁמָה); אוּן אֲפִילוּ ווען אַ אִיד האָט גע'פּוֹעל'ט אוֹיף זִיךְ אַז זַיין גוּף זאָל נִיט פִילְן קֵיין צַעַר פוּן דעם תַּעֲנִית, אָדער נאָךְ מער: אוֹיךְ דער גוּף פִילְט אַ געווִיסְן עוֹנֶג דערְפוּן וואָס דִי נְשָׁמָה האָט תַּעֲנוּג . . . אִיז דאָךְ דאָס אָבּער נִיט קֵיין עוֹנֶג הַגוּף **מִצַד עַצְמוֹ** . . . נאָר מִצַד דער **שְׁלִיטָה** . . . פוּן דער נְשָׁמָה אוֹיפְן גוּף **הֵיפֶךְ** טֶבַע הַגוּף, אֲפִילוּ פוּן גוּף צָרוּף וְקָדוֹשׁ.

The Torah's command that Shabbat (and holidays) must be a time of pleasure for the Jewish people . . . does not mean that only the soul should derive (spiritual) pleasure from Shabbat (or the holiday). The body must (also) derive pleasure from Shabbat (or the holiday). Moreover, the primary objective of the mitzvah [of *oneg*] is specifically (to refine) the body.

Because the natural pleasure of the body is in eating and drinking, the Torah says that the obligation to take pleasure [on Shabbat] is through

RABBI MENACHEM MENDEL SCHNEERSON
1902–1994

The towering Jewish leader of the 20th century, known as "the Lubavitcher Rebbe," or simply as "the Rebbe." Born in southern Ukraine, the Rebbe escaped Nazi-occupied Europe, arriving in the U.S. in June 1941. The Rebbe inspired and guided the revival of traditional Judaism after the European devastation, impacting virtually every Jewish community the world over. The Rebbe often emphasized that the performance of just one additional good deed could usher in the era of Mashiach. The Rebbe's scholarly talks and writings have been printed in more than 200 volumes.

eating. It is only in this way that the pleasure of Shabbat can truly permeate and refine the body.

On the other hand, fasting in order to repent (and so forth) brings no pleasure to the body (although it brings spiritual pleasure to the soul).

Even if someone has refined himself to the point that fasting does not cause his body pain, and even provides his body with the satisfaction of bringing pleasure to the soul . . . nevertheless, this is not a natural pleasure for the body. . . . Rather it is a result of the soul forcing the body . . . to deny its basic nature, even if is a holy and refined body.

Text 11

TALMUD, PESACHIM 101A

אָמַר לְהוּ רַב עָנָן בַּר תַּחְלִיפָא: זִימְנִין סַגִיאִין הֲוָה קָאִימְנָא קַמֵיה דִשְׁמוּאֵל וְנָחִית מֵאִיגְרָא לְאַרְעָא וְהָדַר מְקַדֵשׁ.

Rav Anan bar Tachlifa said, "Many times I would stand before Shmuel. I saw that he would descend from the roof to the ground floor and only then recite *kiddush*."

Figure 4.1

Soul-Centered vs. Body-Centered

	Soul-Oriented	Body-Oriented
Why does the soul descend into the body?	So the body can challenge the soul, allowing the soul to demonstrate its commitment	So the soul can infuse the body with holiness and thus transform it
Why is there a mitzvah to have physical pleasure on Shabbat?	So that the body won't hinder the soul's experience of Shabbat	To permeate the body with the holiness of Shabbat
What type of pleasure is a fundamental part of life?	Spiritual pleasure	Physical pleasure guided by spiritual goals

EXTRA SOUL

Figure 4.2

Four Levels of Soul

Nefesh	Physical
Ruach	Emotional
Neshamah	Intellectual
Yechidah	Oneness

Text 12

RABBI SHNE'UR ZALMAN OF LIADI, *TORAH OR*, VAYAKHEL 87D

בְּשַׁבָּת נִתּוֹסֵף בְּכָל אֶחָד נְשָׁמָה יְתֵירָה . . . וְהַיְינוּ בְּחִינַת אַהֲבָה וְרָצוֹן לַה' שֶׁלְּמַעְלָה מִן הַשֵּׂכֶל וְהַהִתְבּוֹנְנוּת.

כִּי הִנֵּה אִית רָצוֹן וְאִית רָצוֹן. פֵּירוּשׁ אִית רָצוֹן שֶׁנּוֹלַד מֵהַשֵּׂכֶל וְהַהִתְבּוֹנְנוּת . . . אֲבָל אִית בְּחִינַת רָצוֹן הָעֶלְיוֹן שֶׁלְּמַעְלָה מַעְלָה מֵהַחָכְמָה . . . שֶׁזֶּהוּ בְּחִינַת יְחִידָה . . .

וּכְמוֹ עַל דֶּרֶךְ מָשָׁל כַּאֲשֶׁר יַחְפּוֹץ הָאָדָם בְּחֵפֶץ וְרָצוֹן לְאֵיזֶה דָּבָר הַנּוֹגֵעַ לְעֶצֶם הַנֶּפֶשׁ מַמָּשׁ וְגוֹרֵם לוֹ לַעֲשׂוֹת דְּבָרִים שֶׁלֹּא עַל פִּי הַדַּעַת וְהַשֵּׂכֶל כְּלָל כִּי רָצוֹן זֶה עָמוֹק עָמוֹק מֵהַשֵּׂכֶל . . .

וּבְחִינַת אַהֲבָה וְרָצוֹן זֶה לַה' מִתְגַּלֶּה בְּנֶפֶשׁ אָדָם בְּיוֹם הַשַּׁבָּת דַּוְקָא.

On Shabbat everyone has extra soul . . . that is, a love and desire for God that transcends contemplation.

There are two levels of desire. There is the desire that results from contemplation . . . but there is also a desire that is far beyond reason. . . . This is the level called *yechidah*—oneness. . . .

By way of illustration, when we have a desire for something that affects our very essence, we may be driven to nonrational behavior because this desire transcends all reason. . . .

This level of love and desire for God is revealed in our souls on Shabbat.

RABBI SHNE'UR ZALMAN OF LIADI (ALTER REBBE)

1745–1812

Chasidic rebbe, halachic authority, and founder of the Chabad movement. The Alter Rebbe was born in Liozna, Belarus, and was among the principal students of the Magid of Mezeritch. His numerous works include the *Tanya*, an early classic containing the fundamentals of Chabad Chasidism, and *Shulchan Aruch HaRav*, an expanded and reworked code of Jewish law.

LESSON CONCLUSION

Learning Exercise 2

1. Might there be an idea from today's lesson that can help you enhance your Shabbat eating habits?
2. What is one piece of advice that you can give yourself that will help you live a more integrated life, where your purpose and spiritual experiences guide the mundane areas of your life?

KEY POINTS

1. Shabbat angels come to our homes in order to help us overcome the spiritual hesitation we have about greeting the loftiness of Shabbat's sanctity. They also pay this visit to cleanse our souls from the dust of the weekday and to witness the divine presence uniting with the Jewish people. The angels then depart, leaving us alone to be united with God as we recite *kiddush*.
2. Jewish law mandates that we take part in three lavish meals on Shabbat. In fact, we are meant to be on the search all week for special Shabbat delicacies.
3. The emphasis on physical pleasures for a spiritual day seems paradoxical. One way of understanding this is that the physical pleasures ensure that the body does not distract the soul from its spiritual delights. This understanding aligns with the view that the soul descends into the body for the soul's sake, to overcome the obstacles posed by physical living.
4. A deeper understanding is to view the physical pleasure of Shabbat as a way of allowing the body to share the sanctity of Shabbat. This understanding aligns with the view that the soul descends into the body for the body's sake, to elevate and refine the body.
5. The Talmud teaches that we are graced with extra soul on Shabbat. Kabbalah explains that whereas the soul normally relates to God as a separate entity, on Shabbat, the soul's innate connection with God is revealed. Other sources understand "extra soul" in this context as an added appetite. This duality seems to demonstrate the theme of Shabbat—that the physical and spiritual are meant to come together on this special day.

6. We try to engage in the pleasures of Shabbat with appropriate mental focus—by being conscious of the fact that we are doing so to allow the soul to experience Shabbat and to bring the holiness of Shabbat to the body.

ADDITIONAL READINGS

WHAT SHABBOS MEANS TO US

By Rebbetzin Esther Jungreis

From time immemorial Shabbos has kept us going as a people, which is something that even secular Jews concede. The essayist Ahad Ha'am famously wrote, "More than the Jews have kept the Sabbath, the Sabbath has kept the Jews."

The first one to observe Shabbos was our mother Sarah. It is written that in her home the Shabbos candles never went out. They shone brightly from week to week and her challah never became stale. It remained fresh from week to week. How can that be? Is this a fairy tale that cannot be taken seriously by intelligent people?

What if I told you that I personally witnessed this truth come alive in real time? It was in the hell hole called Bergen Belsen, the infamous concentration camp to which my family and I were deported, that I discovered the secret of our mother Sarah's Shabbos candles and challah.

Bergen Belsen was a difficult place for anyone to retain his or her sanity, to breathe without collapsing, to maintain hope when everything seemed hopeless.

But even there, my father, *HaRav HaGaon* Avraham Ha Levi Jungreis, *zt"l,* would make us count the days to Shabbos. Six more days, five more days, four more days, three more days, two more days, one more day.

Every day we would receive a piece of bread. It was putrid, but to those of us who were starving it was delicious. Every day my saintly father would wash for bread, take a *k'zayis,* a miniscule portion that in accordance to Jewish law is adequate for a blessing, and the rest he would save for us and hide it for Shabbos.

When the countdown came to the seventh day—Shabbos—my father would gather us in the middle of night and whisper cajolingly in Yiddish, "*Mach tzi de oiygelech zeese kinderlche*–close your eyes my sweet children–*mir zenen in der heim*—we are at home; Mommy baked challah and it is warm, fresh, and delicious."

And then my father would bring forth those hidden pieces of bread and give them to us. I would actually envision the challah my mother baked and we ate that bread with gusto. Suddenly, mother Sarah's challah became real. Yes, it was fresh. Not only from week to week but from year to year. Similarly, my mother's challah remained forever fresh in our minds, on our palates, and in our hearts. And Mommy's Shabbos *licht* shed their rays of light on all of us. Yes, they remained from week to week and from century to century. The *kedushah*, the sanctity, of those *licht* illuminated our *neshamahs* and our hearts.

One Shabbos night when my father recounted this story, my younger brother tugged at my father's hand and said, "I do not see the lights of Shabbos here. I do not see the challah. I do not see the angels of Shabbos we just greeted and to whom we sang '*Shalom Aleichem.*' "

REBBETZIN ESTHER JUNGREIS
1936–

Born in Szeged, Hungary. She came to the U.S. after surviving the Bergen-Belsen concentration camp. Determined to devote her life to strengthening Judaism in the U.S. and around the world, she founded Hineni, an organization which provides Torah classes and other programs for the Jewish community. Noted lecturer and author of numerous books, including *The Jewish Soul on Fire* and *The Committed Marriage.*

My father's eyes overflowed with tears and in a trembling voice he said, "You, my children, *you* are the angels of Shabbos and the *licht* are your beautiful eyes. As for the Shabbos challah, you just had it. That is why I told you to close your eyes. That challah keeps us alive."

I never forgot those words. When I would stand for roll call, sometimes for hours, in heat, in cold, in rain, in snow, the Nazi keepers flung obscenities at us. I would stand erect and say to myself, "I am an angel of Shabbos. The candles of Shabbos give me light. And the challah of Shabbos energizes me and keeps me alive."

Jewishpress.com, 06.11.2014
http://www.jewishpress.com/judaism/rebbetzins-viewpointrebbetzin-jungreis/what-shabbos-means-to-us/2014/11/06/
Reprinted with permission of the publisher

WHAT ARE ANGELS?

By Rabbi Adin Steinsaltz

The world of formation may be said to be, in its essence, a world of feeling. It is a world whose main substance, or type of experience, is emotion of one kind or another, and in which such emotions are the elements that determine its patterns. The living beings in it are conscious manifestations of particular impulses—impulses to perform one or another act or responding one or another way—or of the power to carry through an incentive, to realize, to fulfill the tendency of an inclination or an inspiration. The living creatures of the world of formation, the beings who function in it as we function in the world of action, are called, in a general way, "angels."

An angel is a spiritual reality with its own unique content, qualities, and character. What distinguishes one angel from another is not the physical quality of spatial apartness but difference of level—one being above or below another—with respect to fundamental causality in terms of some difference in essence. Now as we have said, angels are beings in the world that is the domain of emotion and feeling; and since this is the case, the substantial quality of an angel may be an impulse or a drive—say, an inclination in the direction of love or a seizure of fear, or pity, or the like. To express a larger totality of being, something more comprehensive, we may refer to "a camp of angels." In the general camp of love, for example, there are many subdivisions, virtually innumerable shades and gradations of tender feeling. No two loves are alike in emotion, just as no two ideas are alike. Thus, any general and inclusive drive or impulse is a whole camp, perhaps even a mansion, and is not consistently the same at every level. Whereas among human beings emotions change and vary either as persons change or according to the circumstances of time and place, an angel is totally the manifestation of a single emotional essence. The essence of an angel, therefore, is defined by the limits of a particular emotion, in terms of itself, just as personality and inwardness define the self of each person in our world. An angel, however, is not merely a fragment of existence doing nothing more than just manifesting an emotion; it is a whole and integral being, conscious of itself and its surroundings and able to act and create and do things within the framework of the world of formation. The nature of the angel is to be, to a degree, as its name in Hebrew signifies, a messenger, to constitute a permanent contact between our world of action and the higher worlds. The angel is the one who effects transfers of the vital plenty between worlds.

An angel's missions go in two directions: it may serve as an emissary of God downward, to other angels and to worlds and creatures below the world of formation; and it may also serve as the one who carries things upward from below, from our world to the higher worlds.

The real difference between man and angel is not the fact that man has a body, because the essential comparison is between the human *soul* and the angel. The soul of man is the most complex and includes a whole world of different existential elements of all kinds, while the angel is a being of single essence and therefore in a sense one-dimensional. In addition, man—because of his many-sidedness, his capacity to contain contradictions, and his gift of an inner power of soul, that divine spark that makes him man—has the capacity to distinguish between

---

RABBI ADIN EVEN-ISRAEL (STEINSALTZ)
1937–

Talmudist, author, and philosopher. Rabbi Even-Israel Steinsaltz is considered one of the foremost Jewish thinkers of the 20th century. Praised by *Time* magazine as a "once-in-a-millennium scholar," he has been awarded the Israel Prize for his contributions to Jewish study. He lives in Jerusalem and is the founder of the Israel Institute for Talmudic Publications, a society dedicated to the translation and elucidation of the Talmud.

one thing and another, especially between good and evil. It is this capacity which makes it possible for him to rise to great heights, and by the same token creates the possibility for his failure and backsliding, neither of which is true for the angel. From the point of the view of its essence, the angel is eternally the same; it is static, an unchanging existence, whether temporary or eternal, fixed within the rigid limits of quality given at its very creation.

Among the many thousands of angels to be found in the various worlds are those that have existed from the very beginning of time, for they are an unaltering part of the Eternal Being and the fixed order of the universe. These angels in a sense constitute the channels of plenty through which the divine grace rises and descends in the worlds.

But there are also angels that are continuously being created anew, in all the worlds, and especially in the world of action where thoughts, deeds and experiences give rise to angels of different kinds. Every *mitzva* that a man does is not only an act of transformation in the material world; it is also a spiritual act, sacred in itself. And this aspect of concentrated spirituality and holiness in the *mitzva* is the chief component of that which becomes an angel. In other words, the emotion, the intention, the essential holiness of the act combine to become the essence of the *mitzva* as an existence in itself, as something that has objective reality. And this separate existence of the *mitzva*, by being unique and holy, creates the angel, a new spiritual reality that belongs to the world of formation. So it is that the act of performing a *mitzva* extends beyond its effect in the material world and, by the power of the spiritual holiness within it—holiness in direct communion with all the upper worlds—causes a primary and significant transformation.

More precisely, the person who performs a *mitzva*, who prays or directs his mind toward the Divine, in so doing creates an angel, which is a sort of reaching on the part of man to the higher worlds. Such an angel, however, connected in its essence to the man who created it, still lives, on the whole, in a different dimension of being, namely in the world of formation. And it is in this world of formation that the *mitzva* acquires substance. This is the process by which the specific message or offering to God that is intrinsic in the *mitzva* rises upward and introduces changes in the system of the higher worlds—foremost in the world of formation. From here, in turn, they influence the worlds above them. So we see that a supreme act is performed when what is done below becomes detached from a particular physical place, time, and person and becomes an angel.

Conversely, an angel is sometimes sent downward from a higher world to a lower. For what we call the mission of the angel can be manifested in many different ways. The angel cannot reveal its true form to man, whose being, senses, and instruments of perception belong only to the world of action: in the world of action there are no means of grasping the angel. It continues to belong to a different dimension even when apprehended in one form or another. This may be compared with those frequencies of an electromagnetic field that are beyond the limited range ordinarily perceived by our senses. We know that human vision assimilates only a small fragment of the spectrum; as far as our senses are concerned, the rest of it does not exist. That which is ordinarily invisible is "seen" only through appropriate instruments of transmutation, or interpretation, when, in the language of the Kabbala, they are dressed in clothes or vessels that make it possible for us to apprehend them—as, for example, radio or television waves have to be transmitted through appropriate vessels to be revealed to our senses. In the same way, there are aspects of the reality of the spiritual world of which we are only vaguely conscious. Even animals can sometimes be sensitive, if to a limited degree, to the presence of such a spiritual essence. The ass of Balaam, for instance, who "saw" an angel, did not of course actually see the angel: probably the animal had some obscure sensation of being confronted or threatened by something.

Angels have been revealed to human beings in either of two ways: one is though the vision of the prophet, the seer, or the holy man—that is, an experience by a person on the highest level; the other is through an isolated act of apprehension by an ordinary person suddenly privileged to receive a revelation of things from higher levels. And even so, when such a person or prophet does in some way experience the reality of an angel, his perception, limited by his senses, remains bound to material structures, and his language inevitably tends to expressions of actual or imagined physical forms. Thus, when the prophet tries to describe or to explain to others his experience of seeing an angel, the description verges on the eerie and fantastic. Terms like "winged creature of heaven" or "eyes of the supreme chariot" can be only a pale and inadequate representation of the experience because this experience belongs to another realm with another system of imagery. The description will of necessity tend to be anthropomorphic. Or when, as we know, the angel whom the prophet describes as having the face of an ox does not have any face at all—and certainly not that of an ox—its inner essence, seeking elucidation and reflection within material reality, may express itself in a way that shows a certain likeness between the face of an angel and the face of an ox as the expression of a known spiritual quality.

Thus, all the articulated visions of prophecy are nothing more than ways of representing an abstract formless spiritual reality in the vocabulary of human language; although, to be sure, there may also be a revelation of an angel in quite ordinary form, clothed in some familiar vessel and manifested as a "normal" phenomenon in nature. The difficulty is that the one who sees an angel in this way does not always know that it is an apparition, that the pillar of fire or the image of a man does not belong entirely to the realm of natural cause and effect. And at the same time, the angel—that is to say, the force sent from a higher world—makes its appearance and to a certain extent acts in the material world, being either entirely subject to the laws of our world or operating in a sort of vacuum between the worlds which physical nature is no more than a kind of garment for some higher substance. In the Bible, Manoah, the father of Samson, sees the angel in the image of a prophet; yet he senses in some inexplicable way that it is not a man he sees, that he is witnessing a phenomenon of a different order. Only when the angel changes form completely and becomes a pillar of fire does Manoah recognize that this being, this marvel which he has seen and with whom he has conversed, was not a man, not a prophet, but a being from another dimension of reality—that is to say, an angel. The creation of an angel in our world and the immediate relegation of this angel to another world is, in itself, not at all a supernatural phenomenon; it is a part of a familiar realm of experience, an integral piece of life, which may even seem ordinary and commonplace because of its traditional rootedness in the system of *mitzvot*, or the order of sanctity. When we are in the act of creating the angel, we have no perception of the angel being created, and this act seems to be a part of the whole structure of the practical material world in which we live. Similarly, the angel who is sent to us from another world does not always have a significance or impact beyond the normal laws of physical nature. Indeed, it often happens that the angel precisely reveals itself in nature, in the ordinary common-sense world of causality, and only a prophetic insight or divination can show when, and to what extent, it is the work of higher forces. For man by his very nature is bound to the system of higher worlds, even though ordinarily this system is not revealed and known to him. As a result, the system of higher worlds seems to him to be natural, just as the whole of his two-sided existence, including both matter and spirit, seems self-evident to him. Man does not wonder at all about those passages he goes through all the time in the world of action, from the realm of material existence to the realm of spiritual existence. What is more, the rest of the other worlds that also penetrate our world may appear to us as part of something quite natural. It may be said that the realities of the angel and of the world of formation are part of a system of "natural" being which is as bound by law as that aspect of existence we are able to observe directly. Therefore neither the existence of the angel nor his "mission," taking him from world to world, need break through the reality of nature in the broadest sense of the word.

The domain of angels, the world of formation, is a general system of nonphysical essences, most of them quite simple and consistent in their being. Each angel has a well-defined character which is manifested in the way it functions in our world. This is why it is said that an angel can carry out only one mission, for the essence of an angel is beyond the existing many-sidedness of man. The particular essence of an angel can be evinced in terms of different things and separate forms, but it remains a single thing in itself, like a simple force of nature. Because even though the angel is a being that possesses divine consciousness, its specific essence and function are not altered by it, just as physical forces in the world are specific and single in their mode of functioning and do not keep changing their essences. It follows, then, that just as there are holy angels, built into and created by the sacred system, there are also destructive angels, called "devils" or "demons," who are the emanations of the connection of man with those aspects of reality which are the opposite of holiness. Here, too, the actions of man and his modes of existence, in all their forms, create angels, but angels of another sort, from another level and a different reality. These are hostile angels that may be part of a lower world or even a higher, more spiritual world—this last because even though they do not belong to the realm of holiness, as in all worlds and systems of being, there is a mutual interpenetration and influence between the holy and the not-holy.

The Thirteen Petalled Rose,
(Jerusalem: Koren Publishers, 2010),
excerpt from ch. 1, "Worlds," pp. 3–9

pause
& AFFECT

LESSON 5

Sacred Symbolisms

ROSHCHODESH society

SHABBAT MEMORIES

Text 1

EMMA RUDOLPH, "SHABBAT MEALS: PERFECT ROASTED CHICKEN," *THE FORWARD*, OCTOBER 17, 2012

Every Shabbat, for as long as I can remember, roast chicken had a place at my family's dinner table. . . . Maybe [my mother] chose it because Shabbat came at the end to a very long week of taking care of two young, constantly bickering little girls. Maybe she chose it because she knew she could make an entire dinner, adding whatever vegetables or potatoes were around, in the same pan. Or maybe she chose it because not even the pickiest of eaters can resist the comfort of perfectly roasted chicken.

First, she would surround the chicken with vegetables, sprinkle everything with fresh herbs, and stuff the cavity with a lemon. The kitchen would soon fill with the sweet aroma of caramelizing carrots, onions and leeks. Then came the first bite: crackling golden brown chicken skin spiked with hints of garlic and rosemary. Underneath the skin, tender, juicy meat fell straight off the bone. Follow this bite with a succulent potato, softened and sweetened from the pan juices of the chicken. Welcome to Shabbat roast chicken heaven.

This was the routine that formed the basis for so many of my childhood Shabbat memories. I probably complained a few times about the repetition of chicken on Fridays. I may have even

EMMA RUDOLPH

Editor and food blogger. Emma is the associate editor at Weldon Owen Publishing in San Francisco, California. She is a contributor to *The Forward,* providing flavorful anecdotes and recipes for cooking.

whined for mac 'n' cheese, like "normal" kids. But now, as a college student, there's nothing I crave so deeply on a Friday night as my mom's roasted chicken. . . .

One recent Friday night, in my college apartment a few thousand miles from home, I needed to remember what a "real" Shabbat felt like again. No last minute pasta, sub-par Jewish Student Union dinner, or delivery pizza, but real make-you-feel-good-and-Jewish-to-the-bone Shabbat dinner.

I invited a few friends over, cut up a few vegetables, and popped the chicken in the hot oven. My friends were shocked by how few steps it took me to make a whole, real meal. . . . But that first bite of juicy, moist meat covered in flavorful, crispy skin was all I needed to send me right back in time, to Shabbat dinners with family.

THE SANCTIFICATION PROCLAMATION
A PARTNERSHIP

Text 2
EXODUS 20:8

זָכוֹר אֶת יוֹם הַשַּׁבָּת לְקַדְּשׁוֹ.

Remember the day of Shabbat to sanctify it.

Text 3
GENESIS 1:31–2:3

יוֹם הַשִּׁשִּׁי.
וַיְכֻלּוּ הַשָּׁמַיִם וְהָאָרֶץ וְכָל צְבָאָם.
וַיְכַל אֱלֹקִים בַּיּוֹם הַשְּׁבִיעִי מְלַאכְתּוֹ אֲשֶׁר עָשָׂה.
וַיִּשְׁבֹּת בַּיּוֹם הַשְּׁבִיעִי מִכָּל מְלַאכְתּוֹ אֲשֶׁר עָשָׂה.
וַיְבָרֶךְ אֱלֹקִים אֶת יוֹם הַשְּׁבִיעִי וַיְקַדֵּשׁ אֹתוֹ, כִּי בוֹ שָׁבַת מִכָּל
מְלַאכְתּוֹ אֲשֶׁר בָּרָא אֱלֹקִים לַעֲשׂוֹת.

The sixth day.

The heavens and the earth and all their hosts were completed.

God finished by the seventh day His work that He had done, and He rested on the seventh day from all His work that He had done.

God blessed the seventh day and made it holy, for on it He rested from all His work that He created and fashioned.

Text 4a

GENESIS 1:23

וַיְהִי עֶרֶב וַיְהִי בֹקֶר יוֹם חֲמִישִׁי.

It was evening, and it was morning, a fifth day.

Text 4b

GENESIS 1:31

וַיְהִי עֶרֶב וַיְהִי בֹקֶר יוֹם הַשִּׁשִּׁי.

It was evening, and it was morning, the sixth day.

Text 5

RABBI SAMSON RAPHAEL HIRSCH, GENESIS 1:31

The definite article "the" which precedes a noun presents the thing (or person or entity) as something expected; we are prepared for it, and expect it, due to what was stated before. "Here is *a* man" presents "man" as a new idea, without any preparation, whereas "Here is *the* man" presents "man" as something expected, something we have a right to expect in light of the preceding.

Thus, had Scripture said *yom shishi*, "a sixth day," there would have been no relation to the preceding days, except for the ordinal relation; there would have been no indication that this day was prepared for by all those days that preceded it, and was awaited by all that came before it.

Scripture, however, says, "And it was evening and it was morning, *the* sixth day." The clear implication is that this is the day for which all the preceding days served as preliminaries; all of Creation led up to the sixth day which gave Creation its goal and culmination. . . .

Now the sixth day brought man to earth. On this day the earth was given its master and governor, who would rule it in God's stead. . . . All of Creation hinges on whether this creature—man—will accept and fulfill his exalted mission. . . .

The seventh day . . . was assigned the following task: to remind man, who was created on the sixth day, of the exaltedness of his position and of the dependence of his position—and of the duties that devolve upon him as a result. . . . It

RABBI SAMSON RAPHAEL HIRSCH
1808–1888

Born in Hamburg, Germany; rabbi and educator; intellectual founder of the *Torah Im Derech Eretz* school of Orthodox Judaism, which advocates combining Torah with secular education. Beginning in 1830, Hirsch served as chief rabbi in several prominent German cities. During this period he wrote his *Nineteen Letters on Judaism*, under the pseudonym of Ben Uziel. His work helped preserve traditional Judaism during the era of the German Enlightenment. He is buried in Frankfurt am Main.

is with good reason, then, that we begin the *kiddush* with "The sixth day," etc.

Text 6

TALMUD, SHABBAT 119B

כָּל הַמִתְפַּלֵל בְּעֶרֶב שַׁבָּת וְאוֹמֵר וַיְכֻלּוּ, מַעֲלֶה עָלָיו הַכָּתוּב כְּאִילוּ נַעֲשָׂה שׁוּתָּף לְהַקָדוֹשׁ בָּרוּךְ הוּא בְּמַעֲשֵׂה בְרֵאשִׁית.

One who prays on Friday night and says "*vayechulu*" is considered by Scripture as if he were a partner with God in Creation.

BABYLONIAN TALMUD

A literary work of monumental proportions that draws upon the legal, spiritual, intellectual, ethical, and historical traditions of Judaism. The 37 tractates of the Babylonian Talmud contain the teachings of the Jewish sages from the period after the destruction of the 2nd Temple through the 5th century CE. It has served as the primary vehicle for the transmission of the Oral Law and the education of Jews over the centuries; it is the entry point for all subsequent legal, ethical, and theological Jewish scholarship.

Text 7a

TALMUD, SANHEDRIN 38A

נִכְנַס יַיִן יָצָא סוֹד.

When wine enters, secrets emerge.

Text 7b

RABBI YEHUDAH ARYEH LEIB ALTER, *SEFAT EMET,* KI TISA 5653

בְּשַׁבָּת נִגְלָה הַפְּנִימִיּוּת הַנִסְתָּר. וּכְמוֹ שֶׁהוּא מִצִּדּוֹ יִתְבָּרֵךְ שְׁמוֹ, כֵּן בְּנַפְשׁוֹת בְּנֵי יִשְׂרָאֵל, נִפְתַּח פְּנִימִיּוּת הַלֵּב בְּשַׁבָּת קוֹדֶשׁ . . . וַחֲכָמֵינוּ זִכְרוֹנָם לִבְרָכָה אָמְרוּ (תַּלְמוּד בַּבְלִי, פְּסָחִים קו, א): "זָכוֹר אֶת יוֹם הַשַּׁבָּת - זָכְרֵהוּ עַל הַיַּיִן". הָרֶמֶז הוּא שֶׁבּוֹ נִגְלָה הַסוֹד הַפְּנִימִיּוּת, שֶׁזֶּה פְּעוּלַּת הַיַּיִן.

On Shabbat, the innermost truths are revealed. Just as it is so with respect to God, it is also so for us—the innermost parts of our identities are revealed on Shabbat. . . . Hence, our sages said (Talmud, Pesachim 106a), "Mention the day of Shabbat to sanctify it—mention it over wine." The symbolism of wine is that it is a tool that reveals the inner secrets.

RABBI YEHUDAH ARYEH LEIB ALTER *(SEFAT EMET)*

1847–1905 Chasidic master and scholar. Rabbi Yehudah Aryeh Leib Alter assumed the leadership of the Chasidic dynasty of Gur (Gora), a town near Warsaw, Poland, at the age of 23. He was the grandson and successor of Rabbi Yitschak Meir of Gur, the founder of the Gur dynasty. He is commonly referred to as the *Sefat Emet,* after the title of his commentaries on the Torah and Talmud.

Text 8

RABBI DAVID ABUDRAHAM, *SIDDUR, MA'ARIV SHEL SHABBOS*

עוֹד שָׁמַעְתִּי טַעַם אַחֵר, וְאַתְיָא כְּמַאן דְאָמַר (בְּרָכוֹת מ, א) "עֵץ שֶׁאָכַל מִמֶּנּוּ אָדָם הָרִאשׁוֹן גֶּפֶן הָיָה", וּלְפִיכָךְ נִקְנְסָה עָלָיו מִיתָה. וְלָכֵן הוּא אוֹמֵר "סַבְרִי מָרָנָן?" הֲיֵשׁ בְּדַעְתְּכֶם שֶׁזֶּה הַכּוֹס הוּא לְחַיִּים, וְלֹא לַמָּוֶת כְּאוֹתוֹ שֶׁל אָדָם הָרִאשׁוֹן? וְהֵם עוֹנִים לְחַיֵּי, לְחַיִּים יִהְיֶה וְלֹא יִהְיֶה לַמָּוֶת.

I heard another explanation. It follows the Talmudic view (Berachot 40a) that the forbidden fruit that Adam ate was a grape, and as a result,

RABBI DAVID BEN YOSEF ABUDRAHAM
14TH CENTURY

Resided in Seville, Spain, and is famous for his work on Jewish prayers and blessings. The work—completed around the year 1340—is a commentary on the daily, Shabbat, and festival prayers and collects many customs and laws relating to them. He is believed to have been a disciple of Rabbi Ya'akov ben Asher, author of *Arba'ah Turim.*

death was decreed upon humankind. The reciter of *kiddush* therefore says, "*Savri maranan*? (Do you agree that this cup should be for life, and that it should not be for death as were the grapes that Adam consumed?)" And they all answer "*Lechayei*! (Let it be for life and not for death!)"

CREATION AND EXODUS

Text 9

FRIDAY NIGHT *KIDDUSH*

בָּרוּךְ אַתָּה . . . מֶלֶךְ הָעוֹלָם, אֲשֶׁר קִדְּשָׁנוּ בְּמִצְוֹתָיו וְרָצָה בָנוּ, וְשַׁבַּת קָדְשׁוֹ בְּאַהֲבָה וּבְרָצוֹן הִנְחִילָנוּ, זִכָּרוֹן לְמַעֲשֵׂה בְרֵאשִׁית, תְּחִלָּה לְמִקְרָאֵי קֹדֶשׁ, זֵכֶר לִיצִיאַת מִצְרָיִם . . .

Blessed are You . . . King of the Universe, Who has hallowed us with His commandments, has desired us, and has given us, in love and goodwill, His holy Shabbat as a heritage, in remembrance of the work of Creation. It is the first of the holy festivals, commemorating the Exodus from Egypt. . . .

GOLDEN LOAVES

MODERN MANNA

Text 10

EXODUS 16:22–23

וַיְהִי בַּיּוֹם הַשִּׁשִּׁי לָקְטוּ לֶחֶם מִשְׁנֶה שְׁנֵי הָעֹמֶר לָאֶחָד, וַיָּבֹאוּ
כָּל נְשִׂיאֵי הָעֵדָה, וַיַּגִּידוּ לְמֹשֶׁה.
וַיֹּאמֶר אֲלֵהֶם: הוּא אֲשֶׁר דִּבֶּר ה' שַׁבָּתוֹן שַׁבַּת קֹדֶשׁ לַה' מָחָר,
אֵת אֲשֶׁר תֹּאפוּ אֵפוּ, וְאֵת אֲשֶׁר תְּבַשְּׁלוּ בַּשֵּׁלוּ, וְאֵת כָּל הָעֹדֵף
הַנִּיחוּ לָכֶם לְמִשְׁמֶרֶת עַד הַבֹּקֶר.

On the sixth day, they gathered a double portion of bread, two *omers* for each person. The princes of the community came and reported this to Moses.

Moses said to them, "This is what God said, 'Tomorrow is a holy Shabbat to God. Bake whatever you wish to bake, and cook whatever you wish to cook, and all the rest leave over for safekeeping until morning.'"

Text 11

RABBI YA'AKOV BEN ASHER, *ARBA'AH TURIM, ORACH CHAYIM* 271

וַאֲנִי שָׁמַעְתִּי טַעַם לַעֲשׂוֹת זֵכֶר לַמָּן, שֶׁהָיָה מוּנָּח כְּמוֹ בְּקוּפְסָא טַל לְמַעְלָה וְטַל לְמַטָּה, וְזֵכֶר לָזֶה נוֹתְנִין מַפָּה תַּחַת הַפַּת וְאַחֶרֶת עַל גַּבָּיו.

I have heard that one reason [for covering the bread on Shabbat] is in order to commemorate the manna, which would appear as if it were in a chest, with dew on the bottom and dew on the top. To commemorate this, we put one cloth under the bread and another above it.

RABBI YA'AKOV BEN ASHER (*TUR*, BA'AL HATURIM)
CA. 1269–1343

Halachic authority and codifier. Rabbi Ya'akov was born in Germany and moved to Toledo, Spain, with his father, the noted halachist Rabbeinu Asher, to escape persecution. He wrote *Arba'ah Turim ("Tur")*, an ingeniously organized and highly influential code of Jewish law. He is considered one of the greatest authorities of halachah.

Question for Discussion

Why is it important for us to recall the miracle of the manna specifically on Shabbat? After all, the manna nourished the Jewish people during all seven days of the week.

EXTREME SENSITIVITY

Text 12

DEUTERONOMY 8:7–8

כִּי ה' אֱלֹקֶיךָ מְבִיאֲךָ אֶל אֶרֶץ טוֹבָה . . . אֶרֶץ חִטָּה וּשְׂעֹרָה וְגֶפֶן וּתְאֵנָה וְרִמּוֹן אֶרֶץ זֵית שֶׁמֶן וּדְבָשׁ.

God is bringing you to a good land . . . a land of wheat and barley, vines and figs and pomegranates, a land of oil-producing olives, and honey.

Text 13a

RABBI YA'AKOV BEN ASHER, *ARBA'AH TURIM, ORACH CHAYIM* 271

בִּירוּשַׁלְמִי קָאֲמַר שֶׁלֹּא יִרְאֶה הַפַּת בּוֹשְׁתּוֹ – פֵּירוּשׁ שֶׁהוּא מוּקְדָּם בַּפָּסוּק, וְהָיָה רָאוּי לְהַקְדִּימוֹ בַּבְּרָכָה, וּמַקְדִּימִין בְּבִרְכַּת הַיַּיִן.

The Jerusalem Talmud explains that we cover the bread so that it will not see its own humiliation. The explanation: grain is mentioned first in the verse. Thus, it would be proper to make the blessing first [on bread which is made from grain], yet we make the blessing on the wine first.

Text 13b

REBBETZIN ESTHER JUNGREIS, *THE COMMITTED LIFE* (NEW YORK: CLIFF STREET BOOKS, 1999), P. 19

Obviously, challah does not have feelings, but our sages wanted to impart a lesson to us. If bread, which is inanimate, must be treated with such care and consideration, how much more so must we be on guard not to embarrass or hurt a person.

REBBETZIN ESTHER JUNGREIS
1936–2016

Born in Szeged, Hungary. She came to the U.S. after surviving the Bergen-Belsen concentration camp. Determined to devote her life to strengthening Judaism in the U.S. and around the world, she founded Hineni, an organization that provides Torah classes and other programs for the Jewish community. She was a noted lecturer and author of numerous books, including *The Jewish Soul on Fire* and *The Committed Marriage*.

SHABBAT FISH AND MEAT

A DIFFERENT KETTLE OF FISH

Text 14

EDWARD S. LEVIN, "GEFILTE FISH: A SWEET MEMORY OF MOTHER AT PASSOVER SEDER," *CHICAGO TRIBUNE*, MARCH 31, 1988

Recently, while browsing through the supermarket, a jar of "Mother's" gefilte fish caught my eye and spoke to me in boldface type. . . . It brought me back to the magic of my mother's cooking because my mother's recipe, like their "Mother's" recipe, began with "No sugar added." . . .

Each Passover, as if she were reading a portion of her own personal Haggadah, she told us the story of her gefilte fish. It began with the fact that we were Litvaks—proud, wise, brilliant and generous. Our fish, she explained, was sweet because it was fresh and well prepared. "No sugar added—no sugar needed!"

On the other hand, sugar was an essential ingredient for Galitzianer housewives. They used it to cover a multitude of sins, especially cheap ingredients and poor cooking. Litvaks and Galitzianer were the Hatfields and McCoys of European Jewry, each ascribing to the other traits they'd rather not see in themselves. . . .

By the time the fish was passed a second time she'd get around to the part of her story where she told us that all of our aunts made delicious gefilte fish too, but a couple of them probably added sugar. One in particular was very suspect. Of course it was the one she didn't like, who was, no doubt, a Galiltzianer trying to sugar-coat her past....

A few years after I was married my mother gave my wife her final sign of acceptance. She shared her secret recipe for gefilte fish. Mom was visiting us. Dad was on a business trip. To fill some of the endless hours that develop between mothers-in-law and daughters-in-law, my mother suggested, "Why don't I show you how to make gefilte fish?" Ruth jumped at the chance. Off they went to the fish store to begin the lesson with fish selection and gill reading.

On their return, a cauldron of water was set to boil, awaiting the chopped balls of fish. The room should have been darkened as Mom cast her spell over all of the ingredients. She turned a deep red, blushing, as she said, "Ruth, I swear you to secrecy. Promise you'll never tell anyone so long as I live. Get me the sugar bowl, a tablespoon and a cup of water."

She dipped the spoon in the water and the wet spoon in the sugar and stirred the pulpy mass. Embarrassed, she explained that she really wasn't adding sugar "just the amount that would stick to a wet spoon." Ruth suppressed a giggle but Mom was dead serious.

So it wasn't "No sugar added" after all. It was "almost no sugar added."

Text 15

TALMUD, SHABBAT 118B

בַּמֶּה מְעַנְּגוֹ?
רַב יְהוּדָה בְּרֵיהּ דְּרַב שְׁמוּאֵל בַּר שִׁילַת מִשְּׁמֵיהּ דְּרַב אָמַר: בְּתַבְשִׁיל שֶׁל תְּרָדִין, וְדָגִים גְּדוֹלִים, וְרָאשֵׁי שׁוּמִין.
רַב חִיָּיא בַּר אַשִׁי אָמַר רַב: אֲפִילוּ דָּבָר מוּעָט וְלִכְבוֹד שַׁבָּת עֲשָׂאוֹ, הֲרֵי זֶה עוֹנֶג.
מַאי הִיא? אָמַר רַב פָּפָּא: כָּסָא דְהַרְסְנָא.

How should one have pleasure on Shabbat?

Rav Yehudah son of Rav Shmuel bar Shilat said in Rav's name, "With a dish of beets, large fish, and heads of garlic."

Rav Chiya bar Ashi said in Rav's name, "Even something small—if it is prepared in honor of Shabbat, it satisfies the obligation to take delight."

What is something small?

Rav Papa said, "A pie of fish-hash."

Learning Exercise 1

There are various Jewish ritual laws pertaining to kosher fish and meat. In the left column, list any rule regarding fish; in the right column, list any rule related to meat.

Kosher regulations for fish	Kosher regulations for meat

Text 16

RABBI TSADOK HAKOHEN RABINOWITZ,
PERI TSADIK, PARASHAT EMOR 6

שֶׁעִיקָר עוֹנֶג שַׁבָּת בְּדָגִים, מִשּׁוּם שֶׁאֵין בָּהֶם שׁוּם אִיסוּר חֵלֶב, וְגִיד הַנָּשֶׁה. וּבְעוֹפוֹת יֵשׁ עַל כָּל פָּנִים אִיסוּר דָּם וּנְבֵילָה. מַה שֶּׁאֵין כֵּן בְּדָגִים. מִכְּלָל דְּבִדָגִים אֵין בָּהֶם עִרְבּוּב טוֹב וָרָע.

The primary way to take pleasure on Shabbat is by consuming fish. Unlike animals, there are no prohibited fats in fish nor is there the prohibited sciatic nerve. Although poultry does not have these prohibited elements, the prohibition of blood still pertains to poultry, and it must be slaughtered in a proper manner. None of these laws pertain to fish. With regard to fish, there is no mixture of holy and unholy.

RABBI TSADOK HAKOHEN RABINOWITZ
1823–1900

Chasidic master and thinker. Rabbi Tsadok was born into a Lithuanian rabbinic family and later joined the Chasidic movement. He was a follower of the Chasidic leaders Rabbi Mordechai Yosef Leiner of Izbica and Rabbi Leibel Eiger. He succeeded Rabbi Eiger after his passing and became a rebbe in Lublin, Poland. He authored many works on Jewish law, Chasidism, kabbalah, and ethics, as well as scholarly essays on astronomy, geometry, and algebra.

Question for Discussion

Given these differences between fish and meat, and given what we know about Shabbat, why is there a special requirement to consume fish on this day?

STUFFED FISH

Text 17

ERIC G. FREUDENSTEIN, "SABBATH FISH," *JUDAISM: A QUARTERLY JOURNAL OF JEWISH LIFE AND THOUGHT* 29:4 (1980), PP. 430–431

In the last two hundred years or so, the custom has [become] to eat the Sabbath fish as gefilte fish. That phrase is, of course, the Yiddish for stuffed fish. In the original version of this delicacy, the fish was chopped, mixed with flour and condiments, and this filling was used to stuff the skin of the fish. The whole was then cooked, cut into slices and served. . . .

An important reason why fish, rather than meat, became the preferred Sabbath fish dish was economics. Impoverished Jewish communities could hardly have afforded meat on every ordinary Sabbath, but some kind of fish was usually available at prices that were within reach. The utilization of every morsel was important for a poor community, and in the making of gefilte fish, the housewife could use every ounce. . . .

The Sabbath laws specify the preferred manner in which the edible part of the food shall be separated from the inedible portion, and even the manner in which the residue of the meal, such as the peelings and pits of fruit or the bones and skin of fish, can be removed from the table is laid down in the rules. To do so according to the strictures of *halakhah* requires learning, which not everyone possessed, and which could not be expected from the indigent guests who were often invited to the Sabbath table. All of these

ERIC FREUDENSTEIN
D. 2008

Nutritional scientist and Hebrew scholar. Freudenstein was chief chemist of the Jewish food giant Rokeach for 50 years and was also an ardent Talmudist. His papers have been published in a volume entitled *Yad Gavriel*, that being Eric's Hebrew name.

problems were eliminated by serving the fish in boneless and skinless portions.

"Come and let us give credit to Israel, the holy people," writes a halakhic authority in the name of the Brisker Rav, "for establishing the custom of eating fish on the Sabbath in the form of stuffed fish, thereby eliminating all manner of religious scruples and doubts."

CHOLENT

Text 18

HEINRICH HEINE, "PRINCESS SABBATH," IN *THE STANDARD BOOK OF JEWISH VERSE* (NEW YORK: DODD, MEAD, 1917), P. 256

She denies her lover nothing
Save the smoking of tobacco;
"Dearest, smoking is forbidden,
For to-day it is the Sabbath.

"But at noon, as compensation,
There shall steam for thee a dish
That in very truth divine is—
Thou shalt eat to-day of schalet!

"Schalet, ray of light immortal!
Schalet, daughter of Elysium!"
So had Schiller's song resounded,
Had he ever tasted schalet,

For this schalet is the very
Food of heaven, which, on Sinai,
God Himself instructed Moses
In the secret of preparing . . .

HEINRICH HEINE
1797–1856

German poet. Heine was born Jewish and attended the universities of Bonn, Göttingen, and Berlin. In 1825, in order to open up the possibility of a civil service career, which was closed to Jews at that time, he converted to Protestantism with little enthusiasm and some resentment. Heine's international literary reputation and influence were established by the *Buch der Lieder* (*The Book of Songs*), frequently set to music, though the more somber poems of his last years are also highly regarded.

Text 19

EXODUS 35:3

לֹא תְבַעֲרוּ אֵשׁ בְּכֹל מֹשְׁבֹתֵיכֶם בְּיוֹם הַשַּׁבָּת.

You shall not cause fire to burn in any of your dwelling places on the day of Shabbat.

PERSONAL PREFERENCE

Text 20

RABBI SHNE'UR ZALMAN OF LIADI, *SHULCHAN ARUCH HARAV* 252:2, 7

בַּמֶּה מְעַנְּגוֹ? בִּימֵי חַכְמֵי הַגְּמָרָא הָיוּ מְעַנְּגִין בְּדָגִים גְּדוֹלִים, וּבְתַבְשִׁיל שֶׁל תְּרָדִין, שֶׁמַּאֲכָלִים אֵלּוּ הָיוּ חֲשׁוּבִים עֹנֶג בִּימֵיהֶם. וְכָל מָקוֹם וּמָקוֹם לְפִי מִנְהָגוֹ יַעַנְּגוּהוּ בְּמַאֲכָלִים וּמַשְׁקִים הַחֲשׁוּבִים לָהֶם עֹנֶג.

וְאֵין חִיּוּב לֶאֱכוֹל בָּשָׂר וְלִשְׁתּוֹת יַיִן בְּשַׁבָּת, אֶלָּא לְפִי שֶׁמִּן הַסְּתָם יֵשׁ לְרוֹב בְּנֵי אָדָם עֹנֶג בַּאֲכִילַת בָּשָׂר יוֹתֵר מִבִּשְׁאָר מַאֲכָלִים, וּבִשְׁתִיַּית יַיִן יוֹתֵר מִבִּשְׁאָר מַשְׁקִים, לְכָךְ יֵשׁ לָהֶם לְהַרְבּוֹת בְּבָשָׂר וְיַיִן כְּפִי יְכָלְתָּם וְהַשָּׂגַת יָדָם.

. . . וְטוֹב לִיזָּהֵר לֶאֱכוֹל דָּגִים בְּכָל סְעוּדָה, אֶלָּא אִם כֵּן הַדָּגִים מַזִּיקִים לוֹ לְפִי טִבְעוֹ, אוֹ שֶׁשּׂוֹנְאָם, שֶׁאֵין לוֹ מֵהֶם עוֹנֶג אֶלָּא צַעַר, וְהַשַּׁבָּת לְעֹנֶג נִיתַּן.

How does one have pleasure on Shabbat? In the days of the Talmudic sages they would have pleasure with large fish and a dish of beets. These foods were considered to be delightful in those days, and in every place, one should enjoy the food and drink that are considered delightful in that location.

There is no obligation to eat meat and drink wine on Shabbat. However, because most people enjoy eating meat more than other foods, and in drinking wine more than other drinks, therefore these people should have as much meat and wine as they can enjoy and afford.

. . . It is preferable to be careful about eating fish during all Shabbat meals. This is not true,

RABBI SHNE'UR ZALMAN OF LIADI (ALTER REBBE)
1745–1812

Chasidic rebbe, halachic authority, and founder of the Chabad movement. The Alter Rebbe was born in Liozna, Belarus, and was among the principal students of the Magid of Mezeritch. His numerous works include the *Tanya,* an early classic containing the fundamentals of Chabad Chasidism, and *Shulchan Aruch HaRav,* an expanded and reworked code of Jewish law.

however, if doing so would be harmful, or if one dislikes fish, in which case consuming fish would cause pain instead of pleasure. For Shabbat was given for pleasure.

Learning Exercise 2

Let us wrap up today's lesson by writing down one message that resonated with you from each of the Shabbat foods discussed in this lesson.

	Message
Wine	
Challah	
Fish	
Meat	

Key Points

1. Many of the traditional Shabbat foods are not merely tasty dishes, but they also convey significant symbolisms about Shabbat and life. In this way, our Shabbat meals can become a platform for higher states of consciousness.
2. In *kiddush,* we allude to the fact that the sixth day of Creation brought the human being to Earth. This is because Shabbat is meant to remind the human being of the exaltedness of her position and the duties that devolve upon her as a result.
3. While nature appears to be independent from God, our task is to demonstrate that God is present in and in control of nature. We begin doing so by reciting *kiddush,* and we thereby partner with God in His Creation, allowing the world to reach its desired state.
4. *kiddush* is recited over wine inasmuch as wine is symbolic of revealing that which is normally concealed. There are underlying truths about the world and about us that are normally concealed, and Shabbat allows us to tap these deeper layers and to make them known to us and those around us.
5. While wine can provide us with various benefits, we need to be mindful about its dangers and alert to the fact that we are consuming it for a purpose. This consciousness can help protect against misuse.
6. In *kiddush,* we mention the link between Shabbat and the Creation and Exodus. This invites us to revisit the most important ideas and questions about God: His Creation of the world, His involvement in our lives, and the purpose He set out for us.
7. The two loaves on Shabbat remind us of the biblical story of the manna. The message of this story is that while we need to act, initiate, and plan for our

success, ultimately, "It is the blessing of God that makes us prosper."

8. When on Shabbat we cover the bread for *kiddush*, we remind ourselves of the lengths to which we must go to be sensitive to the dignity of others.
9. One symbolic reason for consuming fish on Shabbat is that fish represent a state of existence that is constantly aware of its Godly source and is thus immune to wrongdoing. On Shabbat, we have the ability to tap into this state of existence.

ADDITIONAL READINGS

THE SYMBOLISM OF CHALLAH

By Yiskah Fantl

There are many beautiful insights on the mitzvah of Challah. While I only have room to encourage a few, I encourage everyone to continue to learn and grow from this extraordinary mitzvah.

Challah embodies the concept of taking something physical and elevating it to the spiritual. Not only are we giving physical nourishment to the people that are eating our challah, they are also being nourished spiritually with the ideas and blessing that we are thinking of and praying for while we are making our challah.

The aroma and taste of warm home baked challah is unparalleled. Making challah is a spiritual experience, and there are a great deal of blessings and insights in each of its ingredients.

There are seven basic ingredients in a challah recipe; water, yeast, sugar, eggs, oil, flour, and salt. There is a special eighth ingredient that is unique to each and every one of us, and that is our souls. When we are making the challah, we are putting our personal energy into the dough. As we add each ingredient we can add a new blessing to our dough, which will enhance the spiritual blessings, for whoever is eating our challah and will also ingest these blessings.

Water: Water represents Torah. Just as we cannot live without water, we also cannot live without Torah. Water brings life and nourishment to all things, so it represents the attribute of *chessed* (kindness). As we add the water, we can think of something in our lives that we want G-d to bless us with in abundant kindness. It should flow down into our lives, just as water flows.

Yeast: Yeast is what enables our dough to rise. Yeast represents growth and expansion. So as we add the yeast, we can think of each one of our family members and friends and pray that they grow and expand in their emotional, physical, and spiritual wellbeing. Yeast also represents rising, rising to our full potentials. We ask that God help all of us rise to who we are meant to be in our fullest potential. Yeast in Hebrew is *shmarim,* which comes from the same root *shomer*, which means protection. As we add the yeast, we should pray for protection for ourselves, our families, Israel, the IDF, and all of the Jewish people.

Eggs: Eggs represent the renewal of the life cycle and the potential of what is about to "hatch." Again, while making the dough, we pray for life, children, and anything going on in our lives that we want God to reveal to us.

Oil: Oil represents anointing. Oil was used to anoint the Jewish kings. When adding your oil, pour a little at a time, "anointing" each one of your loved ones by name and praying for their specific needs.

Sugar: Sugar represents anything sweet in our lives, all the revealed good. We ask G-d for open blessings and open good at this time. Sugar also represents *emunah* (faith). When we have the proper faith, then everything becomes sweet. Even the challenges in our lives, we realize are all from G-d and are all for the best.

Salt: Salt represents discipline or criticism. It is important to have this, but in smaller measure. When adding the salt, we should shake a little off the top. As much as we feel we need to

---

YISKAH FANTL

Yiskah grew up with no Jewish affiliation, until she found antisemitic graffiti in her high school locker. Inspired to learn more about her heritage, Yiskah became a regular attendee of the Chabad at Ohio State University and went on to study in Israel. She is a teacher in a Jewish day school in Cleveland, Ohio, where she lives with her husband and daughter.

rebuke others, we could always give a little less rebuke than we feel is necessary. Salt also represents purification. We pray that anything that is toxic in our lives, minds, souls, and bodies be removed.

Flour: Flour represents sustenance, not only our livelihood, but also our relationships with others. We pray that G-d should bless us with a livelihood that we should use for the right reasons, and that He helps us sustain a relationship that might need some assistance, and thank Him for the relationships we do have that sustain us.

The last step in making the dough is to take all of these essential ingredients that bring their own important blessings and unify them. We think about the oneness of G-d and the oneness of the Jewish people, and as we knead the dough this is also a special time to pray for anything you, your family, friends, or the world needs.

We then let the dough rise.

http://www.shabbosprojectcle.com/the-symbolism-of-challah/
Reprinted with permission of the author

AN ADDITIONAL NOTE ON THE KIDDUSH RITUAL

by Rabbi Adin Steinsaltz

The eve of the Sabbath does not only usher in the day of rest; it has its own particular aspect and significance. Every hour of the preceding afternoon marks another level of an emotionally peaked transition from the six working days of the week to the Sabbath day. The evening before the holy day is therefore itself a climax and a final stage of the transition, to all that the day means, both as a conclusion of the week and as a higher level of existence, beyond the six days of action, beyond time.

This higher level of the Sabbath is bound up with the divine manifestation in the *Sefirah* of *Malkhut* ("kingdom"), which represents the *Shekhinah* and also the totality, the receptacle that absorbs all that occurs, and is also connected with the first *Sefirah*, the Crown. Therefore the quality of Sabbath Eve, which is the summing up of work and events in time, can also be a preparation for the manifestation of the Sabbath as the crown and beginning of time. The *Sefirah* of *Malkhut*, or the *Shekhinah*, represents the divine power as manifested in reality, operating in an infinite variety of ways and means. It has seventy names, each expressing another aspect, another face of this all inclusive *Sefirah*. For *Malkhut* is the seventh of the lower *Sefirot* and, as the last, also includes in itself the entire ten; in other words, it expresses all of the *Sefirot*, each in seven different forms; so that seventy is the key number to the unfolding of the ritual of the evening devoted to *Malkhut* and to the *Shekhinah* which *Malkhut* represents.

What is equivalent in all the manifestations of the *Shekhinah* is that each represents a certain aspect of the feminine. Consequently the symbols and the contents of Sabbath Eve are always oriented to the female, with emphasis on the woman in her universal aspect as well as in terms of the Jewish family.

On entering a home on the eve of the Sabbath, one may see how a dwelling is made into a sanctuary. The table on which are set the white loaves of Sabbath bread and the burning candles recall the Holy Temple with its menorah and its shew bread. The table itself is, as always, a reminder of the altar in the Temple, for eating could and should become an act of sacrifice. In other words, the relation between man and the food he consumes, as expressed in the intention behind the eating of the food, corresponds to the cosmic connection between the material and the spiritual as expressed by every sacrifice on an altar. Especially is this true on the Sabbath, when the Sabbath feast takes on the character of a sacramental act. A sort of communion, in the performance of the *mitzvah* of union of the soul, the body, the food, and the essence of holiness. Therefore at mealtimes the table always has on it a salt container, just as salt had to be on the holy altar as a sign of the covenant of salt. The candles lit by the woman of the house emphasize the light of the Sabbath, the sanctification of the day, and the special task of the woman as representative of *Shekhinah* of *Malkhut*. There are two loaves of special white bread, called *challah* (some houses have twelve *challot*), covered with a cloth; these also recall the bread from heaven, the manna,

---

RABBI ADIN EVEN-ISRAEL (STEINSALTZ)
1937–

Talmudist, author, and philosopher. Rabbi Even-Israel Steinsaltz is considered one of the foremost Jewish thinkers of the 20th century. Praised by *Time* magazine as a "once-in-a-millennium scholar," he has been awarded the Israel Prize for his contributions to Jewish study. He lives in Jerusalem and is the founder of the Israel Institute for Talmudic Publications, a society dedicated to the translation and elucidation of the Talmud.

which on the Sabbath day came down in double portions covered with a layer of dew.

As part of the preparations for the *Kiddush* ("consecration") ceremony, the members of the household sing or recite the song of praise for the "woman of valor" (Proverbs 31:10-31). The song, with its appreciation for the woman, the mother, the housekeeper, has on this Sabbath Eve a double connotation, as praise for the lady of the house and as glorification of the *Shekhinah of Malkhut* who is, in a sense, the mother, the housekeeper of the real world. Following this is the Twenty-third Psalm, expressing the calm trust in God. And one is ready for the *Kiddush* ceremony itself.

In terms of *Halakhah*, the *Kiddush* is the carrying out of the fourth of the Ten Commandments: "Remember the Sabbath Day to keep it holy." At the very beginning of the Sabbath there has to be some act of separation, of consecration, emphasizing the difference between the work days of the week and the holy day and enabling the soul to move into a state of inner tranquility and spiritual receptiveness. To be sure, the words of the consecration are also said at the time of evening prayer and on other occasions; but in Judaism there is a general principle that, to as great an extent as possible, abstract events or processes and all that pertain to them are bound up with specifics and definite actions. Thus the *Kiddush* consecration is connected with the drinking of wine, which, in turn, becomes part of a ceremony and, in turn, is associated with the Sabbath wine sacrifices of the Holy Temple.

The *Kiddush* cup symbolizes the vessel through which, and into which, the blessing comes. The numerical weight of the letters in the word for drinking cup (*kos*) is the same as that of the letters in that name of God expressing the divine revelation in the world, in nature, in law. And into the cup is poured the bounty, the wine that represents the power of the blessing of the word "wine," whose numerical equivalent is seventy, which is also the number of Sabbath Eve. Wine then evokes the bounty, the great plentitude and power; and red wine especially expresses a certain aspect of the *Sefirah* of *Gevurah*, which also has an aspect of severity and justice. Thus after one has poured most of the wine into the cup, a little water, symbol of grace and love, is added to create the right mixture, or harmony, between *Hesed* and *Gevurah*.

After the filling of the cup, which is now the vessel of consecration containing the divine plenty, one places it on the palm of the right hand in such a way that the cup, supported by the upturned fingers, resembles or recalls a rose of five petals. For one of the symbols of *Malkhut* is the rose. And the cup of wine, thus expressing also the *Shekhinah*, stands in the center of the palm and is held by the petal fingers of the rose. The time has come for the recitation of the Kiddush prayer itself.

The Kiddush is composed of two parts. It begins with that part of the Torah (Genesis 2:1-3) where the Sabbath is first mentioned, and then proceeds to the second half which is a prayer composed by the sages especially for the *Kiddush* and in which the various meanings of the Sabbath are poetically and precisely stated. Between the two parts there is the blessing of the vine, or fruit of the grape. In each of these two parts there are exactly thirty-five words, together making seventy, the number of the Eve of the Sabbath. Before reciting the first words from the Torah, two words are added—the last words of the preceding verse: "the sixth day"—because they fit in with the recitation, "Thus the heavens and the earth were finished . . . " and because the first letters of these words form the abbreviation of the Holy Name. In this first section the Sabbath is treated as the day of the summation and cessation of Creation, as God's day of rest.

The second section, selected and determined by the sages, expresses the other side of the Sabbath, the imitation of God by Israel. Before the blessing of the wine, there are two words in Aramaic telling those present to get ready for the blessing. The following words of the *Kiddush* express the primary elements of the Sabbath and the special relation between Sabbath and the nation. There is first the declaration "Blessed art Thou . . . by whose commandments we are sanctified," which is to say that the *mitzvah* is a way of reaching a level of holiness, a way to God. After this the prayer speaks of the chosenness of Israel, as a consequence of which Israel, more than all other nations, has to assume the task of carrying on the act of Creation and its aftermath of rest and holiness. Mention is then made of the exodus from Egypt, as in the version of the Ten Commandments in Deuteronomy (5:15), where the Sabbath, proclaimed as the day of rest from work, recollects the time of slavery in Egypt and likens the Sabbath to the divine act of release from bondage and bestowal of salvation. So that Sabbath is also the weekly day of freedom, celebrating the release and the exodus from Egypt, as well as the concept of salvation which, as the ultimate in time, is the Sabbath of the world.

And out of this emphasis on divine choice and love and out of the need to understand man's obligation to God to continue and to create and to be able to rise above and beyond creation unto the Sabbath rest, the *Kiddush* prayer concludes with the relation of the Jewish people to the Sabbath and thus closes the circle of the relation between God and man. After the recital of the *Kiddush* the one who has performed the ceremony himself drinks from the cup, thereby participating in that communion of the physical with the spiritual which is the essence of all ritual. And from the same cup drink all those gathered at the table. In this way everyone participates in the meaningful act of introducing the Sabbath, represented by the flowering of the rose, which is the cup of redemption of the individual and of the nation and of the world as a whole.

The Thirteen Petalled Rose,
(Jerusalem: Koren Publishers, 2010), ch. 12, pp. 115–119

SABBATH FISH

Eric G. Freudenstein

> *"Your approach," I said, "is too body-oriented. Try to imagine a meta-dinner, not so much a filling occasion as a fulfilling one."*
>
> *—From "When an Invitation Isn't . . . " by Anatole Broyard,* The New York Times, *May 10, 1979.*

INTRODUCTION

When I arrived in the States as a young immigrant, just after the end of World War II, I heard stories of "our boys" in the service who had been stationed in the far corners of the world, cut off from any contact with their families. When the Jewish chaplain was able to get them *gefilte fish* on Friday night or a Jewish holiday, tears would come to their eyes as memories of home were aroused by the sight and taste of the fish. In the smugness and conceit typical of youth and ignorance, I smiled inwardly at these stories. How vulgar, I thought, to associate the love for Judaism with a piece of food. How ignorant, furthermore, to attribute religious significance to *gefilte fish,* something that, to the best of my knowledge, was not even mentioned in the *Shulhan Arukh,* the authoritative book on Jewish laws. As a matter of fact, I had never even heard of *gefilte fish* before my arrival in this country. But fate is often strange and, as Providence would have it, I came to love *gefilte fish,* to develop recipes suitable for mass production and, as Director of Production for the largest manufacturers of kosher fish products for over thirty years, I was probably responsible for serving more servings of *gefilte fish* than anyone else in history.

I decided to take a new look at this custom of fish eating. Leafing through the pages of Jewish lore and history, laws and customs, I became aware of the fact that while *gefilte fish,* as we know it today, may be relatively new (by the standards of our four-thousand-year-old history), the custom of eating fish on the Sabbath and on special occasions goes back to the very origins of our history as a people.

According to an ancient midrash, Miriam's well, stocked with fish, accompanied the Israelites during the forty years of their wanderings in the desert. As if this were an omen, the custom of a fish meal on the eve of the Sabbath accompanied the Jewish people in their wanderings through the millennia and across all continents.

IN ANCIENT EGYPT

The Bible records for us that the Israelites complained to Moses about the lack of variety in the food available to them in the desert:

> In Egypt we had fish for the asking, cucumbers and water-melons, leeks and onions and garlic. Now our throats are parched; there is nothing wherever we look except this manna (Numbers 11:5, 6).

Modern archeological evidence bears out the fact that fish was available for enslaved laborers like the children of Israel in Egypt. There is an Egyptian document concerning a petition addressed to the royal authorities in the 29th year of Ramses III (about 1150-1200 B.C.E.) by the Union of Gravediggers who, as part of their payment, received large amounts of fish four times monthly. The petitioners requested a pay increase, pointing out that they came to the authorities without clothes and ointments, and even without fish, that indispensable food. We know that the ancient Egyptians were able to preserve large quantities of fish for long periods of time by a process of drying and salting, and a

---

ERIC FREUDENSTEIN

D. 2008

Nutritional scientist and Hebrew scholar. Freudenstein was chief chemist of the Jewish food giant Rokeach for 50 years and also an ardent Talmudist. His papers have been published in a volume entitled *Yad Gavriel,* that being Eric's Hebrew name.

warehouse of dried fish was discovered near the Sun Temple of Amarna.

But to the Israelites wandering in the desert, fish meant even more than the free ration handed out to the slaves. There was a beautifully romantic aspect, as told us by the midrash.

> Under the apple-trees I roused thee (Song of Songs 8:5). Rabbi Avira expounded: It was by the merit of the pious women in the generation of the oppression that our ancestors were redeemed from Egypt. The women were determined that the heritage of Abraham, Isaac and Jacob not perish from the earth. When they went to draw water, the Holy One, blessed be He, summoned little fishes into their pitchers. They drew half water and half fish. They came home and placed two kettles on the stove, one to prepare hot water and the other for cooking fish. Then they carried the kettles out to the fields to their husbands and washed them, anointed them, fed them and gave them to drink and lay with them between the kettles.[1]

What species were these little fishes which our ancestors found so delectable during their sojourn in the land of Egypt? To our amazement, the evidence that has been preserved permits us to identify them and to conclude that some of the varieties that are used in the preparation of *gefilte fish* today are the very same species that were present in the Nile delta thousands of years ago. Thus, the Egyptologist Ingrid Gamer-Wallert reaches the following conclusion:

> It appears that the composition of the fish population of Egypt did not substantially change in the last five millennia. More than 30 species can be proven for Ancient Egypt and these still exist today in the waters of the Nile.[2]

These varieties include carp, pike and mullet, and while these carp and pike families are not of the genus used in the Sabbath meal, the mullet (genus Mullet *Mugilidae cephalus)* is exactly the same fish that we use in the preparation of our present-day *gefilte fish* blend. A truly remarkable phenomenon.

The Mishnah records "Egyptian Fish" as an article of commerce,[3] and, according to the commentary of Maimonides, this was a variety of small fish imported from Egypt to Palestine in metal containers and still well known in his own day. We can only speculate whether the popularity of this fish in Palestine[4] was based on ancient traditions.

The starting point of our investigation of the fish meal in ancient Egypt is that passage in Numbers cited above: "In Egypt we had fish, cucumbers, water-melons, and leeks, onions and garlic." Don Isaac Abarbanel, the Jewish Minister of Finance to the Portuguese Court, in his Bible commentary written in the early 16th century, takes the Hebrew word *eth* in the context of our verse to signify "with." The Israelites in Egypt, writes Abarbanel, cooked fish with cucumbers, melons (or better, squash), leeks, onions and garlic in order to improve the poor taste of their ration. In other words, the Bible here gives us the first recorded recipe for fish cookery.

IN THE ERA OF THE TALMUD

Once we come to the period of the Mishnah and Talmud we find a wealth of information about the fishing industry and about the marketing and consumption of fish and fishery products. The main center of fishing was Lake Tiberias, but the Mediterranean and the Jordan River were also known for the bounty of their resources, and their waters were exploited commercially. The coastal town of Acco was the trading center for the commerce in fish, so that "bringing fish to Acco" had the same connotation as "carrying coals to Newcastle." Generally, the fish for sale were attractively spread on leaves and reeds, and they were also served this way at the table,[5] much as the labels on American cans of *gefilte fish* suggest that the

1 *Sotah,* 11b.

2 Aegyptologische Abhandlungen (Wiesbaden, 1970), Vol. 21.

3 Mahshirin 6:3.

4 There was a *Shaar Hadagim,* a fish-gate, in Jerusalem, where the fishermen brought their wares. (See Zeph. 1:10; Neh. 3:3 and 12:39; 2 Chron. 33:14).

5 *Tosefta Shabbat* 13, 16.

portions be served on lettuce leaves. Smaller varieties of fish were sold in metal containers and baskets. Fish were eaten pickled, boiled or fried, and served with vegetables and milk. A popular dish was fish prepared with flour in a type of pie and fish with good, aged wine was considered a meal fit for a king.

The Jews—like the Greeks—loved fish food and were connoisseurs. Said Rabbi Yose ben Halafta (quoted in the famous Bible commentary of Rashi, on Genesis 1:10): "The taste of fish that comes up in Acco cannot be compared to the taste of fish that is caught in neighboring Sidon, and the taste of fish from Sidon does not compare to the taste of fish from neighboring Aspamia." Because of this predilection of the Jews for fish it was the custom to honor the Sabbath with a fish meal on Friday night, at the beginning of the Sabbath.[6]

> Rav Yehudah said in the name of Rav: He who delights in the Sabbath will be granted his heart's desire, as it has been said: "Delight in God and He will grant your heart's desire" (Psalms 37:4). This delight in God shall be understood by reference to the prophet Isaiah: "You shall call the Sabbath a delight," and it concerns, therefore, the delight in the Sabbath. How does one delight in the Sabbath? Rav Yehudah, son of Rav Samuel bar Shilat said in the name of Rav: With a course [of] spinach-beets, large fish and garlic cloves. Rav Hiyya bar Ashi said in the name of Rav: Even a modest meal, if prepared in honor of the Sabbath, is a delight. What might this be? Said Rav Papa: A pie of fish-hash (small fish prepared with flour and fish jelly) (*Shabbat* 118b).

Even the poorest of the poor were entitled to the Friday night fish-meal from the public kitchen: "When may those who possess less than fifty shekels have the dish of vegetables and fish? Every Friday night of the Sabbath."[7]

Talmudic laws regulating the relations of employer and worker take into consideration the need to prepare the Sabbath meal. In general, the worker who is hired for a full day must travel on his own time, so that he can start at his day-break. However, it is understood by both parties that the employer must let him leave *every day* in order to reach his home by night-fall. What about Fridays?

> Rabbi Ammi said in the name of Resh Lakish: On Friday afternoon the employer has to let his workers off in time so that they can draw a barrel of water and fry a fish, before lighting the Sabbath candles (*Genesis Rabba* 72, 3).

No one is to consider himself exempt from the obligation of preparation for the Sabbath. The Talmud records that even the great masters did menial labor to prepare the home in honor of the Sabbath: "Rava (the famous Head of Academy in Mehosa) salted the turbot (he seasoned the fish in honor of the Sabbath)."[8] The custom of honoring the Sabbath with fish is also stressed in the Aggadah, the moral tales of the Sages where we see that people were regarded as especially praiseworthy in the eyes of God if, at any cost, they got fish for sacred occasions. The story of "Joseph, Who Honored the Sabbath"[9] Tells us how a rich pagan was warned that his neighbor, Joseph, would someday eat up all his possessions. To safeguard himself, the pagan sold all that he had and bought a single pearl. Unfortunately he then lost the pearl in a lake where it was swallowed by a fish which was later caught and sold to Joseph. Joseph found the pearl and sold it for a fortune. The moral of the story is pointed out: "He who lends to the Sabbath is repaid by the Sabbath."

A second story[10] brings out the same moral:

> A pious man in Rome held the Sabbaths and festival days much in honor. On the eve of the Day of Atonement he went shopping in the market but found only a fish, which the

---

6 The oldest reference linking fish and the Sabbath is in Neh. 13:16, where we are told that the Tyrians sold fish in Jerusalem on that day until the practice was stopped by Nehemiah.

7 *Tosefta,* end of tractate *Peah,* and Maimonidies, *Laws of Charity* 7, 8.

8 *Shabbat* 119a.

9 Ibid.

10 *Genesis Rabba,* Chapter II also quoted by *Tosafot Ketubot* 5 a; S.V. *ela me-atah.*

servant of the Prefect also wanted to buy. They bid against each other, until finally the Jew got the fish, but at a gold denarius per pound. When, at dinner, the Prefect heard why no fish came to the table he had the Jew who, he presumed, was wealthy, called for him. The Jew came, and represented himself as a tailor.

"And a tailor eats fish at a gold denarius per pound?"

"My lord, permit me to speak!"

"Speak," said the Prefect.

"We have a day which is more precious to us than all days of the year. All the sins which we have committed during the whole year are forgiven us on this day. Therefore we honor this day more than all the days of the year."

Then said the Prefect: "You have justified yourself and are free."

How did God repay the man who thus honored the festival? He had him find a valuable pearl in the fish, from the sale of which he supported himself for the rest of his life.[11]

We know that the Jewish custom of eating fish on the Sabbath eve was noted by the Romans, for it is alluded to in a rather obscure anti-Semitic stanza in a long poem by Perisus:

> But when Herod's birthday is come, and the lamps (like on every Sabbath and Holiday—E. F.), put in the greasy windows along with violets, emit their unctuous clouds of smoke and when the tail of a tunny floats curled round a red dish, and the white jar is bulging with wine, you move your lips in silences and turn pale at the circumcised Sabbath.[12]

Even though Persius' statement is confused, all scholars have connected the passage with the traditional Friday night meal of the Jews. Pliny the Elder, the Roman historian and naturalist who called Jerusalem "the most illustrious city in the East," also comments, in his *Natural History,* on the fish-eating customs of the Jews. In ancient Jewish liturgy, the wish for resurrection in the company of the Just is a frequent motif. It is also found on a tomb inscription, touching in its simplicity, for the nine-year-old daughter of Rabban Gamliel in Bet Shearim: "May she rise again with the Just" (*Tehi amidatah im kesherim*). The desire to be with the saints at the Feast of the Leviathan is the explanation offered to account for the presence of a fish symbol on some Jewish graves in Roman catacombs. The fish meal, fundamentally a festive meal to do honor to the holy days of the year, here becomes a symbol of the good life in the world to come, when legendary Leviathan becomes part of the menu for the ultimate feast in Paradise.[13]

On a more earthy level, fish also served as an aphrodisiac and, especially in later periods, as a symbol of fertility, a protection against the evil eye and as an omen for bringing good luck. All of these ancillary meanings are based on ideas already present in Talmudic literature.

THE AGE OF MYSTICISM: KABBALAH

In the imagery of the Bible and the Talmud, the Royal Table is one of the trappings of kinghood, much as crown and scepter are the insignia of monarchy in the Western tradition. When, in the famous twenty-third psalm, King David sang

> Thou preparest a table before me
> In the presence of mine enemies

The Rabbis comment[14] that this table is the symbol of royalty, parallel to the line that follows, "Thou has anointed my head with oil," which refers to that other symbol of kinghood, the consecration of the king by divine authority. The Royal Table of the ancients was not necessarily one long table, but, rather, a series of small ones: one for the king, with others in the same hall for favorites, friends and the more important servants of the land or of the royal household. In a more general sense, to eat at the king's table came to mean to be supported by the king, regardless of where the meals were physically eaten. The Zohar, the holy book of

---

11 These two stories are rendered here largely as translated by Goodenough, *Jewish Symbols in the Greco-Roman Period,* Vol. 5, p. 44.

12 Persius, *Satire,* V. 180-184.

13 *Baba Batra,* 74b.

14 Midrash *Shohar Tov* to Psalm 23.

the Kabbalah, in a lesson extolling the Sabbath meal, opens the passage by calling Israel "sons of the royal palace."[15] They are guests, as it were, at the Sabbath table, the mystic table of God, the King, and of the Sabbath Queen. In this sense we must understand the severe reprimand and punishment for those who, as *lès majesté,* slight the Sabbath table, and the happiness and reward that, according to the Zohar, await those who honor the Sabbath table. The Holy Shelah,[16] a famous authority among the Kabbalists, prefaces his thoughts on the Sabbath meals with a quotation from Maimonides to the effect that the Sabbath table should be honored with proper good food, including fish. He proceeds to quote an anonymous authority who recommends that fish be included in each of the three obligatory Sabbath meals. The Shelah then develops a *gematria,* a play on the numerical value of Hebrew letters, to indicate that wine, meat and fish at the three Sabbath meals are a desideratum. What follows is a frequently quoted but often neglected call for moderation in food and drink, to which we will refer later.

The *Book of Delight of the Days, (Sepher Hemdat HaYamim)* which has been called the most beautiful book in Lurianic Kabbalah,[17] is a treasury of lore and ethical exhortation concerning the *mitzvot* of Friday night. In the first chapter the author writes:

> The custom is to eat fish on the Sabbath because then there is a proliferation of (mystical) sparks that must be channeled and elevated by the power of the holiness of the Sabbath.

This is a reference to the transmigration of souls in fish. The Holy Or ha-Hayyim, a Sephardic kabbalistic Bible commentator, is also of the view (in his commentary on Genesis 1:26) that the souls of the pious transmigrate into fish. An opposite school of thought, among the believers in the doctrine of transmigration of souls (*gilgul*), prefers to eat fish rather than meat, precisely because souls that have been condemned to be reincarnated in lower forms of life will never enter the body of a fish, but only the bodies of warm-blooded animals. Hence, fish are preferred for the Sabbath meal. An excerpt from the previously mentioned writing of the Holy Shelah will serve to conclude this brief review of kabbalistic thought on the Sabbath meal:

> Those who thoughtlessly fill their bellies, going for the pleasant taste and the intoxicating drink, and then because of the excess of eating fall into a stupor and their mind gets confused—they do not delight *in* the Sabbath, rather they delight *themselves on* the Sabbath. Therefore, one should measure one's actions wisely. A person can eat and drink properly without filling up one's belly, because the latter is not called Rest and Delight, but waste of food and destruction of one's health. It is also harmful to the soul because one is unable to study the Law and perform the commandments after overeating. The idea is to eat and to drink, in good spirit and with joy, food that is wholesome, properly prepared and seasoned and easily digestible—small quantities but good quality, as long as one does not stuff oneself. One may even drink two or three cups of wine to cheer the heart—everything depends on the individual's ability to hold his drink—and then one gets up, with the satisfaction of a good meal, to start an arranged program of study, or to nap briefly in order to rest one's head and limbs a little and then one sits down to study. Abudraham wrote, in the name of a scholar, that one of the reasons for the traditional three Sabbath meals is to avoid stuffing oneself at any one meal. For, by knowing that there will be three meals during the day, there is no need to overindulge at any one of them. It is the holy Sabbath and it shall be used to cling to holiness.[18]

The Hasidic masters, steeped in love for the Jewish people and for every Jewish tradition

15 *Zohar* II, 252.

16 Isaiah ben Abraham haLevi Horowitz, *Shnei Luhot haBrit,* (Jerusalem, 1963), Part I, pp. 97-98.

17 Gershom G. Scholem, *Major Trends in Jewish Mysticism* (New York: Schocken Books, 1961), p. 285.

18 Shelah, *loc cit.*

elaborated on the meaning of the fish course on the Sabbath. Thus it is related by the disciples of the *Zaddik*, Rabbi Simha Bunem of Przysucha:

> Our master—may his merit protect us—said that the custom to eat fish as the first food on the holy Sabbath is based on the fact that fish were the first created living beings, and the holiness of the Sabbath, too, is the root of life; for this reason Israel has the tradition to start delighting in the Sabbath with fish food.[19]

The *Zaddik*, Abraham Joshua Heschel of Apta, adds another thought.[20] The midrash, he says, tell us that the manna of the desert had every conceivable taste that one could wish for, except for the taste of fish. That is why the people murmured: "We remember the fish we ate in Egypt." This lack of fish became the focus of their dissatisfaction with their lot. Israel now has the custom to eat this very food, fish, to demonstrate that we are thankful to God and that our delight in the Sabbath is complete. The symbol of grievance has become the symbol of gratitude.

Rabbi Zevi Elimelekh of Dynow, known as "the *B'nei Yisoskhor"* (the title of his best-known work), refers repeatedly to the custom of serving fish on the Sabbath table.

> We find in the Biblical story of the creation that three things were blessed on three successive days. The fishes were blessed on the fifth day, mankind was blessed on the sixth, and the Sabbath-day was blessed on the seventh day. This is "the three-fold cord that is not quickly broken" (Ecclesiastes). That is why man eats fish on the Sabbath, so that he may be blessed with the triple blessing. This is also alluded to in the twenty-third psalm: "He maketh me to lie down in green pastures," since the Hebrew word for green pastures—*deshe*—consists of three letters that are the initial letters for the words fish, Sabbath and man in Hebrew, and these are joined on the day of rest; hence the verse concludes: "He leadeth me beside the still waters."[21]

Elsewhere, we encounter a more moralistic interpretation of the custom. The Sabbath day shall be devoted to the study of Torah, an act symbolized by the fish meal:

> The element of the fishes is water and the element of Israel is the Torah that has been compared to water. "Ho, everyone that thirsteth, go ye to the water" (Isaiah 55:1). The parable of a fox and the fishes is well-known from the Talmud.[22] And just as the fishes, even though they swim constantly in water, when a drop of rain falls they open their mouths to snap up the drops as if they never tasted water in their life, so Israel—even though their element is Torah all the days of the week—when they hear new interpretations of the Torah on the Sabbath they bend their ears to hear it well. It is written in the *Zohar* that the Sabbath is the day of the Torah par excellence, and the day of the soul—for it was on a Sabbath that the Torah was given to Israel on Sinai.[23]

The custom of eating a piece of *hallah* (white bread) with the fish is a topic of discussion in hasidic literature. Some authors attribute the practice to the requirements of healthy nutrition, while others cite the fact that the Hebrew letters for fish and for grain (*dagim* and *dagan*) have the same numerical value, this making them compatible foods. In conclusion, let us quote the *Bnei Yisoskhor* on this topic:

> The saintly Rabbi Menahem Asariah DeFano (famous Kabbalist and contemporary of the Ari and of Rabbi Moses Cardovero) wrote that, in the world to come, at the banquet of the Leviathan—since there cannot be a religious banquet without breaking bread—they will bring out the flask of manna that had been hidden (Exodus 16:33). Note that Scripture says "for your generations" and that refers to the time when all the generations will gather. This manna is called

19 M. Nirenberg, ed., *Likutei Kol Simhah* (New York, 1955). p. 30.

20 *Sefer Torat Emet*, section *Aykeb.*

21 *Bnei Yisoskhor, Maamarei Hashabbatot* (New York: Chaim Ubracha Pub., 1975) 1:11. 3:16. 8:20.

22 *Berakhot* 61b.

23 *B'nei Yisoskhor*, 1:21.

> "bread," and it is written, "this is the bread that God has given you."[24]

The author adds that the blessing to be pronounced over the manna will be "Blessed art Thou Who bringest forth bread from Heaven," in contrast to our regular benediction, "Blessed art Thou who bringest forth bread from the earth."

The commentators on the *Shulhan Arukh* cite the custom, introduced by the Kabbalists, that after the breaking of the *hallah*-bread at the Friday night meal, the children kiss their mother's hand. It is she who baked and provided the festive meal, fulfilling the task expected of the mistress of the household. In our time, a New York rabbi remembers the custom from his home in Transylvania, a beautiful memory from a world that is no more but that shall not be forgotten.

THE AGE OF ENLIGHTENMENT: OLD VIENNA

When the age of emancipation dawned in Western and Central Europe, the hold of the Jewish religion weakened considerably and some of the intellectuals went so far as to forswear the faith of their ancestors, in order to buy "an admission ticket to European culture." Having spent childhood years in an intensely Jewish milieu, these apostates penned bitter-sweet reminiscences of the Sabbaths of their youth, including meals. Heinrich Heine, the famous German poet, in his *Hebrew Melodies,* describes nostalgically how the simple Jew, with the arrival of the Sabbath, is miraculously transformed from a peddler into a prince who welcomes the Princess Sabbath. Several times, in the *Hebrew Melodies,* he characteristically lapses from lyrical heights to ironical self-ridicule, and after rhapsodizing about the quasi-magical transformation of the lowly work-a-day Jew into the radiant bridegroom of Princess Sabbath, he makes us chuckle about the traditional meals: "Kugel, the beautiful spark of the gods, heavenly ambrosia."

Moritz Gottlieb Saphir was a contemporary of Heine. Born into a Yiddish-speaking, Orthodox family in a small town near Budapest, and having attended *yeshivot* in Pressburg and Prague, he later abandoned traditional Judaism and eventually was baptized as a Lutheran. He settled in Vienna, where he wrote humorous and satirical poems, essays, literary criticism, theater reviews, comedies and short stories. Saphir's popularity and influence were widespread and his witticisms and satirical sketches were frequently reprinted and often quoted. In a nostalgic autobiography he devotes several pages to "Jewish fish." Here follows a slightly condensed English translation:

> Lucullus, (he muses), got quite far in gastronomy. Pompey was no slouch either and he paid to M. Aufidius Lucro, who had invented a technique for fattening peacocks, the sum of 60,000 sesterces; Apicius invented the art of fattening pigs with figs, Vitellius was the first to dine on pies made with nightingale tongues; he paid 2,000 sesterces for a single Swedish nightingale . . . however, none of these virtuosos of culinary art and gluttony had any idea of the *hautgout,* the peculiar charm of the Jewish cuisine. Lord Protector Cromwell once dined with the famous Manasseh Ben Israel and he admitted that he had never eaten so delightful a meal.
>
> Delightful indeed! That must have contained garlic! Whether you call them Brown Carp with Jew-sauce, or Jew-fish, the sweet-sour Jewish fish are world-famous. Once upon a time I tendered a "sweet-sour Jew-fish dinner" to my Gentile literary friends in Munich. I placed a platter of "sour Jew-fish heads" in front of them and I made a little speech:
>
> "Gentlemen! I have invited you all to join me for 'sour Jew-fish heads.' You met here for this *tête-a-tête* and, before we dig in, permit me a few words. Jews and fish have great sympathy for one another. Jews like to eat fish and fish like to eat Jews, as we know from the famous fish that swallowed a whole Jew, from head to toe, for a snack. Of course, he returned him unharmed . . . But the Jews love fish so much because, when they wanted to cross the Red Sea, the fish suddenly started to swallow so much water,

24 Ibid., 3:13.

that the Jews were able to cross dry land, and when Pharaoh arrived, the fish gave all the water off again, drowning the pursuers. "For this reason the Jews, out of gratitude, invite the fish on every Sabbath and holiday. But the Jews themselves have so often been invited guests, only to be fleeced and cleaned out, that they do the same to their own guests, the fish! They remove the scales, they clean them out, and then they finish them off. Look here, gentlemen, these are extraordinarily good fish-heads! For, what is characteristic of a good head? To make life sweet for oneself, even in a sour mess. So one has to sweeten the sour sauce with raisins, almonds, nuts, a little celery and spices to remove some of the bitterness. And then the fish-heads become tasty and inviting!"[25]

The famous satirist ends on a whimsical note: "In order to understand the Jewish national dishes," he writes, "one has to be a scholar; to describe them, one must be a genius; to enjoy them in a mood of sanctity, one must be a Jew; but in order to truly appreciate them, one must be a *meshumed* (an apostate)!"

THE FISH MEAL IN HEBREW AND YIDDISH SONG, IN ART AND LITERATURE

A complete traditional Friday evening table requires Sabbath candles to set the festive mood, the presence of guests (often needy people whom the head of the household would pick up after the synagogue prayer service to join the family circle at the table) and the singing of happy Sabbath songs, the *zemirot*. The lyrics of several of these songs which date back to the early Middle Ages allude to the fish course served on the Sabbath:

How beloved is your tranquility,
Oh, Queen Sabbath,
How do we hasten to receive you.
Come, Crowned Princess,
We welcome you in festive dress,
The candles are lit,
All work and labor has ceased.
We delight in your honor
With all kinds of fowl and fish.
Every manner of delicacy
Has been prepared well ahead . . .
A foretaste of paradise
Is the rest of the Sabbath day.
Oh, let our redemption come quickly,
May lament and suffering disappear.

Leaping across several centuries, we find what may be called a Yiddish song of social protest. The ancient Sabbath hymn just cited glorifies the Sabbath food. But thc words of the song have a different meaning for the poor than for the wealthy. For the rich, the words of the song conjure up a sumptuous fish course, but for us

Kaptsonechlech,
Oi, kaptsonechlech

the poor, oh the despised poor people, the tail of a herring is all that can be anticipated.

Parallel with the dissatisfaction of the impoverished masses with their lot, there is a nostalgic anticipation of Israel's ultimate redemption. The joys of paradise are described in a folk-song that takes the form of a dialogue between a questioning child and the father who must satisfy his offspring's curiosity about all the details of the fascinating *Gan Eden.*

Tatenyu, father dear
What is going to be served at the banquet
that the Messiah has in store for us?
My child,
The Leviathan is going to be served
At the great banquet for the righteous
people of Israel

In Jewish pictorial art, fish often represents this same longing for redemption. On an old pewter Passover Seder-plate (in the Rheinisches Museum, Cologne, Germany) we can see the Star of David surrounded by fishes. The combination is an appropriate messianic symbol because on the night of the Seder the Messiah and the prophet Elijah, who will announce his coming, will arise to prepare the redemption. Again, this time on a pewter Purim-plate dating from 1787 in Bamberg, Germany we find three fishes, the symbol of the zodiac sign for the month of Adar, Pisces. Here the fishes, in addition to the redemption theme, are a sign of good luck. Representations of fish are widespread in the orient as amulets, and in

---

25 M. Saphir, *Meine Memoiren und Anderes* (Leipzig: Phillip Reclam jun.).

Eastern Europe some boys were named Fishl as a good omen against the evil eye.
Representations of fish in ancient Bible manuscripts have been reproduced in the *Encyclopaedia Judaica* (Volume 4, pages 908, 962, 965). These include the Leviathan as the food of the righteous in paradise (the last page of a giant 3-volume Ambrosian Bible written in Ulm, South Germany, in 1236–38), a floral and fish motif in a beautiful Yemenite Bible from the year 1469, and a picture of Jonah and the whale in an Ashkenazi Bible now in the British Museum.
The Jewish Museum in New York has in its collection several paintings on our subject matter. Mention should be made of Hermann Junker's "The Buying of the Fish for Sabbath" (oil on canvas, 1880) which depicts the hustle and bustle of the fish market in a quaint inner city street of old Frankfurt am Main, as Jewish burghers and their womenfolk, dressed in the costume of early eighteen hundreds, go about the business of purchasing food for the Sabbath table. Nahum Tschacbasov's "Family at the Sabbath Table" (oil on canvas, New York, 1946) is an example of modern art. It shows a family partaking of the Sabbath fish course. The Jewish Museum also has a fine specimen of a fish-shaped box (made somewhere in Western Europe in the 18th century) which holds the spices for *havdalah*. Until our own time, the fish has been a favorite form for these spice-boxes. It symbolizes fertility, protection from the evil eye, and good luck for the week to come.
As might be expected, the Sabbath fish-meal finds a place in the descriptions of Jewish life in the literature of the 20th century. Scholem Asch, in his trilogy, *Three Cities*, portrays a traditional Sabbath eve family supper of fish in the home of a *maskil* school teacher at a time of political, social and intellectual ferment of Poland's Jewish masses. Isaac Bashevis Singer, the Nobel laureate, in his masterful short story, "Short Friday," describes an idyllic Sabbath meal complete with a course of *gefilte fish*.
Thus, the old custom of fish-eating on the Sabbath has found its reflection in hymn and folk song, in art and literature. What about the cookbooks? Starting with a recipe in a Yiddish cookbook, *Di Yiddishe Kúch* by B. Shafran (Warsaw, 1930), there has been a veritable explosion of Jewish cookbooks in English that teach the making of traditional Sabbath-fish, whether American, European or Israeli style, as well as such exotic varieties as French, Italian and Chinese-style *gefilte fish*. But how did we make the transition from fish to *gefilte fish*?

GEFILTE FISH

In the last two hundred years or so the custom has taken over to eat the Sabbath fish as *gefilte fish*. That phrase is, of course, the Yiddish for stuffed fish. In the original version of this delicacy, the fish was chopped, mixed with flour and condiments, and this filling was used to stuff the skin of the fish. The whole was then cooked, cut into slices and served. In the modern version, in which the dish has reached this country, the skin is discarded, and *gefilte fish* is the end result of the blending of several varieties of sweetwater fish with onions, eggs, matzo meal and condiments, simmered in a broth of fish trimmings, vegetables and spices. While there are several varieties of the basic recipe, depending on the origin of the cook and his or her skill, there are two main schools of *gefilte fish* cooking: the *litvishe*, the way the Jews from Lithuania or *litvacks* like it, which is unsweetened, but well seasoned with salt and pepper, and the *galitsianer* version, preferred by Jews originating in Austria or Galicia, who like theirs generously sweetened with a heavy dose of sugar.
An important reason why fish, rather than meat, became the preferred Sabbath fish dish was economics. Impoverished Jewish communities could hardly have afforded meat on every ordinary Sabbath, but some kind of fish was usually available at prices that were within reach. The utilization of every morsel was important for a poor community, and in the making of *gefilte fish* the housewife could use every ounce. Moreover, *gefilte fish* was good whether served hot or cold, and since cooking was not permitted on the Sabbath, such a dish could be served either hot on Friday night or for a cold luncheon or supper on the following Sabbath day. We are reminded somehow, of

the baked beans of the New England Puritans. The early American settlers, not permitting themselves to cook on the Christian Sabbath, developed a dish that could be put on the stove the previous day and allowed to simmer until Sunday dinner. Religious requirements and Yankee ingenuity combined to give New England baked beans, just as East European Jews developed *gefilte fish.*

Religious law entered into the picture in yet another way. The Sabbath laws specify the preferred manner in which the edible part of the food shall be separated from the inedible portion, and even the manner in which the residue of the meal, such as the peelings and pits of fruit or the bones and skin of fish, can be removed from the table is laid down in the rules. To do so according to the strictures of *halakhah* requires a learning which not everyone possessed and which could not be expected from the indigent guests who were often invited to the Sabbath table. All of these problems were eliminated by serving the fish in boneless and skinless portions.

"Come and let us give credit to Israel, the holy people," writes a halakhic authority in the name of the Brisker Rav, "for establishing the custom of eating fish on the Sabbath in the form of stuffed fish, thereby eliminating all manner of religious scruples and doubts."[26] During the past thirty years, commercially prepared *gefilte fish* has increasingly filled this demand.

CONCLUSION

And so the saga of our Jewish national dish, *gefilte fish,* continues. It started with the story of the pious women of the land of Egypt, and ever since then the Sabbath fish meal has been a symbol of our will to national self-preservation, the perpetuation of the race, of Jewish identity, and of the love we feel towards our heritage.

Judaism *29:4 (1980)*
Reprinted with the permission of the publisher

---

26 Neuwirth, *Shemirat Shabbat Kehilkhatah* (Jerusalem: Feldheim, 1965), 2. 24.

pause
& AFFECT

LESSON 6

Order from Chaos

ROSHCHODESH society

COMMON QUESTIONS

Learning Exercise 1

From the following list of activities, select those that are most inconsistent with the idea of rest:

1. Lugging a heavy table across the room
2. Tying a knot
3. Brisk walking for one mile
4. Driving a motorcycle
5. Writing a thank you note
6. Gluing together two papers
7. Mixing sand and water at the beach

Question for Discussion

Performing certain difficult tasks is somehow consistent with Shabbat rest, while numerous effortless tasks are not. Why?

Text 1

EXODUS 20:8–11

זָכוֹר אֶת יוֹם הַשַּׁבָּת לְקַדְּשׁוֹ.
שֵׁשֶׁת יָמִים תַּעֲבֹד וְעָשִׂיתָ כָּל מְלַאכְתֶּךָ.
וְיוֹם הַשְּׁבִיעִי שַׁבָּת לַה' אֱלֹהֶיךָ, לֹא תַעֲשֶׂה כָל מְלָאכָה אַתָּה
וּבִנְךָ וּבִתֶּךָ עַבְדְּךָ וַאֲמָתְךָ וּבְהֶמְתֶּךָ וְגֵרְךָ אֲשֶׁר בִּשְׁעָרֶיךָ.
כִּי שֵׁשֶׁת יָמִים עָשָׂה ה' אֶת הַשָּׁמַיִם וְאֶת הָאָרֶץ אֶת הַיָּם וְאֶת
כָּל אֲשֶׁר בָּם וַיָּנַח בַּיּוֹם הַשְּׁבִיעִי, עַל כֵּן בֵּרַךְ ה' אֶת יוֹם הַשַּׁבָּת
וַיְקַדְּשֵׁהוּ.

Remember the Shabbat day to sanctify it.

Six days you shall labor and perform all your work.

But the seventh day is a Shabbat to the Lord your God. On it you shall not do any work, neither you, nor your son or daughter, nor your male or female servant, nor your animals, nor any foreigner residing in your towns.

Because for six days God made the heaven, the earth, the sea, and all that is in them, but He rested on Shabbat. God therefore blessed the day of Shabbat and made it holy.

ORIGINS OF THE LAWS
THE ORAL TORAH

Text 2
LEVITICUS 16:29

וְהָיְתָה לָכֶם לְחֻקַּת עוֹלָם, בַּחֹדֶשׁ הַשְּׁבִיעִי בֶּעָשׂוֹר לַחֹדֶשׁ תְּעַנּוּ אֶת נַפְשֹׁתֵיכֶם, וְכָל מְלָאכָה לֹא תַעֲשׂוּ, הָאֶזְרָח וְהַגֵּר הַגָּר בְּתוֹכְכֶם.

It shall be as an eternal statute for you; in the seventh month, on the tenth of the month, you shall afflict yourselves, and you shall not do any work, neither the native nor the proselyte who dwells among you.

Figure 6.1

Words in the Bible from the Root Word A-N-H

Verse	Context
He said to Abram, "You shall surely know that your seed will be strangers in a land that is not theirs, and they will enslave them and **oppress** [וְעִנּוּ] them for four hundred years." (Genesis 15:13)	God speaks to Abraham and informs him about the future Egyptian exile.
If you **afflict** [תְּעַנֶּה] my daughters, or if you take wives besides my daughters, although no one is with us, behold, God is witness between you and me. (Genesis 31:50)	Laban speaks to his son-in-law, Jacob, and makes a pact with him.
Shechem, the son of Hamor, the Hivvite, the prince of the land, saw her; he took her, lay with her, and **violated her** [וַיְעַנֶּהָ]. (Genesis 34:2)	Shechem rapes Dinah, Jacob and Leah's daughter.
You shall not **oppress** [תְעַנּוּן] any widow or orphan. (Exodus 22:21)	In addition to the overall prohibition against oppressing any person, the Torah here issues an additional prohibition against oppressing the widow and orphan.

Text 3

MAIMONIDES, *COMMENTARY ON THE MISHNAH*, INTRODUCTION

שֶׁכָּל מִצְוָה שֶׁנָּתַן הַקָּדוֹשׁ בָּרוּךְ הוּא לְמֹשֶׁה רַבֵּינוּ נִיתְּנָה לוֹ עִם פֵּירוּשָׁהּ. הָיָה הַקָּדוֹשׁ בָּרוּךְ הוּא אוֹמֵר לוֹ הַמִּקְרָא וְאַחַר כָּךְ אוֹמֵר לוֹ פֵּירוּשׁוֹ וּבֵיאוּרוֹ וְכָל מַה שֶּׁכָּלַל אוֹתוֹ הַמִּקְרָא הַמְחוּכָּם.

Every mitzvah that God gave to Moses was given with its explanation. God would tell Moses the verse and then tell him its meaning, explanation, and all that was contained in the clever wording of the verse.

RABBI MOSHE BEN MAIMON (MAIMONIDES, RAMBAM)
1135–1204

Halachist, philosopher, author, and physician. Maimonides was born in Cordoba, Spain. After the conquest of Cordoba by the Almohads, he fled Spain and eventually settled in Cairo, Egypt. There, he became the leader of the Jewish community and served as court physician to the vizier of Egypt. He is most noted for authoring the *Mishneh Torah,* an encyclopedic arrangement of Jewish law, and for his philosophical work, *Guide for the Perplexed.* His rulings on Jewish law are integral to the formation of halachic consensus.

Text 4

DEUTERONOMY 6:4–9

שְׁמַע יִשְׂרָאֵל ה' אֱלֹקֵינוּ ה' אֶחָד.
וְאָהַבְתָּ אֵת ה' אֱלֹקֶיךָ בְּכָל לְבָבְךָ וּבְכָל נַפְשְׁךָ וּבְכָל מְאֹדֶךָ.
וְהָיוּ הַדְּבָרִים הָאֵלֶּה אֲשֶׁר אָנֹכִי מְצַוְּךָ הַיּוֹם עַל לְבָבֶךָ.
וְשִׁנַּנְתָּם לְבָנֶיךָ וְדִבַּרְתָּ בָּם בְּשִׁבְתְּךָ בְּבֵיתֶךָ וּבְלֶכְתְּךָ בַדֶּרֶךְ וּבְשָׁכְבְּךָ וּבְקוּמֶךָ.
וּקְשַׁרְתָּם לְאוֹת עַל יָדֶךָ וְהָיוּ לְטֹטָפֹת בֵּין עֵינֶיךָ.
וּכְתַבְתָּם עַל מְזֻזוֹת בֵּיתֶךָ וּבִשְׁעָרֶיךָ.

Hear, O Israel, the Lord is our God, the Lord is one.

You shall love the Lord, your God, with all your heart and with all your soul, and with all your might.

And these words that I command you this day shall be upon your heart.

You shall teach them to your sons and speak of them when you sit in your house, when you walk on the way, when you lie down, and when you rise up.

You shall bind them for a sign upon your hand, and they shall be for *totafot* between your eyes.

You shall inscribe them upon the doorposts of your house and upon your gates.

Text 5

DEUTERONOMY 30:11–19

כִּי הַמִּצְוָה הַזֹּאת אֲשֶׁר אָנֹכִי מְצַוְּךָ הַיּוֹם, לֹא נִפְלֵאת הִוא מִמְּךָ,
וְלֹא רְחֹקָה הִוא . . .
כִּי קָרוֹב אֵלֶיךָ הַדָּבָר מְאֹד בְּפִיךָ וּבִלְבָבְךָ לַעֲשֹׂתוֹ.
רְאֵה נָתַתִּי לְפָנֶיךָ הַיּוֹם אֶת הַחַיִּים וְאֶת הַטּוֹב וְאֶת הַמָּוֶת וְאֶת
הָרָע . . . וּבָחַרְתָּ בַּחַיִּים לְמַעַן תִּחְיֶה אַתָּה וְזַרְעֶךָ.

The mitzvah that I am prescribing to you today is not too mysterious or remote from you. . . .

It is something that is very close to you. It is in your mouth and in your heart, so that you can keep it.

See! Today I have set before you [a free choice] between life and good [on one side], and death and evil [on the other]. . . . Choose life, so that you and your descendants will live.

FROM ORAL TO WRITTEN

Text 6

MAIMONIDES, *MISHNEH TORAH*, INTRODUCTION

וְלָמָה עָשָׂה רַבֵּינוּ הַקָּדוֹשׁ כָּךְ וְלֹא הֵנִיחַ הַדָּבָר כְּמוֹת שֶׁהָיָה? לְפִי שֶׁרָאָה שֶׁתַּלְמִידִים מִתְמַעֲטִין וְהוֹלְכִין וְהַצָּרוֹת מִתְחַדְּשׁוֹת וּבָאוֹת, וּמַלְכוּת רוֹמִי פּוֹשֶׁטֶת בָּעוֹלָם וּמִתְגַּבֶּרֶת, וְיִשְׂרָאֵל מִתְגַּלְגְּלִין וְהוֹלְכִין לִקְצָוֹות, חִיבֵּר חִיבּוּר אֶחָד לִהְיוֹת בְּיַד כּוּלָּם כְּדֵי שֶׁיִּלְמְדוּהוּ בִּמְהֵרָה וְלֹא יִשָּׁכַח.

And why did Rebbi do this and did not leave matters as they were? He saw that the number of students was waning, while the instances of Jewish suffering were increasing. The Roman Empire was gaining might and expanding while Jews were scattered across the world. He therefore wrote [the oral law into] one book, so that everyone could learn it quickly and it should not be forgotten.

SHABBAT IN THE MISHNAH

Text 7a

MISHNAH, SHABBAT 7:2

אֲבוֹת מְלָאכוֹת אַרְבָּעִים חָסֵר אֶחָת:
הַזּוֹרֵעַ, וְהַחוֹרֵשׁ, וְהַקּוֹצֵר, וְהַמְעַמֵּר, הַדָּשׁ, וְהַזּוֹרֶה, הַבּוֹרֵר, הַטּוֹחֵן, וְהַמְרַקֵּד, וְהַלָּשׁ, וְהָאוֹפֶה;
הַגּוֹזֵז אֶת הַצֶּמֶר, הַמְלַבְּנוֹ, וְהַמְנַפְּצוֹ, וְהַצּוֹבְעוֹ, וְהַטּוֹוֶה, וְהַמֵּסֵךְ, וְהָעוֹשֶׂה שְׁנֵי בָתֵּי נִירִין, וְהָאוֹרֵג שְׁנֵי חוּטִין, וְהַפּוֹצֵעַ שְׁנֵי חוּטִין, הַקּוֹשֵׁר, וְהַמַּתִּיר, וְהַתּוֹפֵר שְׁתֵּי תְפִירוֹת, הַקּוֹרֵעַ עַל מְנָת לִתְפֹּר שְׁתֵּי תְפִירוֹת;
הַצָּד צְבִי, הַשּׁוֹחֲטוֹ, וְהַמַּפְשִׁיטוֹ, הַמּוֹלְחוֹ, וְהַמְעַבֵּד אֶת עוֹרוֹ, וְהַמּוֹחֲקוֹ, וְהַמְחַתְּכוֹ;
הַכּוֹתֵב שְׁתֵּי אוֹתִיּוֹת, וְהַמּוֹחֵק עַל מְנָת לִכְתֹּב שְׁתֵּי אוֹתִיּוֹת, הַבּוֹנֶה, וְהַסּוֹתֵר, הַמְכַבֶּה, וְהַמַּבְעִיר, הַמַּכֶּה בַפַּטִּישׁ, הַמּוֹצִיא מֵרְשׁוּת לִרְשׁוּת;
הֲרֵי אֵלּוּ אֲבוֹת מְלָאכוֹת אַרְבָּעִים חָסֵר אֶחָת.

There are thirty-nine forbidden "parent labors":

Sowing, plowing, reaping, binding sheaves, threshing, winnowing, selecting, grinding, sifting, kneading, baking;

Shearing wool, washing it, combing it, dyeing it, spinning, stretching [threads], making two loops, weaving two threads, separating two threads, tying, untying, sewing two stitches, tearing in order to sew two stitches;

Capturing a deer, slaughtering it, skinning it, salting it, curing its hide, scraping it [of hair], cutting it up;

MISHNAH

The first authoritative work of Jewish law that was codified in writing. The Mishnah contains the oral traditions that were passed down from teacher to student; it supplements, clarifies, and systematizes the commandments of the Torah. Due to the continual persecution of the Jewish people, it became increasingly difficult to guarantee that these traditions would not be forgotten. Rabbi Yehudah Hanasi therefore redacted the Mishnah at the end of the 2nd century. It serves as the foundation for the Talmud.

Writing two [combined] letters, erasing in order to write two letters, building, demolishing, extinguishing, kindling, striking with a hammer, carrying from one domain to another;

These are the thirty-nine "parent labors."

PROGENY LABORS

Text 7b

TALMUD, BAVA KAMA 2A

גַּבֵּי שַׁבָּת תְּנַן: אֲבוֹת מְלָאכוֹת אַרְבָּעִים חָסֵר אֶחָת; אָבוֹת מִכְּלָל דְּאִיכָּא תּוֹלְדוֹת.

The Mishnah says regarding Shabbat, "There are thirty-nine 'parent labors.'" "Parents" implies that there are "children" as well.

BABYLONIAN TALMUD

A literary work of monumental proportions that draws upon the legal, spiritual, intellectual, ethical, and historical traditions of Judaism. The 37 tractates of the Babylonian Talmud contain the teachings of the Jewish sages from the period after the destruction of the 2nd Temple through the 5th century CE. It has served as the primary vehicle for the transmission of the Oral Law and the education of Jews over the centuries; it is the entry point for all subsequent legal, ethical, and theological Jewish scholarship.

Learning Exercise 2

Try to match the secondary labors listed below in the left column to their root primary labor in the right column:

1. Milking a cow	A. Plowing
2. Gluing together papers	B. Threshing
3. Plucking eyebrows	C. Kneading
4. Mixing water and soil to make mud	D. Shearing
5. Fertilizing a field	E. Sewing

Learning Exercise 3

Consider the following four activities. Which of the primary labors do they most resemble? Is this resemblance sufficient to prohibit it on Shabbat?

Technology	Which Primary Labor Does It Most Resemble?	Status on Shabbat (circle one)
Driving a motorcycle		permitted / prohibited
Velcro		permitted / prohibited
Assembling a Pack 'n Play		permitted / prohibited
Photographing (with a film camera)		permitted / prohibited

DEFINING *MELACHAH*

Question for Discussion

What does it mean that God "rested"? Why would God need to "rest"?

Text 8

GENESIS 2:2–3

וַיְכַל אֱלֹקִים בַּיּוֹם הַשְּׁבִיעִי מְלַאכְתּוֹ אֲשֶׁר עָשָׂה וַיִּשְׁבֹּת בַּיּוֹם
הַשְּׁבִיעִי מִכָּל מְלַאכְתּוֹ אֲשֶׁר עָשָׂה.
וַיְבָרֶךְ אֱלֹקִים אֶת יוֹם הַשְּׁבִיעִי וַיְקַדֵּשׁ אֹתוֹ כִּי בוֹ שָׁבַת מִכָּל
מְלַאכְתּוֹ.

By the seventh day, God completed His *melachah* that He did, and He abstained on the seventh day from all His *melachah* that He did.

And God blessed the seventh day and He hallowed it, for thereon He abstained from all His *melachah*.

Text 9a

RABBI YA'AKOV TSVI MECKLENBURG,
HAKETAV VEHAKABALAH, EXODUS 35:1

דַע כִּי יֵשׁ הֶבְדֵל בֵּין מִלַּת עֲבוֹדָה וּבֵין מִלַּת מְלָאכָה:
עֲבוֹדָה כּוֹלֵל כָּל הַמַּעֲשִׂים שֶׁאָדָם עוֹשֶׂה, וַאֲפִילוּ אֵין בְּמַעֲשֵׂהוּ עִנְיָן הַמִּצְטָרֵךְ לִיְדִיעָה וְחָכְמָה. גַם אֵינוֹ מְשַׁנֶּה דָבָר בְּמַעֲשֵׂהוּ וְלֹא מְתַקֵּן דָבָר. כְּמוֹ לָשֵׂאת מַשָּׂאוֹת אֲבָנִים, לָרוּץ מִמָּקוֹם לְמָקוֹם, לְהוֹלִיךְ כֵּלִים אַחַר רַבּוֹ לְבֵית הַמֶּרְחָץ, לְהַלְבִּישׁוֹ, וְכַיּוֹצֵא מִמַּעֲשִׂים הַלָּלוּ שֶׁהֵם מַעֲשֵׂה עֶבֶד. וְזֶהוּ עִנְיַן הַמִּלָּה עֶבֶד, וְהַשֵּׁם עֲבוֹדָה . . .
וְאֵין שֵׁם מְלָאכָה נוֹפֵל אֶלָּא עַל הַמְחַדֵּשׁ דָבָר בְּעִנְיָנִים הַטִּבְעִים וּמְשַׁנֶּה אוֹתָם בְּמַעֲשֵׂהוּ מִמַּה שֶּׁהָיוּ, וְעַל יְדֵי הַחִדּוּשׁ הַזֶּה יִהְיֶה תִּקּוּן הַדָּבָר, הֵן שֶׁיִּבְנֶה הֵן שֶׁיַּהֲרוֹס, תָּמִיד יְשַׁנֶּה, וּכְשֶׁיֵּשׁ בְּמַעֲשֵׂהוּ תִּקּוּן לְיִישׁוּב הָעוֹלָם הֲרֵי זֶה מְלָאכָה . . . וְכָל מְלָאכָה יֵשׁ לִמּוּד וִידִיעָה בְּאֵיזֶה זְמַן וּבְאֵיזֶה כְּלִי יֵעָשֶׂה . . .
וְיוֹצֵא מִזֶּה עַל דֶּרֶךְ כְּלַל, כִּי כָּל מַעֲשֵׂה אֱלֹקִים שֶׁעָשָׂה בְּשֵׁשֶׁת הַיָּמִים נִקְרָאִים מְלָאכוֹת לֹא עֲבוֹדוֹת. עַל כֵּן כְּתִיב "מִכָּל מְלַאכְתּוֹ" (בְּרֵאשִׁית ב, ב), "כִּי בוֹ שָׁבַת מִכָּל מְלַאכְתּוֹ" (שָׁם, ג) . . .

Know that there is a difference between the word *avodah* and the word *melachah.*

Avodah refers to actions that do not require knowledge or wisdom and where nothing is being changed or fixed by the action. Examples include carrying loads of stones, running from place to place, carrying the clothing of one's master to the bathhouse, dressing him, or any similar work of a slave. These tasks are associated with the words *avodah* and *eved,* which means "slave."

In contrast, the term *melachah* only applies when someone creates something new from raw materials, changing it from its previous state and

RABBI YA'AKOV TSVI MECKLENBURG
1785–1865

German rabbi and biblical exegete. Rabbi Ya'akov served as rabbi in Königsberg, East Prussia. In 1839, he published *Haketav Vehakabalah*, an important commentary that often demonstrates the indivisibility of the Written Torah and the Oral Torah.

> improving it. Whether building or destroying, there must always be a change. When a person's work makes the world more habitable, it is called *melachah*.... And every *melachah* requires learning and knowledge to know when it should be performed, and with what implement....
>
> We now understand why all the work God did during the six days of Creation is called *melachah*, not *avodah*, as we see in the second chapter of Genesis....

Learning Exercise 4

1. Enumerate the differences between *avodah* and *melachah*.

Avodah	*Melachah*
	Act requires knowledge and wisdom
Exhausting	

2. Cite some examples that fit each category:

Avodah	*Melachah*
Running from place to place	Writing

Text 9b

RABBI YA'AKOV TSVI MECKLENBURG, IBID.

וְלָכֵן אֵלֶה הַמְלָאכוֹת כּוּלָם אֲסוּרִים לָנוּ לַעֲשׂוֹת בְּיוֹם הַשַּׁבָּת, כִּי הִזְהִיר "לֹא תַעֲשֶׂה כָל מְלָאכָה". וְלֹא אָסַר עָלֵינוּ הָעֲבוֹדוֹת, כִּי לֹא מָצִינוּ "לֹא תַעֲבוֹד בְּיוֹם הַשַּׁבָּת", אוֹ "לֹא תַעֲשֶׂה בּוֹ עֲבוֹדָה", לְפִי שֶׁלֹא הִזְהִירָנוּ עֲלֵיהֶן.

וְיֹצֵא לָנוּ מִזֶה שֶׁמוּתָּר לְטַלְטֵל בְּשַׁבָּת שׁוּלְחָנוֹת וְכִסְּאוֹת אוֹכְלִים וּמַשְׁקִים . . . כְּשֶׁהֵם לְצוֹרֶךְ עוֹנֶג שַׁבָּת. וְכֵן מוּתָּר לָרוּץ כָּל הַיוֹם מִבַּיִת לְבַיִת וְכַיוֹצֵא, אַף עַל פִּי שֶׁהֵן עָמֵל וְטוֹרַח, לְפִי שֶׁאֵינָן אֶלָא עֲבוֹדוֹת, וְהַשֵׁם יִתְבָּרֵךְ לֹא אָסַר עֲשִׂיַית הָעֲבוֹדָה זוּלַת הַמְלָאכָה.

וְלָכֵן הַחוֹרֵשׁ כָּל שֶׁהוּא, וְהַזוֹרֵעַ כָּל שֶׁהוּא, וְהַכּוֹתֵב שְׁתֵּי אוֹתִיוֹת בַּשַׁבָּת, וְאַף עַל פִּי שֶׁאֵין בְּכָל זֶה עָמָל וְטוֹרַח, כְּבָר חִלֵל אֶת הַשַׁבָּת, לְפִי שֶׁעָשָׂה מְלָאכָה . . .

We are forbidden from performing *melachah* on Shabbat, as it says, "You shall perform no *melachah*." But we do not find a prohibition that says, "You shall perform no *avodah* on Shabbat."

Consequently, it is permitted to carry tables and chairs, food and drink [while indoors] . . . when they are needed to enjoy Shabbat. Similarly, it is permitted to run from house to house all day, and so forth. Despite the fact that there is toil and trouble, it is *avodah*—and God did not forbid *avodah*, only *melachah*.

On the other hand, although there is no toil and trouble when one plows just a bit, plants just a bit, or writes just two letters, these acts desecrate Shabbat because they constitute *melachah*. . . .

Text 9c

RABBI YA'AKOV TSVI MECKLENBURG, IBID.

וְהִנֵּה כָּל הַמַּעֲשִׂים שֶׁהֵכִין הַשֵּׁם יִתְבָּרֵךְ בְּמַעֲשֵׂה בְּרֵאשִׁית לְצוֹרֶךְ הָאָדָם רַבּוֹת מְאֹד, קְצָתָן תְּלוּיִים בָּאֲדָמָה, בַּזְּרָעִים וּבַצְּמָחִים שֶׁהֵן לְצוֹרֶךְ מַאֲכָלוֹ, וּקְצָתָם תְּלוּיִים בִּמְלָאכוֹת שֶׁהֵן לְצוֹרֶךְ כֵּלָיו וּבְגָדָיו, כְּמוֹ מְלֶאכֶת חָרָשׁ וְחוֹשֵׁב, תּוֹפֵר וְצוֹבֵעַ וְכַיּוֹצֵא, וּקְצָתָן לְצוֹרֶךְ דִּירָתוֹ כְּמוֹ מְלֶאכֶת הַבִּנְיָן וְכַיּוֹצֵא. וְאֵלּוּ הֵן ל"ט אָבוֹת מְלָאכוֹת שֶׁקִּבְּלוּ רַזַ"ל הַשְּׁנוּיִים בְּפֶרֶק כְּלָל גָּדוֹל, וְהוּא קַבָּלָתָם עַל דֶּרֶךְ הֲלָכָה לְמֹשֶׁה מִסִּינַי, שֶׁבְּחָכְמַת אֱלֹקִים כְּלוּלִים בְּמִסְפָּר זֶה כָּל הַמְּלָאכוֹת הָרַבּוֹת שֶׁהֵן בִּמְצִיאוּת. כִּי אוֹתָן שֶׁלֹּא נִזְכְּרוּ, הֵן תּוֹלְדוֹת וּכְלוּלוֹת בָּאָבוֹת הַלָּלוּ.

Now, there are many types of *melachot*. Some relate to extracting food from the ground, like plowing. Some relate to the production of garments, like weaving, sewing, and dyeing. Others relate to building homes for shelter. All these are included in the thirty-nine categories of labor that our sages taught in Tractate Shabbat, going all the way back to Moses at Sinai. With divine wisdom, this number includes all potential *melachot*. For anything not included in the thirty-nine would be a corollary of one of the thirty-nine parent labors.

THE DEEPER MESSAGE
REALITY CHECK

Text 10

DAYAN DR. I. GRUNFELD, *THE SABBATH* (JERUSALEM: FELDHEIM PUBLISHERS, 1981), PP. 27–29

Sabbath testifies to God as the supreme Creator of heaven and earth and all they contain. Man, however, is engaged in a constant struggle to gain mastery over God's creation, to bring nature under his control. By the use of his God-given intelligence, skill and energy, he has in large measure succeeded in this. He is thus constantly in danger of forgetting his own creaturehood—his utter and complete dependence on the Lord of all things. He tends to forget that the very powers he uses in his conquest of nature are derived from his Creator, in whose service his life and work should be conducted. . . .

God willed therefore that the Jew, while subduing and controlling his environment like every other human being, must recognize, *and show that he recognizes,* that his powers are derived from One higher that himself. This recognition he is to express by dedicating one day in every week to God, and by refraining on this day from every activity which signifies human power over nature.

On this day we renounce every exercise of intelligent, purposeful control over natural objects and forces, we cease from every act of human power, in order to proclaim God as the Source

DAYAN DR. ISIDOR GRUNFELD
1900–1975

Rabbi and author. Born in Tauberettersheim, Bavaria, Grunfeld studied law and philosophy at the universities of Frankfurt and Hamburg. He settled in England in 1933 where he studied for the rabbinate and was ordained. From 1939 until 1965 he served as *dayan* (chief rabbinical magistrate) of the London Rabbinical Court. Among his numerous communal activities were those on behalf of European Jewish war orphans, and the British Council for Jewish Relief and Rehabilitation. He was also active in Amnesty International and various peace movements. Grunfeld's literary work is chiefly concerned with Rabbi Samson Raphael Hirsch's, editing English translations of his work with extensive introductions and notes. His work, *The Sabbath*, has been a fundamental work for appreciating Shabbat in the modern world.

of all power. By refraining from human creating, the Jew pays silent homage to the Creator....

Melakhah thus includes within its scope any activity of a constructive nature which makes some significant change in our material environment—significant, that is, in relation to its usefulness for human purposes. Any act, however small, which demonstrates man's mastery of nature in this way is a *melakhah*, be it striking a light or washing clothes, tying a knot or building a house.

FOOD, SHELTER, CLOTHING

Figure 6.2

The Thirty-Nine *Melachot*

Baking	Cloth and Leather Making		Constructing	Other
1. Sowing	12. Shearing	25. Trapping	32. Writing	39. Carrying (from a private domain to a public domain and vice versa)
2. Plowing	13. Bleaching	26. Slaughtering	33. Erasing	
3. Reaping	14. Combing	27. Skinning	34. Building	
4. Binding Sheaves	15. Dyeing	28. Tanning	35. Breaking Down	
5. Threshing	16. Spinning	29. Smoothing	36. Striking the Final Hammer's Blow	
6. Winnowing	17. Stretching the Threads	30. Scoring	37. Extinguishing a Fire	
7. Selecting	18. Making Loops	31. Cutting	38. Kindling a Fire	
8. Grinding	19. Weaving			
9. Sifting	20. Separating the Threads			
10. Kneading	21. Tying a Knot			
11. Baking	22. Untying a Knot			
	23. Sewing			
	24. Tearing			

CARRYING

Text 11

DAYAN DR. I. GRUNFELD, IBID., P. 36

If the other *melakhoth* show us man mastering and controlling his natural environment, this one shows him active in the social realm, carrying on the intercourse of the community, circulating its material good between house and house, through street and thoroughfare; not for trade only, but also for the personal and social ends of everyday life. "Carrying" is the characteristic *melakhah* by which man pursues and attains his purposes in society. By ceasing from each of the other *melakhoth,* we proclaim God as the source of our power over nature. By ceasing from "carrying" we acknowledge Him our Master in the social organization—the world of house, street and city—needs above all else the realization of God's presences and God's purpose, the sanctification and dedication which ceasing from *melakhah* expresses. The community whose members refrain from "carrying" on Sabbath places the seal of God upon its social life.

CONCLUSION

Learning Exercise 5

1. Did you have any questions about Shabbat observance that have been answered by this lesson?
2. Do you have any questions about Shabbat observance that have not been answered by this lesson?
3. What is one idea from this lesson that you think might be beneficial to a particular area of your life?

Key Points

1. Every mitzvah that God gave to Moses was given with an explanation. God would tell Moses the verse, which was to become part of the Written Torah, and then tell him its explanation, which was passed down orally from one generation to the next. It is impossible to perform the *mitzvot* without the explanations provided by the Oral Torah.

2. The Written-Oral dynamic continued for centuries, but due to the oppression and dispersion that existed around the year 200 CE, Rabbi Yehudah wrote the Mishnah so that the Oral Torah would not be forgotten.

3. The Mishnah teaches that the words in the Torah "do not work" refer to thirty-nine "parent" *melachot* (labors). These include "progeny" as well—acts that serve similar functions and that share similar properties with one of the thirty-nine *melachot*. This system has allowed Jews to apply the laws of Shabbat to emerging technologies.

4. The common denominator between the thirty-nine *melachot* is that they are activities requiring a degree of wisdom to effect a change in nature. Indeed, through the dual system of "parents" and "progeny," all activities requiring wisdom to effect a change in nature are included in the thirty-nine categories of labor.

5. Because we are resting to commemorate God's rest, the kind of work from which we refrain is the kind of work from which God refrained. God rested not from toil but from changing nature with His wisdom, and so our rest ought to mirror this. This is why things that aren't strenuous labor can be forbidden on Shabbat and things that entail much toil might not be forbidden.

6. When we are in a mode of creating, it is hard to think of ourselves as created beings, and so it is easy to forget the One who gave us the talents and resources to achieve success. Once a week, therefore, we stop creating and take time to focus on the fact that God orchestrated our creative successes.
7. The goal is for our weekday lives to be infused with some degree of the Shabbat mind-set, an endeavor powered by Shabbat observance. However, like all *mitzvot*, Shabbat is not an all-or-nothing proposition; the important thing is to start somewhere.

ADDITIONAL READINGS

ORTHODOX ANSWERS TO UNUSUAL QUESTIONS: RABBI RULES ON SABBATH SKATING AND OTHER ISSUES

By Brian Murphy

CAESAREA, ISRAEL

The full scope of Jewish texts and traditions couldn't help the rabbi sort this one out: Could he skate to synagogue on the holy day of rest and prayer?

Dov Kaplan decided he should go straight to the top for an answer—a religious sage in Jerusalem who rules on what's acceptable, and what's not, under Orthodox Jewish law. His verdict on the in-line skates? Roll on, including Saturdays.

The recent case was more than just a quirky display of Torah scholarship.

The modern world of gadgets and hobbies makes being true to faith increasingly difficult for Jews who strictly observe Shabbat, or the Sabbath, and its detailed list of forbidden activities. The ban includes any type of commercial labor, nearly all modes of transportation and anything construed as igniting or extinguishing "fire," such as cooking or even flicking a light switch.

Any Shabbat problem—like the roller-skating question—probably will find its way to a crammed wedge of offices on a Jerusalem hilltop. The space serves as a kind of one-stop answer factory: the staff responding to letters and e-mails, the head rabbi issuing religious decrees, and amateur inventors tinkering at work tables to find Shabbat-acceptable devices. Among the latest projects is a doorbell that uses air pressure instead of electricity.

"We believe the Torah is a living document and needs to address modern issues, especially with the incredible pace of change," said Rabbi Levi Yitzchak Halperin, who directs the Institute for Science and Halacha, Halacha being the body of Jewish law. "But we are not an institute that is looking for loopholes."

On roller-skating? "That wasn't a real hard one," he said with a smile.

Kaplan's problem arose after plans were made for a second synagogue in Caesarea, a town of 5,000 people on the Mediterranean coast that has the feeling of a Florida resort, right down to bike paths and an 18-hole golf course.

Cars are out on Shabbat. Bicycles are banned because of the risk of fixing a chain or flat, which would be considered work. So Kaplan thought of zipping between the two synagogues using in-line skates—even though he needs beginner-level lessons.

"We must have respect for Jewish law and traditions," said Kaplan, 45, who was raised in Long Beach, N.Y., and immigrated to Israel when he was 11. "But we also have to show that Orthodox rabbis are not distant, unapproachable and closed to new ideas. Who knows if I'll actually skate. It's more about making a point."

Halperin saw no problem. He decided that skates can't break down the way bikes do.

The institute is a mix of library, workshop and warehouse. In one room, Orthodox rabbinical

---

BRIAN MURPHY

1959–

Murphy is a journalist at the *Washington Post*. He served as the international religion correspondent for the Associated Press from 2004–2006, and prior to that, he served as an AP correspondent in more than 40 countries. He has authored several nonfiction books, including, *81 Days Below Zero* (2015) and *The Root of the Wild Madder* (2005)

students pore over books. Next door is a workshop loaded with switches and wires, a place to experiment with ways around using electricity on Shabbat. Other Jewish groups in Israel and abroad also offer guidance on Shabbat and other matters, but Halperin is widely considered the definitive voice.

When the institute opened in the 1960s, electricity was the main source of inquiries and innovations—which some ultra-Orthodox dismissed as diluting Jewish law. About a third of Israel's Jewish population either strictly adheres to Shabbat codes or follows them to some degree, such as not watching television on the holy day but traveling by car to synagogue. In the United States, about 7 percent of Jews identify themselves as Orthodox.

Under Orthodox views, it's forbidden to "close" an electrical circuit on Shabbat—for example turning on a light, dialing a phone or hitting an elevator button.

The solution was developing appliances, phones and other electrical devices with preset open-and-close cycles. The institute's Shabbat phone is a prime example: It has a constant "on-off" cycle so the caller is not directly dialing a number, but allowing the phone to make the connection.

It's no longer so straightforward. Halperin is peppered with requests of all kinds.

Can the institute develop a TV remote for Shabbat? Not interested in even trying.

Is stem cell research acceptable? Yes, Halperin says, as long as the process will not alter the genetic makeup of the patient. Cloning, however, is considered wrong.

The use of sperm banks? There are many obstacles, Halperin says. But in some cases—such as a husband who froze his sperm before he died or was rendered sterile—it's allowable because reproduction remains within the family.

The queries have even reached beyond this world.

Shabbat questions about space travel were raised when Israeli astronaut Ilan Ramon was aboard the space shuttle *Columbia*, which broke apart during reentry in 2003. When, it was asked, is Shabbat in outer space, given that the observance begins and ends with sunset? Halperin's conclusion: Calculate when Shabbat would occur at the launch pad.

Other solutions require a bit more elbow grease. One of them was tucked into a corner: an attempt to create a Shabbat wheelchair that uses pneumatic power as an alternative to electric power. There are still some bugs, said the institute's key researcher, Rabbi Shmuel Strauss.

"It still doesn't have the efficiency of a battery," Strauss said. "We're working on it."

The Washington Post, October 29, 2005

STEALING A DAY OUT OF LIFE TO LIVE

By Chief Rabbi Warren Goldstein

We are assailed by the constant obsession with communication through ubiquitous screen devices

The late Oliver Sacks, famed professor of neurology and best-selling author recently wrote these emotional words for *The New York Times* days before he died, reflecting on the Shabbat of his childhood:

> The peace of the Sabbath, of a stopped world, a time outside time, was palpable, infused everything, and I found myself drenched with a wistfulness, something akin to nostalgia, wondering...

His words reminded me of those of Justice Louis Brandeis, one of the most celebrated judges in American history, who wrote many decades before:

> In the home of my parents, there was no Jewish Sabbath, nor in my own home. But I recall vividly the joy and awe with which my uncle, Lewis Dembitz welcomed the arrival of the day and the piety with which he observed it. I remember the extra delicacies, lighting of candles, prayers over a cup of wine, and quaint chants, and Uncle Lewis poring over the books most of the day. I remember more particularly an elusive something about him which was spoken of as "Sabbath Peace" and which later brought to my mind a passage from Addison in which he speaks of "stealing a day out of life to live".

Sacks and Brandeis were both profoundly drawn to the "peace of the Sabbath". For Sacks it is "a stopped world, a time outside time" and Brandeis turns to the words of the great seventeenth-century British poet, Joseph Addison, who spoke of "stealing a day out of life to live."

Brandeis goes on to complain about the restrictions of Shabbat, the fact that there are certain activities that Jewish law prohibits on the day—we don't write, work, cook, garden, drive cars, use the phone, turn on lights, activate electrical appliances, amongst other things.

It is important to understand the philosophy behind these restrictions—rather than impeding our enjoyment of the day, they actually create the magic and inspiration of the Shabbat experience, what Sacks calls a "stopped world" and a "time outside of time."

To understand this idea, let's go back to that inspiring phrase Brandeis used to describe Shabbat of, "stealing a day out of life to live". What does it mean to live? Living is really about connecting—connecting to our family, friends and community, connecting to G-d, and ultimately connecting to ourselves. We know from personal experience that there is no joy in life comparable to the joy of connection.

And yet, because there is so much that we do, day in and day out, in order to get by—to survive and to achieve in this world—that in the end we spend so little time actively connecting. The pace of modern life, and the tasks and responsibilities that consume our lives morning until evening, are an intrusion; they distract us and prevent us from really connecting with our family and friends, with G-d, and with ourselves. Shabbat is a day on which we are not overwhelmed with operational and functional matters; it is a day dedicated to living.

CHIEF RABBI WARREN GOLDSTEIN, PHD
1971–

Chief Rabbi of South Africa. Rabbi Goldstein was elected chief rabbi in 2005, making him the youngest to ever hold the post, and the first to have been born in South Africa. Rabbi Goldstein received his rabbinic training in Johannesburg and Jerusalem, and he also earned a PhD in constitutional law and human rights from the University of the Witwatersrand. In 2013, he founded the Shabbat Project, bringing thousands of Jews together in Shabbat observance for one weekend. He has authored a number of books, including, *Defending the Human Spirit: Jewish Law's Vision for a Moral Society* (2006).

But why do we need so many rigid rules for a day of connection? Duke University Professor of Psychology and Behavioural Economics, Dan Ariely, explains it best:

> Shabbat isn't just about relaxing. It's also about keeping a list of rules and restrictions—things that make the day different from all others. Rules offer relief, because somebody else (in this case, God) is doing the driving, and you can doze off in the passenger seat. Shabbat isn't just about relaxing, it's about keeping a list of rules and restrictions—things that make the day different from all others . . . When we have to make lots of decisions with no rules to guide us, nothing is automatic and we have to invest some energy in every one of those decisions. All of those decisions sap our moral energy, making us more likely to yield to temptation. But when we have rules—particularly strict rules—we don't have to make the same number of decisions, and we are left with much more moral energy . . . The rules link us to other people, to some other larger purpose, or to a deep belief.

So here is the exquisite irony. The restrictions of Shabbat are actually liberating. It is the things we can't do on Shabbat which free us to do the things we can. Take, for example, the restriction on driving. It may seem as if it infringes on our ability to move around. But actually it frees us—to walk together as family and friends, really connecting and talking in peace and tranquility, side-by-side, instead of talking into the speaker-phone of a car as we negotiate traffic. The restriction on cell phones and computers is another example. We are assailed by the constant obsession with communication through ubiquitous screen devices. Shabbat frees us from these devices, so that we actually have the space to really connect with one another, face-to-face, without interruption or interference.

Modern life has fragmented; we are constantly pulled in different directions by distractions, demands and onerous responsibilities that pile up with increasing speed. We seldom get the chance to be truly present. In a world of distraction and disconnection, Shabbat enters to offers us that chance to connect, to revisit, reinvigorate and reinvest in our most important relationships. And so, in an unexpected twist, at this point of the greatest technological and civilizational development in history, it turns out that we moderns need the ancient biblical institution of Shabbat more than ever.

Shabbat grants the gift of a profound tranquility and a truly refreshing break that can only come from a non-negotiable day off. Professor Ariely points out that most stress in life comes from mental stress—buckling under a list of "to do's"; knowing that right now, we could be doing this, or ought to be doing that. But on Shabbat we have the freedom and peace of mind that comes with knowing all our work is done. The Torah says: "six days you shall labour and complete all of your work . . . and the seventh is a Shabbat to the L-rd your G-d." What is meant by "complete all your work"? Who can finish all their work? And in six days! The Talmud says that on Shabbat we feel as if all our work is done. Once a week, when Shabbat comes in, we really can feel as if all our work is done, because, on Shabbat, work is not even an option. . . . And because of that, we have to step back and let go. There is a real sense of peace and tranquility in accepting that all our work that can be done, has been done.

And from inner peace we find purpose and meaning. The cacophony of life recedes so that we can actually discern our true purpose in the world.

As Sacks reflects:

> And now, weak, short of breath, my once-firm muscles melted away by cancer, I find my thoughts, increasingly, not on the supernatural or spiritual, but on what is meant by living a good and worthwhile life—achieving a sense of peace within oneself. I find my thoughts drifting to the Sabbath, the day of rest, the seventh day of the week, and perhaps the seventh day of one's life as well, when one can feel that one's work is done, and one may, in good conscience, rest.

And so, G-d created the Shabbat and made it an integral part of the fabric of the world. He created one day a week when the noise fades. He stopped creating and so do we. The world goes quite. And once the noise and distraction dissipate—the hidden, spiritual, miraculous reality of the world emerges for us all.

http://www.chiefrabbi.co.za/2015/10/stealing-a-day-out-of-life-to-live/
Reprinted with permission of the publisher

pause

& AFFECT

LESSON 7

The Farewell

ROSHCHODESH society

THE RELUCTANT FAREWELL

Text 1

ELIE WIESEL, *WISE MEN AND THEIR TALES: PORTRAITS OF BIBLICAL, TALMUDIC, AND HASIDIC MASTERS* (NEW YORK: SCHOCKEN BOOKS, 2003), PP. 329–330

The end of Shabbat was signaled by mother and grandmother. Shortly before the Havdalah ceremony, which separates light from darkness and the sacred from the profane, the Shabbat from the weekdays, both women, like all mothers, would recite the special prayer attributed to the great Rebbe Levi-Yitzhak of Berditchev: "*Gott fun Avrohom, Yitzhok un Yankev . . .*" God of Abraham, Isaac, and Jacob, extend your protection over Thy children and ours . . . When the prayer ends, the Havdalah begins.

Whereupon another song takes hold of my memory: "*Bobeshi, zog nokh nit God fun Avrohom . . .*" It's a little child pleading with his grandmother not to recite her prayers, not yet, let her wait a bit longer, the sun hasn't set yet in the west, let Shabbat last a while longer . . . The little child loves the Shabbat and refuses to leave it behind—or to be left behind.

ELIE WIESEL
1928–2016

Writer, professor, and political activist. Wiesel was born in Sighet, Romania, and was deported by the Nazis to Auschwitz when he was 15. He is the author of more than 40 books of fiction and non-fiction, including the acclaimed memoir *Night*, which has been published in more than 30 languages. In 1986, Wiesel won the Nobel Prize for Peace. He has received numerous awards, including the Presidential Medal of Freedom and the U.S. Congressional Gold Medal.

Text 2

RABBI YOSEF CARO, SHULCHAN ARUCH, *ORACH CHAYIM* 293:1

מְאַחֲרִין תְּפִלַּת עַרְבִית, כְּדֵי לְהוֹסִיף מֵחוֹל עַל הַקּוֹדֶשׁ.

We postpone the evening service on Saturday night to add from the weekday to Shabbat.

RABBI YOSEF CARO (MARAN, *BEIT YOSEF*)
1488–1575

Halachic authority and author. Rabbi Caro was born in Spain, but was forced to flee during the expulsion in 1492 and eventually settled in Safed, Israel. He authored many works including the *Beit Yosef*, *Kesef Mishneh*, and a mystical work, *Magid Meisharim*. Rabbi Caro's magnum opus, the Shulchan Aruch (Code of Jewish Law), has been universally accepted as the basis for modern Jewish law.

LOSS AND APPREHENSION

Text 3a

TALMUD, BEITSAH 16A

נְשָׁמָה יְתֵירָה נוֹתֵן הַקָּדוֹשׁ בָּרוּךְ הוּא בְּאָדָם עֶרֶב שַׁבָּת, וּלְמוֹצָאֵי שַׁבָּת נוֹטְלִין אוֹתָהּ הֵימֶנּוּ.

On the eve of Shabbat, God gives a person extra soul; at the close of Shabbat it is withdrawn from the person.

BABYLONIAN TALMUD

A literary work of monumental proportions that draws upon the legal, spiritual, intellectual, ethical, and historical traditions of Judaism. The 37 tractates of the Babylonian Talmud contain the teachings of the Jewish sages from the period after the destruction of the 2nd Temple through the 5th century CE. It has served as the primary vehicle for the transmission of the Oral Law and the education of Jews over the centuries; it is the entry point for all subsequent legal, ethical, and theological Jewish scholarship.

Text 3b

TALMUD, IBID.

כֵּיוָן שֶׁשָּׁבַת, "וַוי אָבְדָה נֶפֶשׁ".

Once Shabbat is concluded, [we cry]: "Woe, the [extra] soul has been lost!"

Text 4

RABBI JOSEPH B. SOLOVEITCHIK, QUOTED IN *THE RAV: THE WORLD OF RABBI JOSEPH B. SOLOVEITCHIK*, VOL. 1, AARON RAKEFET-ROTHKOFF, ED. (JERSEY CITY, NJ: KTAV PUBLISHING HOUSE, 1999), PP. 159–161

In Warsaw we lived three houses away from the Modzhitzer shtiebel. Generally, I would go to the Modzhitzer shtiebel for the seudah shlishit [third meal] of the Sabbath. They would sing all the zemirot for the seudah shlishit. Poor Jews would be seated around the table in the shtiebel.

The Modzhitzer shteibel was located in a poor district in Warsaw called the Grzybowska district. My father could not afford to live in a more affluent district. This was a neighborhood where many of the Jews worked as porters. . . .

I knew these Jews well and I constantly spoke with them. They were sincerely pious Jews who willingly sacrificed for their spiritual commitments. I once spoke with one of them who was frail and short. He constantly carried heavy metal pieces and I wondered where he got the physical strength to support this weight. His load was always tied around him with a thick cord and he totally resembled a "coolie." On the Sabbath, I saw this very Jew and I did not recognize him. He came over to me in his tattered kapote. It was covered with endless patches, and even the patches had patches. Yet his face shone with the joy of the Sabbath. I recognized in a tangible fashion that a person's Sabbath countenance is totally different than his weekday appearance.

RABBI JOSEPH B. SOLOVEITCHIK
1903–1993

Talmudist and philosopher. A scion of a famous Lithuanian rabbinical family, Rabbi Soloveitchik was one of the most influential Jewish personalities, leaders, and thinkers of the 20th century. In 1941, he became professor of Talmud at RIETS—Yeshiva University; in this capacity, he ordained more rabbis than anyone else in Jewish history. Among his published works are *Halakhic Man* and *Lonely Man of Faith*.

So, I asked him: When will we daven Ma'ariv [pray the evening prayer for the conclusion of the Sabbath]?

He answered: What is with you? Are you already longing for the weekdays to begin? What do you mean when will we daven Ma'ariv, are we lacking anything now?

When these Jews would sing the *"Bnei Heikhalah"* ["The dwellers of the Sanctuary who wish to experience the Divine Presence"] at the end of the seudah shlishit, they were singing about themselves. When they sang "He maketh me lie down in green pastures" [from the twenty-third Psalm (23:2)], they knew that there were no "green pastures" outside of the shtiebel. There were many vicious Poles out there who were anxious to participate in pogroms against the Jews. They were desirous of taking away any chance for the Jews to earn a livelihood. The Jews knew all this and therefore they could not depart from the Sabbath. They sang a refrain and repeated it. They only wanted to remain with the Sabbath.

HAVDALAH
INTRODUCTORY VERSES

Text 5
HAVDALAH, OPENING VERSES

הִנֵּה אֵל יְשׁוּעָתִי אֶבְטַח וְלֹא אֶפְחָד, כִּי עָזִּי וְזִמְרָת יָ-הּ ה', וַיְהִי לִי לִישׁוּעָה.
וּשְׁאַבְתֶּם מַיִם בְּשָׂשׂוֹן מִמַּעַיְנֵי הַיְשׁוּעָה.
לַה' הַיְשׁוּעָה, עַל עַמְּךָ בִרְכָתֶךָ סֶּלָה.
ה' צְבָאוֹת עִמָּנוּ, מִשְׂגָּב לָנוּ אֱלֹהֵי יַעֲקֹב סֶלָה.
ה' צְבָאוֹת, אַשְׁרֵי אָדָם בֹּטֵחַ בָּךְ.
ה' הוֹשִׁיעָה, הַמֶּלֶךְ יַעֲנֵנוּ בְיוֹם קָרְאֵנוּ.
לַיְּהוּדִים הָיְתָה אוֹרָה וְשִׂמְחָה וְשָׂשׂוֹן וִיקָר, כֵּן תִּהְיֶה לָנוּ.
כּוֹס יְשׁוּעוֹת אֶשָּׂא וּבְשֵׁם ה' אֶקְרָא.

Indeed, God is my deliverance; I am confident and shall not fear, for God is my strength and my praise, and He has been my salvation (Isaiah 12:2).

You shall draw water with joy from the well-springs of salvation (ibid., 3).

Deliverance is God's; may Your blessing be upon Your people forever (Psalms 3:9).

The God of the many heavenly and worldly beings is with us; the God of Jacob is our everlasting stronghold (ibid., 46:8).

God of the many heavenly and worldly beings—happy is the man who trusts in You (ibid., 84:13).

God deliver us; may the King answer us on the day we call (ibid., 20:10).

For the Jews, there was light and joy, gladness and honor (Esther 8:16). And so let it be with us.

I will raise a cup in thanks over my salvation and invoke God's name (Psalms 116:13).

Questions for Discussion

1. Considering what you have learned during this course about Shabbat, why do we recite this seemingly random collection of verses at the conclusion of Shabbat?
2. Is there a theme (or themes) to this collection of verses?

MULTISENSORY EXPERIENCE

Text 6

HAVDALAH, BLESSINGS RECITED OVER WINE, SPICES, AND FIRE

בָּרוּךְ אַתָּה ה' אֱלֹקֵינוּ מֶלֶךְ הָעוֹלָם בּוֹרֵא פְּרִי הַגָּפֶן.
בָּרוּךְ אַתָּה ה' אֱלֹקֵינוּ מֶלֶךְ הָעוֹלָם בּוֹרֵא מִינֵי בְשָׂמִים.
בָּרוּךְ אַתָּה ה' אֱלֹקֵינוּ מֶלֶךְ הָעוֹלָם בּוֹרֵא מְאוֹרֵי הָאֵשׁ.

Blessed are You . . . King of the Universe, Who creates the fruit of the vine.

Blessed are You . . . King of the Universe, Who creates various kinds of spices.

Blessed are You . . . King of the Universe, Who creates the lights of fire.

Question for Discussion

How might this consumption of wine, smelling of aromatic spices, and glancing at fire match the theme(s) of the verses mentioned above?

Text 7a

MIDRASH, *BEREISHIT RABAH* 11:2

ל"ו שָׁעוֹת שִׁימְּשָׁה אוֹתָהּ הָאוֹרָה: שְׁנֵים עָשָׂר שֶׁל עֶרֶב שַׁבָּת, וי"ב שֶׁל לֵילֵי שַׁבָּת, וי"ב שֶׁל שַׁבָּת. כֵּיוָן שֶׁשָּׁקְעָה הַחַמָּה בְּמוֹצָאֵי שַׁבָּת הִתְחִיל הַחוֹשֶׁךְ מְמַשְׁמֵשׁ וּבָא, וְנִתְיָרֵא אָדָם הָרִאשׁוֹן.

The sublime light shone [for Adam and Eve] for thirty-six hours: twelve hours on Friday, twelve hours on Friday night, and twelve hours on Shabbat day. When the sun set on Saturday night and darkness became increasingly palpable, Adam was frightened.

BEREISHIT RABAH

An early rabbinic commentary on the Book of Genesis. This Midrash bears the name of Rabbi Oshiya Rabah (Rabbi Oshiya "the Great") whose teaching opens this work. This Midrash provides textual exegeses and stories, expounds upon the biblical narrative, and develops and illustrates moral principles. Produced by the sages of the Talmud in the Land of Israel, its use of Aramaic closely resembles that of the Jerusalem Talmud. It was first printed in Constantinople in 1512 together with four other Midrashic works on the other four books of the Pentateuch.

Text 7b

TALMUD, AVODAH ZARAH, 8A

אָמַר: אוֹי לִי, שֶׁבִּשְׁבִיל שֶׁסָּרַחְתִּי עוֹלָם חָשׁוּךְ בַּעֲדִי.

Adam said, "Woe is me, for because of my sin the world has gone dark on me."

Text 7c

TALMUD, PESACHIM 54A

וּבְמוֹצָאֵי שַׁבָּת נָתַן הַקָדוֹשׁ בָּרוּךְ הוּא דֵיעָה בְּאָדָם הָרִאשׁוֹן מֵעֵין דוּגְמָא שֶׁל מַעְלָה, וְהֵבִיא שְׁנֵי אֲבָנִים וּטְחָנָן זוֹ בְּזוֹ וְיָצָא מֵהֶן אוֹר.

On Saturday night, God imparted to Adam a glimpse of His wisdom. Adam took two [flint] stones and rubbed them together, and fire sprang forth.

Question for Discussion

How does this explain why we kindle a flame at the conclusion of Shabbat?

DO NOT FEAR, JACOB

Text 8

AL TIRA AVDI YA'AKOV, SATURDAY NIGHT LITURGY

אָמַר ה' לְיַעֲקֹב. אַל תִּירָא עַבְדִּי יַעֲקֹב.
בָּחַר ה' בְּיַעֲקֹב. אַל תִּירָא עַבְדִּי יַעֲקֹב.
גָּאַל ה' אֶת יַעֲקֹב. אַל תִּירָא עַבְדִּי יַעֲקֹב.
דָּרַךְ כּוֹכָב מִיַּעֲקֹב. אַל תִּירָא עַבְדִּי יַעֲקֹב.

God spoke to Jacob; fear not My servant Jacob.

God chose Jacob; fear not My servant Jacob.

God redeemed Jacob; fear not My servant Jacob.

A star shall rise from Jacob; fear not My servant Jacob.

Text 9a

RABBI SHNE'UR ZALMAN OF LIADI, *LIKUTEI TORAH*, BALAK 72A

בְּשַׁבָּת כְּתִיב (בְּרֵאשִׁית ב, ב): "וַיְכַל אֱלֹקִים", פֵּירוּשׁ שֶׁכָּלְתָה בְּחִינַת וּמַדְרֵגַת מִדַּת הַצִּמְצוּם וְהַהֶסְתֵּר דְּשֵׁם אֱלֹקִים . . . שֶׁבְּשַׁבָּת מִתְגַּלֶּה בְּנַפְשׁוֹ בְּחִינַת אֱלֹקוּת בִּבְחִינַת גִּילּוּי מַמָּשׁ.

With regard to Shabbat it says (Genesis 2:2), "And Elokim ceased," meaning, the level of Elokim, concealment, ceased. . . . Our souls are graced with a perceivable divine manifestation on Shabbat.

RABBI SHNE'UR ZALMAN OF LIADI (ALTER REBBE)
1745–1812

Chasidic rebbe, halachic authority, and founder of the Chabad movement. The Alter Rebbe was born in Liozna, Belarus, and was among the principal students of the Magid of Mezeritch. His numerous works include the *Tanya*, an early classic containing the fundamentals of Chabad Chasidism, and *Shulchan Aruch HaRav*, an expanded and reworked code of Jewish law.

Text 9b

RABBI SHNE'UR ZALMAN OF LIADI, IBID., 72B

וְזֶהוּ מַה שֶּׁאוֹמְרִים בְּמוֹצָאֵי שַׁבָּת "אַל תִּירָא עַבְדִּי יַעֲקֹב" כו'. כִּי בְּשַׁבָּת אָנוּ בִּבְחִינַת יִשְׂרָאֵל, שֶׁאֵין צָרִיךְ לִבְחִינַת עֲבוֹדָה וִיגִיעָה לְבָרֵר בֵּרוּרִים . . . רַק אָנוּ אָז בִּבְחִינַת בֵּן, בָּנִים לַמָּקוֹם . . .

וְאַחַר כָּךְ בְּמוֹצָאֵי שַׁבָּת שֶׁמִּסְתַּלֶּקֶת הַנְּשָׁמָה יְתֵירָה, וְצָרִיךְ לַחֲזוֹר וְלֵירֵד לִהְיוֹת בִּבְחִינַת יַעֲקֹב עַבְדִּי בְּכָל שֵׁשֶׁת יְמֵי הַמַּעֲשֶׂה . . . לְכָךְ אוֹמֵר "אַל תִּירָא עַבְדִּי יַעֲקֹב" כו' מִלֵּירֵד שָׁם. וּבָזֶה נוֹתְנִים כֹּחַ וְעוֹז כו'. וְהִיא יְרִידָה צוֹרֶךְ עֲלִיָּיה בְּשַׁבָּת שֶׁאַחַר כָּךְ.

As Shabbat ends, we chant, "Fear not, My servant Jacob."

During Shabbat, we are in a higher spiritual state, which is indicated by the name Israel. On this level, there is no need for laborious spiritual toil. . . . In this state, we are referred to as God's children. . . .

However, after Shabbat, when our extra soul departs, we revert to the lower spiritual state of Jacob, the servant who must engage in six days of spiritual labor. . . . We therefore say at this time, "Be not afraid of descending to the state of Jacob, My servant."

These reassuring words provide us with the strength to contend with the weekday challenges. And this descent leads to heretofore unreached spiritual heights to be experienced on the following Shabbat.

BRIDGE OF SEPARATION

Text 10

HAVDALAH BLESSING, SATURDAY NIGHT LITURGY

בָּרוּךְ אַתָּה ה' אֱלֹקֵינוּ מֶלֶךְ הָעוֹלָם, הַמַּבְדִּיל בֵּין קֹדֶשׁ לְחוֹל, בֵּין אוֹר לְחֹשֶׁךְ, בֵּין יִשְׂרָאֵל לָעַמִּים, בֵּין יוֹם הַשְּׁבִיעִי לְשֵׁשֶׁת יְמֵי הַמַּעֲשֶׂה. בָּרוּךְ אַתָּה ה' הַמַּבְדִּיל בֵּין קֹדֶשׁ לְחוֹל.

Blessed are You . . . King of the Universe, Who makes a distinction between sacred and mundane, between light and darkness, between Israel and the nations, between the seventh day and the six days of labor. Blessed are You . . . Who makes a distinction between sacred and mundane.

Text 11

THE LUBAVITCHER REBBE, RABBI MENACHEM MENDEL SCHNEERSON, *LIKUTEI SICHOT* 36:76

שֶׁזֶּהוּ הַתּוֹכֶן הַפְּנִימִי דִסְעוּדַת מְלַוֶּה מַלְכָּה . . . כִּי בִּסְעוּדָה זוֹ יֶשְׁנוֹ הַחִיבּוּר דְשַׁבָּת וְחוֹל, דְמֵחַד גִּיסָא הֲרֵי הוּא לְאַחֲרֵי גְמַר קְדוּשַּׁת שַׁבָּת, אֲבָל לְאִידָךְ יֵשׁ בָּהּ הַבְּרָכָה (וְהַהַמְשָׁכָה) דְיוֹם הַשַּׁבָּת, שֶׁעַל יְדֵי זֶה נִמְשָׁךְ הַכֹּחַ דְשַׁבָּת גַּם בִּסְעוּדָה שֶׁל חוֹל.

This is the deeper meaning of the *melaveh malkah* meal. . . . It serves to connect Shabbat with the weekday. On the one hand, this meal begins only after the holiness of Shabbat has departed. On the other hand, it is an extension of Shabbat [inasmuch as the Jews in the desert ate for this meal manna that had fallen on Friday for Shabbat]. Thus, the spirit, power, and blessing of Shabbat are drawn into a weekday meal.

RABBI MENACHEM MENDEL SCHNEERSON
1902–1994

The towering Jewish leader of the 20th century, known as "the Lubavitcher Rebbe," or simply as "the Rebbe." Born in southern Ukraine, the Rebbe escaped Nazi-occupied Europe, arriving in the U.S. in June 1941. The Rebbe inspired and guided the revival of traditional Judaism after the European devastation, impacting virtually every Jewish community the world over. The Rebbe often emphasized that the performance of just one additional good deed could usher in the era of Mashiach. The Rebbe's scholarly talks and writings have been printed in more than 200 volumes.

COURSE CONCLUSION
FEMININE SHABBAT

Text 12a
TALMUD, AVODAH ZARAH 3A

מִי שֶׁטָּרַח בְּעֶרֶב שַׁבָּת יֹאכַל בְּשַׁבָּת, מִי שֶׁלֹּא טָרַח בְּעֶרֶב שַׁבָּת מֵהֵיכָן יֹאכַל בְּשַׁבָּת?

Those who labor before Shabbat shall eat on Shabbat; but those who do not labor before Shabbat, from whence shall they eat?

Text 12b

RABBI KALONYMOS KALMAN HALEVI EPSTEIN,
MA'OR VASHEMESH, KI TISA

יֵשׁ הַשְׁרָאַת קְדוּשָּׁה לְכָל אָדָם בְּשַׁבָּת . . . רַק יֵשׁ בְּנֵי אָדָם אֲשֶׁר מַרְגִישִׁים כָּל כַּךְ רַק מְעַט מִן הַמְעַט, וְיֵשׁ שֶׁיֵּשׁ לָהֶם הַרְבֵּה קְדוּשָּׁה מְאֹד . . . וְהַכֹּל הוּא לְפִי הֲכָנַת בְּנֵי אָדָם, אֲשֶׁר מוּכָן מֵעֶרֶב שַׁבָּת לְשַׁבָּת . . . וְכָל שֶׁכֵּן מֵחַד בְּשַׁבָּת לְשַׁבָּת אֲשֶׁר מַמְשִׁיךְ עַל עַצְמוֹ קְדוּשַּׁת שַׁבָּת בְּכָל שֵׁשֶׁת יְמֵי הַמַּעֲשֶׂה.

On Shabbat, holiness rests upon every person. . . . However, some people sense only the smallest measure [of holiness] while others experience much more. . . . It all depends upon our preparation during the week . . . and on how much we bring upon ourselves the holiness of Shabbat during the six days of the week.

RABBI KALONYMOS KALMAN HALEVI EPSTEIN
1751–1823

A native of Cracow, Poland, he was a disciple of Rabbi Elimelech of Lizensk, the Seer of Lublin, and other great Chasidic leaders. He authored a Chasidic classic titled *Ma'or Vashemesh*, first published in 1842.

Text 13

ZOHAR 2:63B

כָּל שִׁיתָּא יוֹמִין מִתְבָּרְכָאן מִיּוֹמָא שְׁבִיעָאָה.

All six days are blessed [with manna] from the seventh.

ZOHAR

The seminal work of Kabbalah, Jewish mysticism. The *Zohar* is a mystical commentary on the Torah, written in Aramaic and Hebrew. According to Arizal, the *Zohar* contains the teachings of Rabbi Shimon bar Yocha'i who lived in the Land of Israel during the second century. The *Zohar* has become one of the indispensable texts of traditional Judaism, alongside and nearly equal in stature to the Mishnah and Talmud.

COURSE REVIEW

Learning Exercise 1

Choose one teaching, law, idea, or quote from this course for each of the criteria below.

Value

Surprising fact

Action item

Favorite quote or sound bite

Controversial concept

Concept that resonated

Concept I will share with others

Key Points

1. Shabbat is a delightful time and we are reluctant to part with it. This is why Jews have always tried to prolong Shabbat by postponing its ending and "stealing" some weekday time to add to Shabbat.
2. The extra soul that we are given during Shabbat departs when Shabbat ends. This leaves us with a painful sense of apprehension and loss. The words of the Havdalah prayer comfort us during this time of loss, and the wine and spices serve to lift our spirits.
3. Kindling a flame during Havdalah reminds us that God provided fire and light to Adam and Eve during their time of apprehension. Just as God provided them with the tools to help them overcome their fears, so will He provide us with similar tools to navigate the week.
4. During Shabbat, we sense the oneness between God and us. During the week, we lose that sense and serve God as if we are external to Him. The Shabbat mode is described by the name Israel and the weekday mode is described by the name Jacob.
5. The transition from Israel to Jacob makes the soul apprehensive. We soothe its fears by singing to it and encouraging it not to fear the Jacob mode. It will only strengthen us for the coming Shabbat, when we will reenter the Israel mode on an even higher level.
6. Although the Havdalah highlights the distinction between Shabbat and the week, it also serves to build a bridge between the two. Once we appreciate the difference between them, we can work to bring the sanctity of Shabbat into the mundane week.
7. Shabbat receives the work that we invested all week to prepare for Shabbat, and turns it into a blessing for the coming week. This is one of the reasons that Shabbat is described as a feminine day.

ADDITIONAL READINGS

THE KABBALAH OF *HAVDALAH*

By Rabbi Yanki Tauber

If there is no daat *(discriminating intelligence), how can there be differentiation? (Jerusalem Talmud, Berachot 5:2)*

In the Jewish home, the close of the Shabbat is marked with a special ceremony, called *Havdalah* ("differentiation"). Over a brimming cup of wine, to the multi-flamed light of a braided candle and the smell of aromatic spices, we recite: "Blessed are You, L-rd our G-d . . . Who differentiates between the holy and the mundane, between light and darkness, between Israel and the nations, between the seventh day and the six days of work."

Differentiation is at the heart of what we call morality. If theft or adultery are wrong, it is only because there is a real difference between mine and yours and between the wedded and the unwedded state. If ceasing work on Shabbat or eating matzah on Passover are meaningful deeds, this is only because Shabbat is truly different from Friday and matzah is truly different from leavened bread. If there is meaning and purpose to our actions, there must be true significance to the differences between things.

Differentiation, however, also implies a sameness to the things being differentiated. If Shabbat and Sunday looked, smelled and tasted differently to our physical senses, there would be no need to actively differentiate between them. Indeed, when the Torah employs the verb "to differentiate" (*lehavdil*), it is to distinguish between things that are essentially similar. A case in point is the concluding verse of Leviticus 11, the chapter which lays down the kashrut dietary laws. The verse reads: "To differentiate between the pure and the impure; between the animal that may be eaten and the animal that may not be eaten," regarding which our sages remark:

Need this be said regarding the difference between a donkey and a cow?. . . Rather, this is to tell us to differentiate between the animal which had half its windpipe cut [during the slaughtering] and the animal which had most of its windpipe cut. . . . Need this be said regarding the difference between a wild ass and a deer? Rather, this is to tell us to differentiate between an animal in which there developed a defect yet remains fit to be eaten and an animal in which there developed a defect which renders it unfit to be eaten (Rashi on verse, from Torat Kohanim*).*

In other words, *havdalah* requires the ability to look at two similar things and appreciate that, despite their elementary similarity, they are to be differentiated and held apart. In the words of our sages, "If there is no *daat* (discriminating intelligence), how can there be *havdalah*?"

A WORLD OF WORDS

The capacity to differentiate, as we have noted, is the basis for any moral vision of life. Chassidic teaching takes this a step further, demonstrating how *havdalah* is the essence of the created existence, of what we call reality. An axiom of the Jewish faith is that G-d is infinite—without beginning and without end.

RABBI YANKI TAUBER

1965–

Chasidic scholar and author. A native of Brooklyn, NY, Rabbi Tauber is an internationally renowned author who specializes in adapting the teachings of the Lubavitcher Rebbe. He is a member of the JLI curriculum development team, and has written numerous articles and books, including *Once Upon a Chassid* and *Beyond the Letter of the Law*.

This raises the problem, addressed by all major Jewish philosophers, of how our world can possibly exist, since a truly infinite being precludes the existence of anything other than itself. Indeed, the Torah asserts that "There is nothing else besides Him." But what about ourselves, our world, our reality? Are these not existences besides Him?

In his *Tanya,* Rabbi Schneur Zalman of Liadi lays the groundwork for a resolution of this problem by defining the created reality as divine speech. In the first chapter of Genesis, G-d's creation of the world is described as a series of (ten) utterances: G-d said, "Let there be light!" and there was light; G-d said, "Let the earth send forth vegetation," "Let there be luminaries in the heavens," "Let the waters spawn living creatures," and plants, stars and fish emerged into existence. Citing teachings from the Midrash, the Kabbalist Rabbi Isaac Luria and Chassidism's founder Rabbi Israel Baal Shem Tov, Rabbi Schneur Zalman deduces that these divine utterances are not merely the cause of these existences—they *are* these existences. What we experience as "light" is but the embodiment of G-d's articulated desire that there be light; what we experience as a "tree" is but the embodiment of G-d's articulated desire that there be a tree.

So the created reality is not, in truth, something else besides Him, any more than our spoken words are things distinct from ourselves. Speaking is a creative act; but when we speak we are not creating anything that is other than ourselves—we are giving vocal form to our own ideas, feelings and desires. In describing G-d's creation of the world as a series of divine utterances, the Torah wishes to convey the idea that the world is not something distinct from its Creator, but His spoken words—His articulation of concepts and potentials which are an integral part of His being.

The implications of such a conception of ourselves and our world—of reality as divine speech—are numerous and manifold. One is the realization that the differences between things are secondary to a primary sameness that embraces them all. A language might include millions of words, but these are all variations on a handful of consonants and vowels. On a more basic level, these consonants and vowels are just variations on how a minute expulsion of breath is bounced off the speaker's vocal cords, tongue, palate, teeth and lips.

A tree might seem very different from a ray of light, as might a fish from a star. But each of these objects is, in essence, the same thing: a divine word, an articulation of divine will. In origin, they share a singular essence; their differentiation occurs at a later stage, as they pass through the divine mouth that imparts to them their respective forms and characteristics.

Thus the Torah relates how, on the first day of creation, "G-d differentiated between light and darkness." What can be more different than light and darkness? What differentiation is necessary between such obviously different phenomena? But light and darkness are both creations of G-d; both are divine words, formulations of the same surge of divine will. Their distinction is the product of a divine act of *havdalah,* of a deliberate differentiation between two essentially synonymous realities.

DAAT

In light of this, we can better understand the above-quoted Talmudic dictum regarding the connection between *daat* and *havdalah.* The Talmud is discussing the fact that in the evening prayers recited after the close of Shabbat, the text of the *Havdalah* is inserted in the prayer which begins: "You grant *daat* to man, and teach the human being understanding; grant us, from You, wisdom, understanding and knowledge . . ." The reason for this placement, says the Talmud, is that "If there is no *daat,* how can there be *havdalah*?"

On the most basic level, the Talmud is saying that an act of *havdalah* requires the discriminating intelligence of *daat*. On a deeper level, it is saying that *havdalah* is possible only because "*You* grant *daat* to man"—only because G-d Himself grants us the capacity to differentiate between various elements of His creation.

For if the world is divine speech, if all created things are essentially the same, how can we differentiate between them? And if we do differentiate, what significance can there be to our differentiation? We might discern light and darkness; we might identify certain things as holy and others as mundane; we might designate the first six days of the week for material achievement and its seventh day for spiritual rest; but if all of these are, in essence, divine words, what power have we to differentiate between them?

But G-d wanted a moral world—a world in which the deeds of man are purposeful and meaningful. So He imparted variety, diversity and distinction to His creation, decreeing that the differences between things should possess import and significance. His act of creation was an act of *havdalah*—of differentiating between essentially similar entities. And He granted the human being a mind capable of appreciating the paradox of *havdalah*—the paradox of meaningful difference imposed upon intrinsic synonymy—thereby empowering us to implement, through our awareness and our actions, the differentiations He decreed in His world.

THE SECOND PARADOX

Havdalah carries another paradox—that its ultimate function is to join and unite the very things it comes to differentiate.

The Torah commands us to remember and to preserve the day of Shabbat—to distinguish it, in mind, word and deed, from the six days of work. Yet Shabbat is integrally bound to the other days of the week. It is the culmination of our weekday endeavors—the day on which all that we labored for and achieved in the preceding six days ascends on high, attaining its most complete and perfect realization. And Shabbat is the day from which all days are blessed—the source of the fortitude and energy that drives our efforts of the workweek that follows it.

We are told to preserve our uniqueness as Jews—to safeguard the delineation between Israel and the nations. Yet the people of Israel are designated to serve as "a light unto the nations," as the conveyers of the ethos and ideals of Torah to all inhabitants of the earth.

We are instructed to differentiate between the holy and the mundane—to embrace what is sacred and G-dly in our lives while exercising wariness and restraint in the material aspects of life. At the same time, we are told that "the purpose of man's creation, and of the creation of all worlds, spiritual and material is to make for G-d a dwelling place in the lowly realms"—to involve our everyday material pursuits in the quest to know and serve G-d, thereby making Him at home in the lowliest, most mundane stratum of creation.

For it is only through our awareness and enforcement of the boundaries within creation that these objectives can be achieved. Only if Shabbat is preserved in its distinctiveness and transcendence can it elevate and empower the other six days of the week. Only in their uniqueness as G-d's chosen people does the nation of Israel have anything of true value to offer the peoples of the world. Only when our spiritual life is kept inviolably apart from the coarsening influence of the material can it in turn sanctify the material by enlisting it to serve its spiritual aims.

FROM UNITY TO SYMPHONY

Havdalah is the substance of our daily lives, as every hour and moment confronts us with the challenge to define and differentiate—to distinguish between right and wrong, between holy and mundane. But these delineations are merely a means to an end, a process springing from a primordial unity and leading toward a future synthesis.

In origin and essence, all is one. But an even deeper unity is achieved when differentiations and demarcations are imposed upon the primordial oneness, and its component parts are each given a distinct role in creation's symphonious expression of the goodness and perfection of its Creator.

Based on the teachings of the Lubavitcher Rebbe, Rabbi Menachem Mendel Schneerson
Week in Review, Published by The Meaningful Life Center
Reprinted with permission of the publisher

NIGHT OF THE RIGHTEOUS

by Meir Michel Abehsera

It is a prevalent custom among observant Jews to gather on Saturday night, singing and dancing and telling stories until dawn. We extend the Shabbat that has technically passed, carrying some of its holiness with us into days of the week, the realm of the profane. It is the ideal time to speak about the righteous (in Hebrew, "*tzadikim*"). Any story or anecdote about them is a Shabbat in itself, a rest-stop for the Jew who is preparing to confront the weekdays. It is a place of transition where the mind is given ample time to ready itself for the mundane.

The spiritual forces of darkness have been starving during the entire length of the Shabbat. Therefore, you can only expect that as soon as Shabbat draws to its end, these forces will reach out to devour the defenseless. They lie in wait by the doors of every house of prayer and grab congregants by the dozen. One bite from the beast, and they are infused with an acute sense of the Saturday night blues.

Saturday night is a most sacred time, when exile is boxed in by redemption. It is a time when the nourishment of the spirit is most varied, when all duality is resolved. Intelligence is heightened, and everyone who celebrates the occasion is instantly wise. Doubts wane. Impossible questions are easily answered.

The night exhausts itself, depositing a block of resolutions.

It is the night when the true face of the Jew emerges. The subtle mixture of light and darkness gives a brightly hued, vibrant luminosity to the ambient air in which the face reveals ancient wisdom. The image is somewhat grainy, because neither light nor darkness is yet settled in their respective vessels. But in their eager jockeying for position, in that play of volatile contrasts, the true face is exposed.

Shabbat bathes the Jew in a bright and homogenous light which is not necessarily conducive to revelations of individual character. Shabbat is much too full, and therefore permits no contrast. Shabbat is the reservoir, not the conduit. It is contained within specific limits which allow no explosions to occur. Saturday night's light however, flickers relentlessly. It is a black fire whose pulsating luminescence disturbs and disperses the obtrusive layers that camouflage the soul. The Jew is never more conscious of his mission than during these hours. It is on this night that the world was created and on the very same night that light was made. Now, light is again renewed through our actions. As Shabbat draws to its end, and the obscurity of night begins to cover us with its black mantle, we burn a braided candle, whose variegated and animated flame rekindles the light of Creation. Our holy masters say that the feeling of sadness we experience at Shabbat's end is caused by our subconscious sense of the primordial Shattering of the Vessels—that timeless, spaceless juncture in the history of Creation when the divine light fell into the lower worlds. We are given a taste of that decline. The light of Shabbat has flown back to its nest, and we search for it within. Some mystical writings compare that departure of the light to a deer fleeting from its pursuer, running with its head tilted under and to the side, staring back into your eyes. In that look of the deer, as the light recedes swiftly in the distance, we are given to retroactively appreciate the hidden reality of Shabbat.

MEIR NISSIM "MICHEL" ABEHSERA

1934–2014

Born in Morocco to the prominent Abuchatzeira family, Meir Nissim's family relocated to France when he was 10 years old. He was a civil engineer until he discovered the emerging field of macrobiotics, which he began to study and teach. He authored 8 books on the subject, and he eventually moved to New York where he opened the first macrobiotic restaurant in the city and became a sought-after lecturer nationwide. He lived his final years in Jerusalem.

It is said that at the beginning of Creation—meaning on Saturday night—the vessels prepared to hold the infinite light of Creation broke. On that same night, the repair of the vessels also began. Thus, we can only assume that there is no more opportune time to repair our own. Darkness was formed when work was left undone. The mundane week lies before us like an open abyss, auguring a reprise of that tragedy. The abyss beckons, and its pull is far out of proportion to our fragilities. The disparity is the main cause of Saturday night melancholia. The threat is real.

The threat is so real in fact, that one cannot possibly remain insensitive to it, since all of us descend from Adam, who was the first to experience the fall. It is said that upon seeing the sun set for the first time, he experienced a great anguish, certain that darkness had settled on the world because of his sin. That very same night, he took two stones and struck them one against the other until sparks flew. Though such a simple act seemed to hold little promise of transcendence, it was, in fact, the initial stroke that impelled him to return to the Garden of Eden. Poor though it may have been, the light of the fire gave him comfort, and so he blessed it. The memory of that past makes of Saturday night a most opportune time for new beginnings. Anticipation of something new happening is never so great, which is the reason why this night is known as the "Night of the Redeemer." According to tradition, the Redeemer (*Mashiach*) will reveal himself in the wink of an eye, even when all the signs and estimations will concur to proclaim his coming. He will surprise everyone, wicked or wise, and also the cautious, those who prefer not to speak about him, from fear of exacerbating other's skepticism, or from taking the risk of spoiling the suspense of his coming. Above all, he will most likely surprise those who think and speak of him constantly, even those who serve him. In accordance with that, we are left with no other alternative than to opt for the obvious. The Redeemer will surprise primarily those who expect him the most—as a mother is surprised by the presence of her child, the same with couples, or true friends—for the simple reason that true surprise hits more strongly those who have much life in them. Others, who have less, will most likely find it hard to react enthusiastically to the news.

It is precisely in such an atmosphere of anticipation—namely, that we could at any moment be taken unaware by something already known—that past faults can be corrected. If folly so treacherously intrudes inside us, to have us commit an error, it is perfectly sensible, therefore, to utilize such means which would take the intruder by surprise. What better scheme is there than to confront the faults during moments that seem so uncertain as to confound them? Being that a fault is, on the whole, of an accidental nature, it is logical that it be exposed to an atmosphere that suits its character. Saturday night's incomplete light makes it an ideal host. No judgment is passed. But take heed. Don't be so readily fooled by such a display of leniency. The diminished light does not indicate some sort of deficiency or weakness. In truth, the reason why the light has dimmed is because it has traveled a distance to gather momentum, before coming back with a force that renews Creation. Kabbala calls such a light "*Or Chozer,*" "Returning Light." It comes to wake us up from sleep. It says, "Where were you while I was there in your midst? I was a willing guest and you were such a distracted host." It is Shabbat speaking. Distance makes it talk; it has divested itself of its clothing of effervescent gold, and donned a humbler robe to travel lightly.

As the night advances, our faults change aspect. The deeds that are performed for selfish gain are released from bondage. There is no visible trace of corruption in any of them. This occurs because the night makes us more compassionate on ourselves. Or else it is making us so wise that we can discern some of the workings of redemption. In any event, the fact is that at such times, faults greatly contribute to enriching the atmosphere, while the night kindly obliges by returning the favor with a gift all its own. It broadens the scope of each fault as far as the twilight of Creation. There the fault becomes deed, the instant it re-enters its original mold. You can imagine how much such a moment of good-will can benefit anyone, stranger or friend. What appears to him most improbable will resolve itself in the warmth of companionship. His faults experience a loss of identity. They have become new entities altogether. They are enriching reality. The interaction between each fault and the specific hour of the night, formulates the mode of the celebration at hand.

On Saturday night, it is quite visible that the guests experience change the moment they enter the house. However, no transmutation will really begin to take place before the food is served. The animation of the voices generates enough warmth to fecundate the most sterile of thought. The multitude of bodies produces more than enough pressure to wring out bothersome ruminations. The heart is jolted by Chasidic chanting. Music, which usually follows, tears all worries apart. But nothing appears more catalyzing than dance, when every remnant of pain—that of dancer and onlookers alike—is shaken off with each change of cadence. The highlight of the celebration, however, will take place in the calm before dawn, when most people have left. By then everyone is weary. Words are few and the movements slow. Silence prevails in spite of the resonance of voices or the fracas of pots being washed. Not even the dissonant chords played by dilettante musicians are able to disrupt the quiescence of the moment. At this stage, incidental noises are put at the service of silence to give it a new depth. Thus nested, thought is given to witness how the passing of time has fulfilled the night's promises—the cycle of transmutations is virtually completed—and that subsequently, the slowest of metabolism has benefited as well. At any moment, all this abundance of human exchange ignites time, which shoots back far into the past, to redeem it. The past, in turn, redeems the present. Creation has just begun.

www.kabbalaonline.org
Reprinted with permission

ACKNOWLEDGMENTS

Seldom does one have the opportunity to seamlessly fuse a life's mission and a labor of love. These acknowledgments are a public affirmation of the incredible blessings I experience daily.

Extreme appreciation is owed to the course editor, **Rabbi Mordechai Dinerman,** for his dedication, talent, and skillful ability in bringing this project to fruition. I am deeply grateful to our gifted writers, **Rabbi Zalman Abraham, Mrs. Malky Bitton,** and **Rabbi Lazer Gurkow** for contributing to this course with wisdom, wit, and brilliant insight, and to **Rabbi Michoel Shapiro** for his assistance with the writing of Lesson Six. **Rabbis Yakov Gershon** and **Shmuel Raskin** stand out for their excellent research assistance. **Rabbis Shloime Chein, Dov Greenberg,** and **Dubi Rabinowitz,** we credit you for your valuable input into Lesson One. To each of you I say: thank you for so generously sharing your expertise. It has been a true pleasure and joy to collaborate with you every step of the way, and I consider myself exceedingly fortunate to reap the rewards of this quintessential dream team. The **Rosh Chodesh Society** is indeed blessed.

This course has benefitted and draws heavily from the past JLI course *Oasis in Time,* edited by **Dr. Chana Silberstein, PhD** and the **Rosh Chodesh Society** is honor-bound for this largesse.

Mrs. Malky Bitton, Mrs. Shula Bryski, Mrs. Rochel Holzkenner, and Mrs. Chanie Wilhelm graciously agreed to lend their expertise and experience—from reviewing curricula, to aiding in general course development, to piloting the course so that others may benefit. We acknowledge their pedagogic and instructional skills and thank them on behalf of the entire **Rosh Chodesh Society**.

Our talented teams have expended numerous hours to bring our materials to production. **Mrs. Rachel Witty, Mrs. Ya'akovah Weber,** and **Lynne Clamage** meticulously copyedited and proofread the texts with attention and dedication. **Rabbi Zalman Abraham** created the beautiful book design. **Shternie Morozow** is responsible for the wonderful and professional book layout and **Raizel Shurpin**, we make note of your skilled and generous assistance, as well. To **Mrs. Rivki Mockin**, our curriculum coordinator, your sensibilities in every aspect of book production are commendable and worthy of special mention. I am deeply thankful to all of you. You always rise to the occasion.

We laud our marketing and design team headed by **Rabbi Zalman Abraham,** for producing all our beautiful marketing materials with creative vision and attentiveness to the finest of detail. Thank you **Mrs. Mush Kanner, Mrs. Shevi Rivkin, Raizel Shurpin,** and **Rikkie Winner** for your artfulness, proficiency, and grace. Great appreciation goes to **Rabbi Mendy Elishevitz** and **Rabbi Sholom Cohen,** who oversee and ensure the integrity of our cyberspace field.

Special mention must be made regarding our very gifted multimedia team. Thank you, **Mushka Pruss,** for the magnificent PowerPoint presentations—a wonderful asset to each lesson. Having the good fortune to work with **Moshe and Getzy Raskin** of Swish Media, who are simply so good at all things video, is a blessing I'm sure many would wish for.

Many thanks to **Mr. Shimon Leib Jacobs** and to **Mary Stevens** for the printing and distribution of our books. Much gratitude to **Rabbi Mendel Sirota**, who oversees production, shipping, and handling. You always go the extra mile and we acknowledge your efforts.

Kudos to **Baila Pruss,** an administrator and single-handed project manager *par excellence*. She is much more than her title can ever tell you and my appreciation for her knows no bounds. Your contributions are immeasurable. Allow me an additional shout-out to **Fraydee Kessler**: you have carried our ship in this capacity for many years, and your imprint remains with us even as we wish you great success in your family's move.

We acknowledge our chief of operations, **Rabbi Levi Kaplan**, a master at everything he does—there are too many tasks and favors to enumerate, but each one is always completed to perfection. Your efforts on behalf of everything **RCS** do not go unnoticed.

The **Rosh Chodesh Society** is enormously grateful for the encouragement of **Rabbi Moshe Kotlarsky,** chairman of the **Rohr Jewish Learning Institute** and vice chairman of *Merkos L'Inyonei Chinuch*—Lubavitch world headquarters.

We are fortuitously blessed with the unwavering support of **JLI**'s principal benefactors, **Mr. George and Mrs. Pamela Rohr**, who have staunchly spearheaded and invested in the growth of the organization with an unparalleled commitment. Their dedication is evident and alive within the tens of thousands of Jewish students studying Torah around the globe. May your merit stand you—and all of us—in good stead, and may you reap bountiful blessings all the days of your long, happy, healthy, and auspicious lives.

Heartfelt acclamation to **Mr. Yitzchak and Mrs. Julie Gniwisch** for their steadfast support and resolute belief in us, always. May the goodness you bring to the world be returned to you ten thousandfold.

Our deepest gratitude to **Mr. Pablo and Mrs. Sara Briman** for their devoted friendship and support. May you enjoy unceasing goodness, kindness, and unbridled joy forever.

JLI's devoted executive board—**Rabbi Chaim Block**, **Rabbi Hesh Epstein**, **Rabbi Ronnie Fine, Rabbi Yosef Gansburg**, **Rabbi Shmuel Kaplan**, **Rabbi Yisrael Rice,** and **Rabbi Avrohom Sternberg**—give countless hours to the development of **JLI**. Their dedication, commitment, and sage advice have helped the organization grow and flourish.

Rabbi Shmuel Kaplan, chairman of the **Rosh Chodesh Society**, has been instrumental in formulating its vision since its inception and continues to be a source of guidance as we are blessed to experience tremendous growth within our sisterhood.

The constant progress of **JLI** is a testament to the visionary leadership of our director, **Rabbi Efraim Mintz**, who is never content with the status quo, boldly encourages unbridled innovation and forward thinking, and embodies successful accomplishment. You are an example to many. On this auspicious day, I thank you publicly, both personally and professionally, for this benevolent, outstanding, and truly wonderful opportunity. Directing the **Rosh Chodesh Society** is the calling of my heart and the journey of my soul. It is a gift that keeps on giving eternal blessings. May all who read this be equally blessed. Your merit is great. Thank you for sharing it with me.

The **Rosh Chodesh Society**, **JLI**'s women's division, was launched on the anniversary of the first *yahrtzeits* of **Rabbi Gavriel Noach** and **Rebbetzin Rivkah Holtzberg, *H"YD***, devoted Chabad emissaries to Mumbai, India. May the merit of the countless Jewish women who are engaged in these Torah studies serve as a testament to the heroic life they led, and continue to perpetuate their noble deeds.

On behalf of all the individuals who play a role in the **Rosh Chodesh Society**, particularly our affiliates out there on the front lines fulfilling their positions, I offer up a prayer to Almighty G-d: May He actualize the hope of the Jewish nation, as repeatedly expressed by the Lubavitcher Rebbe, of righteous memory, and may we very soon experience the world as it will be, filled with the knowledge of G-d as the waters cover the sea. Amen.

Shluchos! It is solely thanks to you that we will merit the fulfillment of our mandate, *No Jewish Woman Will Be Left Behind*. We could never do it without you. You continue to change the world for the better. Thank you for allowing us to partner with you. You are the heart and soul of the Jewish nation. Indeed, this is the ultimate acknowledgment.

Shaindy Jacobson
Director, **Rosh Chodesh Society**
Brooklyn, New York

Vav (6) Tishrei 5778

The Rohr Jewish Learning Institute

An affiliate of **Merkos L'Inyonei Chinuch**

The Educational Arm of **The Chabad Lubavitch Movement**

822 Eastern Parkway, Brooklyn, NY 11213

ROSHCHODESH society FACULTY

UNITED STATES

BIRMINGHAM, AL
Mrs. Frumie Posner
Chabad of Alabama
205.970.0100
cyfposner@aol.com

FOUNTAIN HILLS, AZ
Mrs. Tzipi Lipskier
Chabad of Fountain Hills
480.776.4763
tzipi@jewishfountainhills.com

TUCSON, AZ
Mrs. Feigie Ceitlin
Chabad Lubavitch of Tucson
520.869.4971
FeigieCeitlin@gmail.com

LITTLE ROCK, AR
Mrs. Estie Ciment
Lubavitch of Arkansas
501.221.7940
Estie@arjewishcenter.com

ARCATA, CA
Mrs. Mushkie Cowen
Chabad of Humboldt
412.390.6481
mushkiecowen@gmail.com

BAKERSFIELD, CA
Mrs. Esther Malka Schlanger
Chabad of Bakersfield
661.835.8381
estherm@bak.rr.com

BERKELEY, CA
Mrs. Miriam Chaya Ferris
Chabad of the East Bay
510.684.5292
miriamferris@gmail.com

CALABASAS, CA
Mrs. Shaina Friedman
Chabad of Calabasas
818.222.3838
shaini@jewishcalabasas.com

ENCINO, CA
Mrs. Chana Herzog
Chabad of Encino
818.784.9986
JLI@chabadofthevalley.com

FOLSOM, CA
Mrs. Goldie Grossbaum
Chabad Folsom
916.608.9811
info@jewishfolsom.org

FREMONT, CA
Mrs. Chaya Fuss
Chabad of Fremont
510.300.4090
chaya@chabadfremont.com

FRESNO, CA
Mrs. Chanie Zirkind
Chabad of Fresno
559.432.2770
chabadfresno@sbcglobal.net

GLENDALE, CA
Mrs. Shterny Backman
Chabad of Glendale
818.240.2750
shterny@chabadcenter.org

GOLETA, CA
Mrs. Devorah Loschak
Chabad of S. Barbara
805.324.3584
dloschak@gmail.com

HUNTINGTON BEACH, CA
Mrs. Susha Alperowitz
Chabad of West Orange County
714.846.2285
chabadhb@verizon.net

IRVINE, CA
Mrs. Binie Tenenbaum
Chabad of Irvine
949.786.5000
binie@chabadirvine.org

LAGUNA NIGUEL, CA
Mrs. Kreinie Paltiel
Chabad of Laguna Niguel
949.831.7701
Krein-ie@ChabadLagunaNiguel.com

LONG BEACH, CA
Mrs. Amina Newman
Congregation Lubavitch
562.596.1681
info@longbeachshul.com

LOS ALTOS, CA
Mrs. Nechama Schusterman
Chabad Los Altos
650.858.6990
nechama@bayareafc.org

LOS ANGELES, CA
Mrs. Channa Hecht
Chabad Jewish Center of Brentwood
310.826.4453
channa@chabadbw.com

LOS ANGELES, CA
Mrs. Dvonye Korf
Chabad of Greater Los Feliz
323.660.5177
rabbi@chabadlosfeliz.org

LOS ANGELES, CA
Mrs. Shterny Gurary
Chabad Jewish Center of Hancock Park
323.939.5138
rabbi@jewishhp.com

MALIBU, CA
Mrs. Sarah Cunin
Chabad of Malibu
310.456.6588
sarah@ganmalibu.com

MILL VALLEY, CA
Mrs. Chana Scop
Chabad of Mill Valley
415.419.7296
chanascop@comcast.net

NEWBURY PARK, CA
Mrs. Tzippy Schneerson
Chabad of Newbury Park
805.499.7051
sschneerson@gmail.com

NEWHALL, CA
Mrs Frumi Marozov
Chabad of SCV
6616445734
frumim@gmail.com

OAKLAND, CA
Mrs. Shulamis Labkowski
Chabad of Oakland
510.545.6770
info@jewishoakland.org

OCEANSIDE, CA
Mrs. Nechama Greenberg
Chabad Jewish Center Oceanside
760.806.7765
info@jewishoceanside.com

PACIFIC PALISADES, CA
Mrs. Zisi Cunin
Chabad of Pacific Palisades
310.454.7783
info@chabadpalisades.com

PALO ALTO, CA
Mrs. Devory Levin
Chabad Palo Alto
650.561.6013
devory@chabadpaloalto.com

PASADENA, CA
Mrs. Chana Hanoka
Chabad of Pasadena
626.564.8820
hanoka@sbcglobal.net

PLEASANTON, CA
Mrs. Fruma Resnick
Chabad of the Tri-Valley
925.846.0700
Fruma@JewishTriValley.com

RANCHO MIRAGE, CA
Mrs. Chaya Posner
Chabad of Rancho Mirage
760.770.7785
info@chabadrm.com

REDONDO BEACH, CA
Mrs. Sara Mintz
Chabad Jewish Community Center
310.871.5940
saralemintz@aol.com

REDWOOD CITY, CA
Mrs. Ella Potash
Chabad of Redwood City
650.232.0995
ella@jewishredwoodcity.com

SACRAMENTO, CA
Mrs. Dinie Cohen
Chabad of Sacramento
916.455.1400
chabadsac@aol.com

S. DIEGO, CA
Mrs. Leah Fradkin
Chabad of S. Diego
858.547.0076
lfradkin@chasd.org

S. DIEGO, CA
Mrs. Nechama Dina Carlebach
Chabad of Downtown
619.702.8518
Info@chabaddowntown.com

S. FRANCISCO, CA
Mrs. Sara Hecht
RTC-Chabad
415.386.8123
office@rtchabad.org

S. FRANCISCO, CA
Mrs. Mattie Pil
Schneerson Center
415.933.4310
mattieplot@gmail.com

S. MONICA, CA
Mrs. Sara Levitansky
Bais Chabad of Simcha Monica
310.829.5620
soriandisaac@gmail.com

S. MONICA, CA
Mrs. Rivka Rabinowitz
Chabad Living Torah Center
310.394.5699
rabbi@livingtorahcenter.com

S. ROSA, CA
Mrs. Altie Wolvovsky
Chabad Jewish Center
707.577.0277
rabbi@jewishsonoma.com

SEAL BEACH, CA
Mrs. Bluma Marcus
Chabad of Cypress
714.828.1851
shmuelmarcus@yahoo.com

SIMI VALLEY, CA
Mrs. Bassie Gurary
Chabad of Simi Valley
805.577.0573
bassie@chabadsimi.org

TEMECULA, CA
Mrs. Dina Hurwitz
Chabad Jewish Center Temecula Valley
951.813.1401
jewishtemecula@gmail.com

THOUSAND OAKS, CA
Mrs. Shula Bryski
Chabad of Thousand Oaks
805.493.7776
shula@jewishto.org

TOLUCA LAKE, CA
Mrs. Michal Carlebach
Chabad of Toluca Lake
818.308.4118
chabadtl@gmail.com

VACAVILLE, CA
Mrs. Aidel Zaklos
Chabad of Solano County
707.592.5300
rabbi@jewishsolano.com

VENTURA, CA
Mrs. Sarah Miriam Latowicz
Chabad of Ventura
805.658.7441
chabadventura@aol.com

DENVER, CO
Mrs. Elka Popack
Chabad Lubavitch of Colorado
303.780.0537
elkapopack@gmail.com

LONE TREE, CO
Mrs. Hindy Mintz
Chabad Jewish Center - South Metro Denver
303-694-9119
Hindy@DenverJewishCenter.com

WESTMINSTER, CO
Mrs. Leah Brackman
Chabad of NW Metro Denver
303.429.5177
Leahbrackman9@gmail.com

GREENWICH, CT
Mrs. Maryashie Deren
Chabad Lubavitch of Greenwich
203.629.9059
info@chabadgreenwich.org

MILFORD, CT
Mrs. Chanie Wilhelm
Chabad Jewish Center of Milford
203.878.4569
chanie@jewishmilford.com

ORANGE, CT
Mrs. Bluma Hecht
Chabad of Orange
203.795.5261
blumahecht@gmail.com

WILMINGTON, DE
Mrs. Rochel Flikshtein
Chabad of Delaware
302.529.9900
Office@ChabadDE.com

BOCA RATON, FL
Mrs. Ahuva New
Chabad of East Boca Raton
561.417.7797
Office@chabadbocabeaches.com

BOCA RATON, FL
Mrs. Rivkah Denburg
Mrs. Chani Bukiet
Chabad of Boca Raton
561.994.6257
ikaden@aol.com

BOYNTON BEACH, FL
Mrs. Dina Ciment
Chabad of Boynton
561.732.4633
ciments@gmail.com

BRADENTON, FL
Mrs. Chanie Bukiet
Chabad of Bradenton and Lakewood Ranch
941.752.3030
Chanie@chabadofbradenton.com

FORT LAUDERDALE, FL
Mrs. Rochel Holzkenner
Chabad of Las Olas
954.224.7162
rochelholzkenner@gmail.com

JUPITER, FL
Mrs. Chaya Sarah Barash
Chabad Jewish Center of Jupiter
561.694.6950
csbarash@yahoo.com

LAKE MARY, FL
Mrs. Chanshy Majesky
Chabad-Lubavitch of North Orlando
407.878.3011
chanshy@JewishNorthOrlando.com

LAKE WORTH, FL
Mrs. Leah Rosenfeld
Chabad Lake Worth
561.649.8468
Chabadlakeworth@gmail.com

LAKELAND, FL
Mrs. Libby Lazaros
Chabad of Lakeland
863.510.5968
mendel@chabadlakeland.org

MIAMI, FL
Mrs. Chana Gopin
Chabad at Midtown
305.573.9995
info@maormiami.org

MIAMI, FL
Mrs. Gutal Fellig
Chabad of South Dade
305.445.5444
info@chabadmiami.com

MIAMI BEACH, FL
Mrs. Chani Katz
Chabad House in Miami Beach
305.505.9065
rabbi@mbjewish.com

MIAMI BEACH, FL
Mrs. Tzippy Mann
Chabad of Venetian & Sunset Islands
305.674.8400
tzippymann@gmail.com

PALM BEACH, FL
Mrs. Hindel Levitin
Chabad of Northern Palm Beach Island
561.659.3884
hindelle@gmail.com

PALM HARBOR, FL
Mrs. Mushky Adler
Chabad of Pinellas County
248.305.0462
emailmushka@gmail.com

PALMETTO BAY, FL
Mrs. Chani Gansburg
Chabad of Palmetto Bay
786.282.0413
chabadpalmettobay@gmail.com

PUNTA GORDA, FL
Mrs. Sheina Jacobson
Chabad of Charlotte County
941.833.3381
chabadpg@yahoo.com

ROYAL PALM BEACH, FL
Mrs. Leah Schtroks
Chabad of Royal Palm Beach
561.795.1534
rabbizevis@gmail.com

S. PETERSBURG, FL
Mrs. Chaya Korf
Chabad Jewish Center
727.344.4900
chaya@chabadsp.com

SARASOTA, FL
Mrs. Sara Steinmetz
Chabad of Sarasota
941.925.0770
steinmetz.sara@gmail.com

SUNNY ISLES BEACH, FL
Mrs. Chanie Kaller
Chabad Russian Center
305.803.5315
Rabbi@chabadrc.org

SURFSIDE, FL
Mrs. Chani Lipskar
The Shul of Bal Harbour
305.868.1411
info@theshul.org

TAMPA, FL
Mrs. Sulha Dubrowski
Chabad of Tampa Bay
813.963.2317
lamplightersd@gmail.com

VALRICO, FL
Mrs. Tzippy Rubashkin
Chabad of Brandon
813.571.8100
tzipsor@gmail.com

WESLEY CHAPEL, FL
Mrs Chanie Yarmush
Chabad of East Pasco & New Tampa
813-642-3244
mmy613@aol.com

ATLANTA, GA
Mrs. Dassie New
Chabad of Georgia
404.843.2464 ext.102
office@chabadga.com

ATLANTA, GA
Mrs. Leah Sollish
Mrs. Dena Schusterman
Chabad In-town
404.898.0434
leah@chabadintown.org

KENNESAW, GA
Mrs. Nechami Charytan
Chabad Jewish Center
678.460.7702
info@jewishwestcobb.com

PEACHTREE CORNERS, GA
Mrs Esther Lerman
Chabad of Gwinnett
6785950196
esther@chabadofgwinnett.org

BOISE, ID
Mrs. Esther M. Lifshitz
Chabad Lubavitch of Idaho
208.841.9927
esther@jewishidaho.com

CHICAGO, IL
Mrs. Chaya Epstein
Women to Women
773.875.9147
w2wchaya@gmail.com

CHICAGO, IL
Mrs. Dinie Cohen
Jewish Women's Group
773.262.1381
ndcohen@sbcglobal.net

DEERFIELD, IL
Mrs. Dena Brody
Chabad House
305.335.9770
denabrody1@gmail.com

GLENVIEW, IL
Mrs. Sara Benjaminson
Rohr Chabad Center of Glenview
847.998.0770
Chabad@ChabadofGlenview.com

HIGHLAND PARK, IL
Mrs. Michla Schanowitz
North Suburban Chabad
847.433.1567
yschanow@sbcglobal.net

NORTHBROOK, IL
Mrs. Esther Rochel Moscowitz
Lubavitch Chabad of Northbrook
847.564.8770
info@chabadnorthbrook.com

DAVENPORT, IA
Mrs. Chana Cadaner
Chabad Lubavitch of the Quad Cities
563.355.1065
Chana@Chabadquadcities.com

IOWA CITY, IA
Mrs. Chaya Blesofsky
Chabad Lubavitch of Iowa City
319.358.1323
chabadiowa@msn.com

OVERLAND PARK, KS
Mrs. Blumah Wineberg
Neshei Chabad of KC
913.649.4852
nesheichabad@gmail.com

LEXINGTON, KY
Mrs. Shoshi Litvin
Chabad of the Bluegrass
502.576.0392
chabadofthebluegrass@gmail.com

METAIRIE, LA
Mrs. Chanie Nemes
Chabad Jewish Center
504.957.4987
chanienemes@gmail.com

ANNAPOLIS, MD
Mrs. Hindy Light
Chabad of Anne Arundel County
443.321.9859
hindy@chabadaac.com

BALTIMORE, MD
Mrs. Rochelle Kaplan
Aleph Learning Institute
410.486.2666 ext.2
alephjli@gmail.com

BEL AIR, MD
Mrs. Fraida Malka Schusterman
Chabad of Harford County
443.353.9718
Chabad@HarfordJewish.com

COLUMBIA, MD
Mrs. Chaya Sufrin
Lubavitch Center of Howard County
443.474.0340
rabbi@chabadclarksville.org

GAITHERSBURG, MD
Mrs. Chana Raichik
Chabad Upper Montgomery County
301.537.0068
chana@ourshul.org

OLNEY, MD
Mrs. Devorah Stolik
Chabad of Olney
301.660.6770
info@jewisholney.com

OWINGS MILLS, MD
Mrs. Chanie Katsenelenbogen
chabad Owings Mills
410.356.5156
chanie@chabadom.com

POTOMAC, MD
Mrs. Chana Kaplan
Chabad of the Village
301.433.4524
villagechabad@gmail.com

POTOMAC, MD
Mrs. Sarale Bluming
Chabad of Potomac
240.621.0770
sara@chabadpotomac.com

SILVER SPRING, MD
Mrs. Chaya Wolvovsky
Chabad of Silver Spring
301.593.1117
chayawolvovsky@gmail.com

ANDOVER, MA
Mrs Faigy Bronstein
Chabad Lubavitch Jewish Center of Merrimack Valley
978-470-2288
Bronstein08@gmail.com

CHESTNUT HILL, MA
Mrs. Grunie Uminer
Chabad at Chestnut Hill
617.738.9770
grunie@chabadch.com

NATICK, MA
Mrs. Chanie Fogelman
Chabad Center of Natick
508.202.2283
education@chabadnatick.com

PEABODY, MA
Mrs. Raizel Schusterman
Chabad of Peabody
978.977.9111
raizel@jewishpeabody.com

STOUGHTON, MA
Mrs. Chana Gurkow
Shaloh House
781.344.6334
rabbi@shalohhouse.com

SUDBURY, MA
Mrs. Shayna Freeman
Chabad Center of Sudbury
978.443.0110
info@chabadsudbury.com

WELLESLEY, MA
Mrs. Geni Bleich
Wellesley Weston Chabad House
781.239.1076
JewishWomenRgr8@aol.com

COMMERCE, MI
Mrs. Estie Greenberg
Chabad Jewish Center of Commerce
248.363.3644
estie@jewishcommerce.org

SOUTHFIELD, MI
Mrs. Tzippy Misholovin
FREE of Michigan
248.569.8514
free.michigan@yahoo.com

WEST BLOOMFIELD, MI
Mrs. Itty Shemtov
The Shul
248.788.4000
itty@theshul.net

MINNETONKA, MN
Ms. Rivkie Grossbaum
Chabad Minneapolis
952.929.9922
rivka@ChabadMinneapolis.com

S. PAUL, MN
Mrs. Nechama Bendet
Chabad Lubavitch of Greater S. Paul
651.998.9298
jewishspaul@gmail.com

KANSAS CITY, MO
Mrs. Chana'le Itkin
Chabad on the Plaza
816.645.6610
chana@plazachabad.com

S. LOUIS, MO
Mrs. Shiffy Landa
Chabad of Greater St. Louis
314.725.0400
chaim@showmechabad.com

BOZEMAN, MT
Mrs. Chavie Bruk
Chabad-Lubavitch of Montana
406.585.8770
chavs84@yahoo.com

MISSOULA, MT
Mrs. Shayna Nash
Chabad Lubavitch of Missoula
406.529.3196
berrynash@gmail.com

MANCHESTER, NH
Mrs. Shternie Krinsky
Lubavitch of New Hampshire
603.647.0204
shterniekrinsky@gmail.com

CHERRY HILL, NJ
Mrs. Dinie Mangel
Chabad Lubavitch in Cherry Hill
856.874.1500
Dinie@TheChabadCenter.org

CLINTON, NJ
Mrs. Rachel Kornfeld
Chabad of Hunterdon County
908.238.9002
rachel@jewishhunterdon.com

FRANKLIN LAKES, NJ
Mrs. Mimi Kaplan
Chabad of NW Bergen County – Franklin Lakes
201.848.0449
kaplanmimi@gmail.com

FREEHOLD, NJ
Mrs. Zisi Bernstein
Chabad of Freehold
732.972.3687
zisinj@gmail.com

HOBOKEN, NJ
Mrs. Shaindel Schapiro
Chabad Hoboken
201.386.5222
chabadhoboken@gmail.com

MONTVILLE, NJ
Mrs. Chaya Schera Spalter
Chabad of Montville
973.727.8824
Chabadmontville@aol.com

MORRISTOWN, NJ
Mrs. Gani Goodman
Morristown RCA
917.860.0146
jdomber@gmail.com

RANDOLPH, NJ
Mrs. Chava Bekhor
Chabad of Randolph
973.895.3070
info@chabadrandolph.com

TOMS RIVER, NJ
Mrs. Chanie Gourarie
Chabad Toms River
732.349.4199
chanie@chabadtomsriver.com

VINELAND, NJ
Mrs. Nechama Rapoport
Chabad of Cumberland County
856.207.3797
yohama1@verizon.net

WEST ORANGE, NJ
Mrs. Altie Kasowitz
Lubavitch Center
973.486.2362
altiekas@yahoo.com

WOODCLIFF LAKE, NJ
Mrs. Hindy Drizin
Valley Chabad
201.476.0157
hindy@valleychabad.org

LAS CRUCES, NM
Mrs. Chenchie Schmukler
Chabad of Las Cruces
575.524.1330
chenchie@ymail.com

BEDFORD HILLS, NY
Mrs. Sara Wolf
Chabad of Bedford & Pound Ridge Towns
914.666.6065
sara@chabadbedford.com

BRONX, NY
Mrs. Sorah Shemtov
Chabad Lubavitch of Riverdale
718.549.1100 ext. 15
sorahshmtv@gmail.com

BRONXVILLE, NY
Mrs. Mushka Deitsch
Chabad of Bronxville
347.623.0449
mushka@jewishbronxville.com

BROOKLYN, NY
Mrs. Chana'le Levin
Chabad of Ditmas Park
347.850.2255
ChabadofDitmasPark@gmail.com

BROOKLYN, NY
Mrs. Chanel Lipskier
Mrs. Dvora Lakein
The Beis Medrash Women's Circle
718.778.6712
WC@thebeismedrash.com

BROOKLYN, NY
Mrs. Devorah Marosov
Chabad of Midwood
718.338.3324
dmarsow@gmail.com

BROOKLYN, NY
Mrs. Esther Abramowitz
Chabad-Lubavitch of Clinton Hill
718.974.9472
esther@greenechabad.com

BROOKLYN, NY
Mrs. Esther Winner
Chabad Neshama
718.946.9833 ext.104
estherwinner@gmail.com

BROOKLYN, NY
Mrs. Sarah Hecht
Chabad of Park Slope
718.965.9836
shconquer@aol.com

BROOKLYN, NY
Mrs. Tzippy Vigler
Mayan Yisroel Chassidus Center
718.677.0030
tv@mayanyisroel.net

CEDARHURST, NY
Mrs. Chana Wolowik
Sara Blau
Chabad of the Five Towns
516.295.2478
chanie@chabad5towns.com

FLUSHING, NY
Mrs. Chanie Zalmanov
Chabad of Eastern Queens
718.464.0778
chaniezalmanov@gmail.com

FOREST HILLS, NY
Mrs. Mushky Mendelson
Congregation Machane Chodosh
347.867.8672
rabbi@machanechodosh.org

GREAT NECK, NY
Mrs. Chanie Geisinsky
Chabad of Great Neck
516.528.6033
cgeisinsky@gmail.com

MAMARONECK, NY
Mrs. Chana Silberstein
Jewish Women's Circle
914.834.8000
chana@jewishlarchmont.com

NEW YORK, NY
Mrs. Chana Paris
Chabad of Tribeca
212.566.6764
info@chabadoftribeca.com

NEW YORK, NY
Mrs. Chanie Krasnianski
Chabad Upper East Side
212.717.4613
ckrasnianski@gmail.com

NEW YORK, NY
Mrs. Devora Wilhelm
Chabad Young Professionals UES
347.451.4375
chabadyp@gmail.com

NEW YORK, NY
Mrs. Frumie Weitman
Chabad Jewish Latin Center
646.678.3569
jewishlatincenternyc@gmail.com

NEW YORK, NY
Mrs. Gillie Shanowitz
New York Hebrew
646.573.6773
gillie@nychebrewschool.org

NEW YORK, NY
Mrs. Mushka Zaklos
Chabad of Battery Park
646.770.3636
jewishbpc@gmail.com

NEW YORK, NY
Mrs. Rachel Benchimol
Aleph Learning
646.827.9181
info@alephlearning.org

NEW YORK, NY
Mrs. Raizy Metzger
Upper Midtown Chabad
212.758.3770
raizymetzger@yahoo.com

ROCHESTER, NY
Mrs. Chany Mochkin
Chabad Lubavitch of Rochester
585.981.0477
chanymo@yahoo.com

STONY BROOK, NY
Mrs. Chanie Cohen
Neshei Chabad Woman's Club
631.585.521
chanie@chabadsb.com

SUFFERN, NY
Mrs. Esty Weber
NCFJE
443.418.4336
Estherweber7@gmail.com

CINCINNATI, OH
Mrs. Chana Mangel
Chabad Jewish Center
513.793.5200
office@chabadba.com

CLEVELAND, OH
Mrs. Estie Marozov
Friendship Circle
216.377.3000
RabbiYossi@ChabadofCleveland.com

DAYTON, OH
Mrs. Devorah Leah Mangel
Chabad of Greater Dayton
937.643.0770
chabad@chabaddayton.com

NEW ALBANY, OH
Mrs. Esther Kaltmann
Chabad of Columbus
614.610.4293
esther.kaltmann@sbcglobal.net

SALEM, OR
Mrs. Fruma Perlstein
Chabad Jewish Center of Salem
503.383.9569
Fruma@chabadsalem.com

ALLENTOWN, PA
Mrs. Devorah Halperin
Chabad of the Lehigh Valley
610.351.6511
Rabbi@chabadlehighvalley.com

FORT WASHINGTON, PA
Mrs. Devorah Leah Deitsch
Lubavitch of Montgomery County
215.591.9310
devorah@jewishmc.com

MERION STATION, PA
Mrs. Michal Sherman
Chabad of the Main Line
610.660.9900
michal@chabadmainline.org

NEWTOWN, PA
Mrs. Rosie Weinstein
Lubavitch of Bucks County
215.497.9925
rosie@jewishcenter.info

PITTSBURGH, PA
Mrs Batya Rosenblum
Chabad of the South Hill
4123442424
batya812@gmail.com

PITTSBURGH, PA
Mrs. Chani Altein
Chabad of Pittsburgh
412.421.3561
jli@chabadpgh.com

RYDAL, PA
Mrs. Nechama Dina Gurevitz
Chabad Lubavitch Jewish Center
267.536.5757
zusheg@gmail.com

STATE COLLEGE, PA
Mrs. Miri Gourarie
Chabad of the Undergrad
814.409.8130
mirigourarie@gmail.com

STATE COLLEGE, PA
Mrs. Sarah Meretsky
Chabad of Penn State
814.861.8063
sarahitameretsky@comcast.net

ASHVILLE, SC
Mrs. Chana Susskind
Chabad House of Ashville
828.505.0746
chana@chabadasheville.org

COLUMBIA, SC
Mrs. Devorah Leah Marrus
The Chabad-Alef House
803.237.6084
devorahld@gmail.com

MYRTLE BEACH, SC
Mrs. Leah Aizenmen
Chabad of Myrtle Beach
843.448.0035
laizenman@gmail.com

MEMPHIS, TN
Mrs. Rivky Klein
Chabad Lubavitch of Tennessee
901.754.0404
Info@JewishMemphis.com

NASHVILLE, TN
Mrs. Esther Tiechtel
Chabad of Nashville
615.646.5750
rabbi@chabadnashville.com

ARLINGTON, TX
Mrs. Risha Gurevitch
Chabad of Arlington
817.451.1171
rishi@arlingtonchabad.org

AUSTIN, TX
Mrs. Mussy Levertov
Chabad Young Professionals
512.905.2778
Mendyaustin@gmail.com

BELLAIRE, TX
Mrs. Esty Zaklikofsky
The Shul of Bellaire
713.484.9887
estyzak@gmail.com

DALLAS, TX
Mrs. Michal Shapiro
Chabad of Dallas
972.818.0770
moshenaparstek@gmail.com

FORT WORTH, TX
Mrs. Chana Tovah Mandel
Chabad of Fort Worth
817.263.7701
Cgi@chabadfortworth.com

HOUSTON, TX
Mrs. Leah Marinovsky
Chabad Lubavitch
713.541.1774
leahfeige2@aim.com

HOUSTON, TX
Mrs. Rochel Lazaroff
Chabad at Rice
713.522.2004
Rochel@aishelhouse.org

MISSOURI CITY, TX
Mrs Chaya Feigenson
Chabad of Sugar Land
8327580685
cbfeigenson@gmail.com

S. ANTONIO, TX
Mrs. Rivkie Block
Chabad Lubavitch
210.492.1085
chabadsa@sbcglobal.net

SALT LAKE CITY, UT
Mrs. Sheina Zippel
Chabad Lubavitch of Utah
801.414.3377
sheina@jewishutah.com

BURLINGTON, VT
Mrs. Draizy Junik
Chabad of Vermont
802.658.5770
chabad@chabadvt.org

NORFOLK, VA
Mrs. Rashi Brashevitzky
Chabad of Tidewater
757.616.0770
Rabbilevi@chabadoftidewater.com

MERCER ISLAND, WA
Mrs. Devorah Kornfeld
Chabad of Mercer Island
206.679.9117
y-kornfeld2@yahoo.com

OLYMPIA, WA
Mrs. Chava Edelman
Chabad of Olympia
360.584.4306
info@jewisholympia.com

SPOKANE, WA
Mrs. Chaya Sarah Hahn
Chabad of Spokane
509.443.0770
rabbihahn@gmail.com

VANCOUVER, WA
Mrs. Tzivie Greenberg
Chabad Jewish Center
360.326.5923
info@jewishclarkcounty.com

KENOSHA, WI
Mrs. Rivkie Wilschanski
Chabad of Kenosha
262.359.0770
rabbitzali@jewishkenosha.com

MADISON, WI
Mrs. Henya Matusof
Rohr Chabad House at University of Wisconsin-Madison
608.257.1757
Info@jewishuwmadison.com

MEQUON, WI
Mrs. Dinie Rapoport
Center for Jewish Life
262.242.2235
dinie@chabadmequon.com

US VIRGIN ISLANDS

S. THOMAS
Mrs. Henya Federman
Chabad Lubavitch of the Virgin Islands
340.714.2770
henya@jewishvirginislands.com

AUSTRALIA

ROSE BAY, NSW
Mrs. Henya Milecki
South Head Synagogue
61.4.2361.3770
henyam@me.com

Mrs Esther Feldman
Beis Menachem Chabad - Dover Heights Shule
61-2-9731-8682
esterke_f@hotmail.com

SYDNEY, NSW
Mrs. Sara-Tova Yaffe
CBD Chabad
61.4.2247.0655
saratova613@gmail.com

SYDNEY, NSW
EAST ST KILDA, VIC
Mrs. Sara Rosenfeld
Beis Chabad Ohel Devorah
61.3.9525.9014
rivkah.groner@gmail.com

BELGIUM

BRUSSELS
Mrs. Nehama Tawil
EJCC
32.2.231.1770
ntawil@ejcc.eu

BRUSSELS
Mrs. Shulamit Pinson
Ohel Menachem
32.47.621.7445
info@ganihai.com

EDEGEM, ANTWERPEN
Mrs. Chaya Hertz
Chai Center
32.3.288.7970
chajah@gmail.com

BRAZIL

MANAUS
Mrs. Dvorah Lea Raichman
Chabad-Lubavitch of Manaus
55.92.3088.3302
Zagudeby@hotmail.com

S. PAULO
Mrs. Rivka Rosenfeld
Sinagoga Beit Menachem
55.11.3816.6216
rivkyrosenfeld@hotmail.com

S. PAULO
Mrs. Sarah Steinmetz
Beit Chabad Central
55.11.3081.3081
sarah.a.steinmetz@gmail.com

CANADA

RICHMOND, BC
Mrs. Chanie Baitelman
Chabad of Richmond
604.277.6427
admin@chabadrichmond.com

VANCOUVER, BC
Mrs. Chaya Rosenfeld
Lubavitch of British Columbia
604.266.1313
esti@lubavitchbc.com

VANCOUVER, BC
Mrs. Malky Bitton
Chabad of Downtown
778.688.1273
malky@chabadcitycentre.com

HAMILTON, ON
Mrs. Shaina Rosenfeld
Chabad Lubavitch Hamilton
905.529.7458
shaina@chabadhamilton.com

MAPLE, ON
Mrs. Toby Bernstein
Chabad Romano Centre
905.303.1880
chabad@chabadrc.org

OTTAWA, ON
Mrs. Devora Caytak
Jewish Youth Library of Ottawa
613.729.1619
Dev18@sympatico.ca

S. CATHARINES, ON
Mrs. Perla Zaltzman
Chabad at Brock
905.401.6281
perla@Jewishniagara.com

THORNHILL, ON
Mrs. Chanah Leah Beckerman
Chabad at York

THORNHILL, ON
Mrs. Chanie Hildeshaim
Chabad Russian Center of Thornhill Woods
905.326.9258
chanie@jewishthornhillwoods.org

THORNHILL, ON
Mrs. Faygie Kaplan
Chabad @ Flamingo
905.763.4040
faygie@chabadflamingo.com

THORNHILL, ON
Mrs. Goldie Plotkin
Chabad Lubavitch of Markham
905.886.0420
rabbi@chabadmarkham.org

TORONTO, ON
Mrs. Chana Gansburg
Chabad on the Avenue
416.546.8770
chana@chabadavenue.com

TORONTO, ON
Mrs. Mushky Blau
JRCC South Thornhill
6477095770
Mushka.Blau@jrcc.org

TORONTO, ON
Mrs. Nechama Dina Jacobson
JRCC West Thornhill
416.902.9254
ndjacobson@rogers.com

TORONTO, ON
Mrs. Rivka Gansburg
Chabad Lubavitch of York Mills
416.551.9391
rivky@chabadyorkmills.com

TORONTO, ON
Mrs. Yehudis Steiner
Uptown Chabad
416.635.9696
yehudissteiner@gmail.com

WATERLOO, ON
Mrs. Rivky Goldman
Chabad Lubavitch of the Waterloo Region
519.725.4289
rmg@jewishwaterloo.com

WHITBY, ON
Mrs. Chana Borenstein
Chabad Jewish Centre of Durham Region
905.493.9007
info@jewishdurham.com

MONTREAL, QC
Mrs. Chanie Gansbourg
Chabad of Old Montreal
514.907.8778
chabadofoldmtl@gmail.com

MONTREAL, QC
Mrs. Rashi Weiss
Chabad Student Centre
514.845.4443
rashi@chabadmcgill.com

MONTREAL, QC
Mrs. Simcha Fine
Chabad Zichron Kedoshim
514.738.3434
simchafine@gmail.com

MONTREAL, QC
Mrs. Zeldie Treitel
Montreal Torah Center
514.739.0770
zeldie@themtc.com

VILLE S. LAURENT, QC
Mrs. Leah Silberstein
Chabad Ville S. Laurent
514.747.1199
info@chabadvsl.com

CAYMAN ISLANDS

GRAND CAYMAN
Mrs. Rikal Pewzner
Chabad Cayman
717.798.1040
rikal@jewishcayman.com

CHINA

PUDONG
Mrs. Nechama Greenberg
Chabad of Pudong
86.21.1780.0791
nechamieg@gmail.com

DENMARK

COPENHAGEN
Mrs. Rochel Loewenthal
ChabaDanmark
45.3316.1850
Info@chabad.dk

FRANCE

MARSEILLE
Mrs. Vivi (Rivka) Altabé
Beth Habad Marseille 8ème
33.6.11.600.305
loubavitch13008@gmail.com

PARIS
Mrs. Mushky Lachkar
Habad Bercy 13
33.6.63.025.430
mushky92@gmail.com

PAU
Mrs. Shayna Matusof
Habad des Pyrenees-Atlantiques
33.6.22.107.549
habadpyrenees@gmail.com

GUATEMALA

GUATEMALA CITY
Mrs. Yael Pelman
Chabad of Guatemala
718.504.7344
yaell@hotmail.com

ISRAEL

JERUSALEM
Mrs. Chana Canterman
Chabad Center of Talbiya
972.54.682.3737
chabadtalbiya@gmail.com

ITALY

FIRENZE
Mrs. Sonia Wolvovsky
Chabad of Tuscany
39.38.9595.2034
jewishtuscany@gmail.com

RUSSIAN FEDERATION

MOSCOW
Mrs. Rivky Wilansky
Chabad of Moscow
7.495.645.5000
doamitzvah@gmail.com

SOUTH AFRICA

SEA POINT, CAPE TOWN
Mrs. Avigail Popack
Chabad Center of Cape Town
27.21.434.3740
avipopack@gmail.com

SWEDEN

MALMÖ
Mrs. Reizel Kesselman
Chabad Malmo
46.40.979.358
chabadmalmo@gmail.com

SWITZERLAND

LUGANO
Mrs. Yuti Kantor
Chabad Lugano
41.91.921.3720
Yuti@jewishlugano.com

LUZERN
Mrs. Rivky Drukman
Chabad of Central Switzerland
41.41.361.1770
Info@ChabadLuzern.com

UNITED KINGDOM

BIRMINGHAM, ENGLAND
Mrs. Rivky Cheruff
Chabad on Campus Birmingham
44.78.05092236
dercheruff@gmail.com

EDGWARE, MIDDX, ENGLAND
Mrs. Sarah Jacobs
Lubavitch of Edgware
44.20.8905.4141
sarahjacobs@loe.org.uk

EDGWARE, MIDDX, ENGLAND
Mrs. Shterna Sudak
Lubavitch Foundation
44.20.8800.0022
Shternasudak@yahoo.com

ILFORD, ESSEX, ENGLAND
Mrs. Devorah Sufrin
Chabad Lubavitch Centres Essex
44.20.8554.1624
mrssufrin@chabadilford.co.uk

LEEDS, ENGLAND
Mrs. Dabrushy Pink
Chabad Lubavitch of Leeds
0113 266 3311
jwc@judaismlive.com

LONDON, ENGLAND
Mrs. Chai Cohen
Chabad-Lubavitch of Shoreditch
44.77.7261.2661
cohenchai@gmail.com

LONDON, ENGLAND
Mrs. Devora Lew
Chabad of Bloomsbury - Central London
44.20.7060.9770
info@bloomsburychabad.org

LONDON, ENGLAND
Mrs. Devorah Leah Weisz
Chabad of Hampstead Village
44.79.7652.2807
Shulinhampstead@gmail.com

LONDON, ENGLAND
Mrs. Hadasa Korer
Chabad Lubavitch of Islington
44.20.7688.0169
mkorer@gmail.com

LONDON, ENGLAND
Mrs. Kezi Levin
Brondesbury Park Synagogue
44.20.8451.0091
kezi@bark.org

MANCHESTER, ENGLAND
Mrs. Shaina Cohen
Lchaim Chabad Manchester
44.16.1792.6335
Shaina@Lchaim.org.uk

WESTMINSTER, LONDON, ENGLAND
Mrs. Chana Kalmenson
Chabad of Belgravia
44.75.8592.0195
jewishbelgravia@gmail.com

URUGUAY

MONTEVIDEO
Mrs. Musya Shemtov
Beit Jabad Uruguay
598.2709.3444
rmusyashemtov@gmail.com

VENEZUELA

CARACAS
Mrs. Chani Rosenblum
Hogar Jabad Lubavitch
58.212.264.7011
chaniros1@gmail.com

JEWISH LEARNING INSTITUTE

THE JEWISH LEARNING MULTIPLEX

Brought to you by the Rohr Jewish Learning Institute

In fulfillment of the mandate of the Lubavitcher Rebbe, of blessed memory, whose leadership guides every step of our work, the mission of the Rohr Jewish Learning Institute is to transform Jewish life and the greater community through the study of Torah, connecting each Jew to our shared heritage of Jewish learning.

While our flagship program remains the cornerstone of our organization, JLI is proud to feature additional divisions catering to specific populations, in order to meet a wide array of educational needs.

THE ROHR JEWISH LEARNING INSTITUTE,
a subsidiary of *Merkos L'Inyonei Chinuch*,
is the adult education arm of the Chabad-Lubavitch Movement.

Torah Studies provides a rich and nuanced encounter with the weekly Torah reading.

MyShiur courses are designed to assist students in developing the skills needed to study Talmud independently.

IN PARTNERSHIP WITH CHABAD ON CAMPUS

This rigorous fellowship program invites select college students to explore the fundamentals of Judaism.

IN PARTNERSHIP WITH CTEEN: CHABAD TEEN NETWORK

Jewish teens forge their identity as they engage in Torah study, social interaction, and serious fun.

The Rosh Chodesh Society gathers Jewish women together once a month for intensive textual study.

TorahCafe.com provides an exclusive selection of top-rated Jewish educational videos.

This yearly event rejuvenates mind, body, and spirit with a powerful synthesis of Jewish learning and community.

Participants delve into our nation's rich past while exploring the Holy Land's relevance and meaning today.

Select affiliates are invited to partner with peers and noted professionals, as leaders of innovation and excellence.

Machon Shmuel is an institute providing Torah research in the service of educators worldwide.

NOTES

NOTES

NOTES